Scott Kolecki

CORVETTE Concept Cars

Developing America's Favorite Sports Car

CarTech®

CarTech®

6118 Main Street
North Branch, MN 55056
Phone: 651-277-1200 or 800-551-4754
Fax: 651-277-1203
www.cartechbooks.com

Edit by Wes Eisenschenk
Layout by Connie DeFlorin

ISBN 978-1-61325-713-5
Item No. CT686

Library of Congress Cataloging-in-Publication Data Available

Written, edited, designed, and printed in the U.S.A.
10 9 8 7 6 5 4 3 2 1

DISTRIBUTION BY:

Europe
PGUK
63 Hatton Garden
London EC1N 8LE, England
Phone: 020 7061 1980 • Fax: 020 7242 3725
www.pguk.co.uk

Australia
Renniks Publications Ltd.
3/37-39 Green Street
Banksmeadow, NSW 2109, Australia
Phone: 2 9695 7055 • Fax: 2 9695 7355
www.renniks.com

Canada
Login Canada
300 Saulteaux Crescent
Winnipeg, MB, R3J 3T2 Canada
Phone: 800 665 1148 • Fax: 800 665 0103
www.lb.ca

TABLE OF CONTENTS

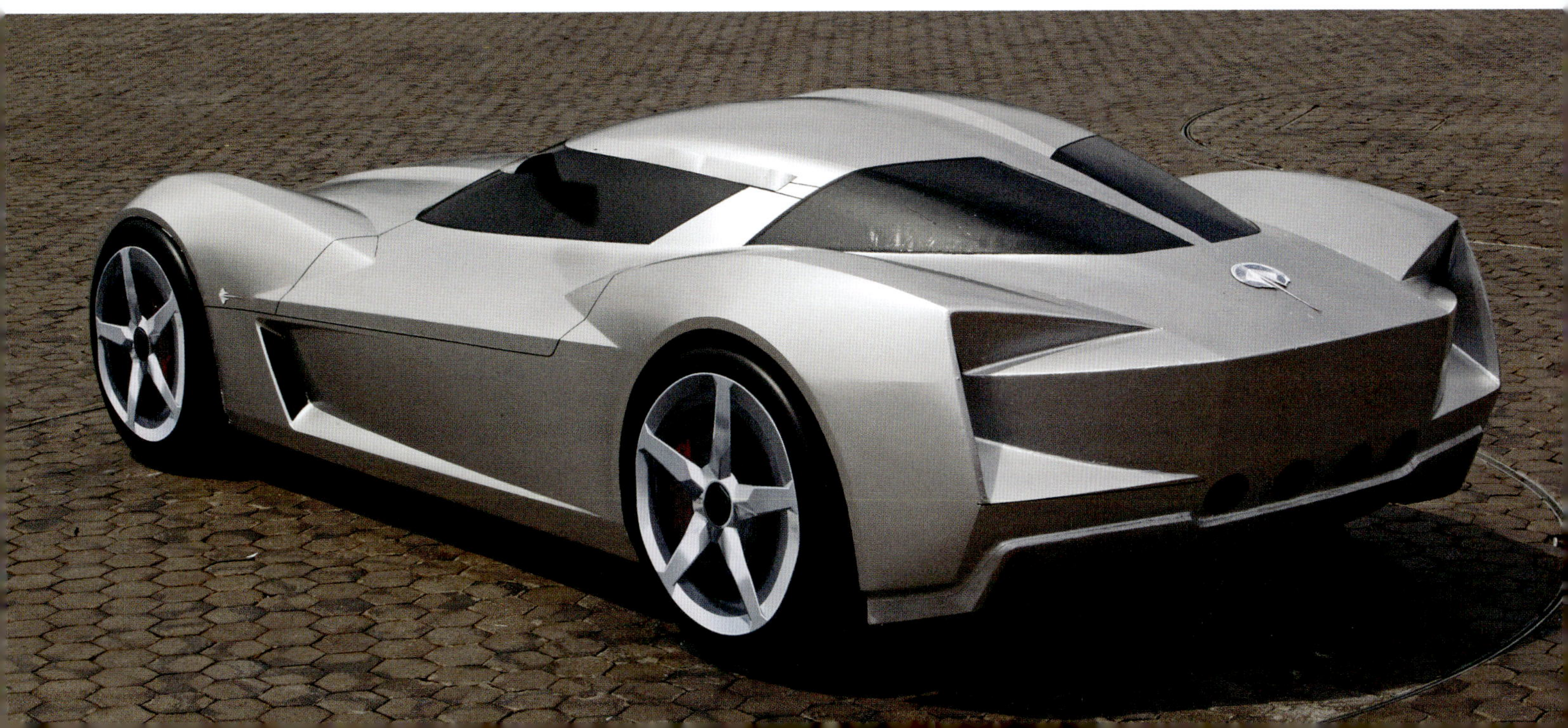

DEDICATION

This book is respectfully dedicated to two very special people in my life: Raymond Hontert and Erika Kolecki.

As a child, Grandpa Ray taught me all about classic cars. He, along with Grandma Ruth, took me and my brothers to one of the local Friday night car shows or cruise-ins, where he introduced us to a seemingly endless variety of classic, sport, and muscle cars. It wasn't long before his passion for these beautiful machines became my own. Grandpa, I am forever grateful to you for kindling my love affair with the American automobile and most especially the Chevrolet Corvette.

Today, I am immensely blessed to share that same passion with my amazing wife. Although our opinions on our "favorite car of all time" differ (Erika is a Jeep Wrangler girl at heart), she has always been the first to encourage and support my Corvette lifestyle, including the countless hours I've spent throughout our marriage writing about them.

I love you, E, and I always will.

ACKNOWLEDGMENTS

I would like to thank the following people who helped make this book possible.

John Kyros at the GM Heritage Center, for the many hours spent assembling preview slides and emailing me the incredible photographs contained in this book. I could not have done this project without your help, and I am forever grateful for the friendship that we formed along the way.

Derek E. Moore, Bob Bubnis, Betty Hardison, and Daniel Decker of the National Corvette Museum, a massive thank you for sharing your combined insights into the rich history of the Corvette, for the in-person/in-depth tour of the museum, for all the time spent pulling information from the archives, and for allowing me to bring a photographer into the museum to photograph so many of the amazing cars on display there.

Richard Earl, thank you for sharing your personal perspectives on the Corvette, for the images of your father and grandfather, and for trusting me to share a bit of your family's incredible story. Dan Vaughn, thank you for sharing your amazing photographs with me and for your insight on Corvette concept cars.

Joe Bortz and the Bortz Auto Collection, thank you for your generosity throughout this project. Your insights on the Banshee, Biscayne, and the LaSalle II were incredibly valuable, and I am honored that you were interested enough in this project to share some of your own stories with me. Geoffrey R. Hacker, PhD, thank you for your expertise on the Alembic I and the early years of fiberglass cars, including the Corvette.

Joe Kolecki, thank you for traveling all the way to Bowling Green to photograph Corvette concept cars at the National Corvette Museum. I love you, brother!

Don Spisak, thank you for sharing your exceptional skills behind the camera lens, for being the very first to read this book in its entirety, and for the constant words of encouragement from you and Daina over the past year.

Cliff Wanner, thank you for proofreading the early sections of this book while I was writing it. Your feedback has been invaluable, as were our long discussions about Corvette concept cars while we were out cruising the backroads of Tennessee and southern Kentucky.

Jonny Bens, thank you for being the first to share your photos of the XP-987 GT with me when I began this project. Bonnie Wolf and *Vette Vues* magazine, thank you for coming to my rescue at the last minute with some beautiful images of the E85 Concept.

To all of the writers and automotive historians who have published books, written magazine articles, and created websites, videos, podcasts, or other media about the history of the Corvette, this book would not have been possible without each of your individual perspectives on and knowledge of the people and cars contained

ACKNOWLEDGMENTS

Continued

herein. I especially want to recognize Jerry Burton (*Zora Arkus-Duntov: The Legend Behind Corvette*), David W. Temple (*The Cars of Harley Earl*), Dave McLellan (*Corvette from the Inside*), and Karl Ludvigsen (*Corvette: America's Star-Spangled Sports Car*).

To Nick Dellis, Cameron Martel, Chris Tulumba, and the entire team at A07Online, thank you for your encouragement and support throughout this project. Having access to corvsport.com and supercars.net was incredibly valuable. I hope you enjoy the results!

Thank you to my entire family, but most especially Erika, Kendyll, Sophie, and Ella, for being my biggest cheerleaders and for giving me the time to write, especially on weekend afternoons when we could have been out on the lake. I love you all so very much.

Finally, to the team at CarTech Publishing, and especially Wes Eisenschenk, for taking a chance on me and for all your encouragement along the way. Writing this book has been a dream come true, and I am immensely grateful to have had this amazing opportunity.

INTRODUCTION

The dream of the potential buyer must be discovered and satisfied, and the buyer must be awakened with his dreams turned into cars that he can and will buy.

—Harley J. Earl

For nearly 70 years, the Chevrolet Corvette has been a defining and inseparable part of the American automotive landscape. Since the arrival of Harley Earl's "Project Opel" Corvette concept in January 1953, this automotive icon has been transformed time and again from a well-intentioned but underpowered "sporty car" and boulevard cruiser into the world-class, mid-engine supercar we know and love today.

Although it might be difficult to imagine, there was a time when the word *Corvette* was not synonymous with anything resembling a high-performance sports car. Despite creating a great deal of excitement when it was introduced, the Corvette's long-term future seemed unlikely throughout its first decade of existence. Even in recent years, there have been a variety of outside influences—political, economic, and environmental—that threatened to bring the brand to its knees.

The Corvette's ongoing success has required the unwavering inspiration, imagination, perseverance, and often sheer daring of its engineers, designers, mechanics, racers, managers, and corporate executives. They have had to continuously reinvent the car from its earliest stigma as a "rolling bathtub" (a nickname it earned after a single year of production) into one of the most sought-after sports cars of all time.

This book is an introduction to three of Corvette's leading men, Harley Earl, Zora Arkus-Duntov, and Bill Mitchell, as well as a look at their contributions to the "form and function" of the Corvette throughout their careers with Chevrolet and General Motors.

It is also a tribute to the dozens of creative minds, including Larry Shinoda, Frank Winchell, Dave McLellan, and Tom Peters (to name but a few) who contributed their design and engineering talents to advance the evolution of "America's Favorite Sports Car" through each of its eight successive generations.

Ultimately, this book is an exploration of the Corvette concept ("dream") cars designed by these innovative thinkers over the past 70 years. From turnstile beauty queens to purpose-driven research vehicles and test mules, we'll look at the good, the bad, and the "ugly" concepts from each generation to better understand how their creation helped shape the production models they inspired.

CHAPTER 1

MAKING "DREAM CARS" A REALITY

The stylist's real pride lies in the creativeness of his hands—hands which mold the offerings of a dreamer's mind into an automobile design which is aesthetically pleasing to the public.
—Harley J. Earl

At the end of World War II, America was enjoying a prolonged period of economic growth and prosperity. The automobile industry contributed significantly to that growth. In less than 10 years' time, the number of vehicles produced annually in the United States had quadrupled. American automobile manufacturers resumed building large and flashy family sedans that offered would-be owners reliable transportation with plenty of space for a growing family.

At the same time, American automotive enthusiasts, many of them servicemen who had been stationed in Europe during the War, returned home with a fascination for the smaller, two-seat sports cars they had been introduced to and driven while overseas. Because American automobile manufacturers had nothing comparable to offer consumers domestically, an increasing number of British sports cars (most notably the MG TC Roadster, Jaguar XK 120, Triumph TR, and Austin Healey) began entering the US automotive market from "across the pond."

On the West Coast, there were a handful of independent coachbuilders who had begun designing, driving, and racing their own custom, two-passenger sporty cars. While increasing numbers of these homegrown racers began appearing across the United States, nothing of the sort was being considered, let alone developed, in Detroit. Most US automobile manufacturers doubted the market potential of a mass-produced, American-built sports car until Harley Earl introduced his concept for a low-priced "sporty car" in the summer of 1952.

Nearly four times as many Americans bought an automobile after World War II as had either before or during it. Many consumers felt compelled to purchase vehicles from US companies, such as this 1948 Buick Super Sedanette, as an outward acknowledgment of national pride.

The 1947 MG TC Roadster was one of the most frequently imported European sports cars after World War II. It has been credited with starting the sports car craze in America and was regularly raced at Watkins Glen and Pebble Beach speedways.

Harley Earl: The Early Years

Harley Jefferson Earl was a pioneer of automobile design and one of the leading automotive stylists of the 20th century. His immeasurable contributions to the industry included the creation of clay modeling as a design standard (one that is still used today) and the introduction and evolution of the concept automobile.

Earl's start in the automotive industry occurred when he left Stanford University to work for the family-owned Earl Automotive Works in Hollywood, California. The company, which specialized in custom-built automobiles for stars of the silver screen, provided young Harley with the opportunity to hone his skills as a designer and custom coach builder. When his father sold Earl Automotive Works in 1919 to Donald Lee, a successful West Coast Cadillac distributor, 25-year-old Harley stayed on as lead designer and director of Lee's newly acquired body shop.

Lawrence P. Fisher, general manager of Cadillac, discovered Earl while visiting Don Lee's Coach &

Best remembered as the "Father of the Corvette," Harley J. Earl's extensive contributions to automobile styling helped produce some of the most beautiful and extravagant automobiles the world has ever seen. (Photo Courtesy Richard Earl, automotive historian and grandson of Harley Earl)

The Project Opel prototype is on display in GM's styling auditorium in 1952. Look closely at the fender badging. There was a brief period when GM's marketing team considered other names for the car, including "Corvair" and "Cougar." This is one of only a few photos in existence that shows the Motorama Corvette with the "Cougar" moniker on its front fenders. (Photo Courtesy General Motors LLC)

GM President Alfred P. Sloan (standing) and a young Harley Earl pose with the 1927 LaSalle roadster, the first mass-produced automobile to be intentionally "stylized." (Photo Courtesy General Motors LLC)

Body Corporation during a business trip to California. Fisher had been immensely impressed by the originality of Earl's coach designs. Upon returning to Detroit, he convinced General Motors President Alfred P. Sloan they needed to hire Earl to help with the development of a sporty-yet-elegant companion car that Sloan had envisioned to fill the gap between the Buick and Cadillac models. Earl joined General Motors in 1926 as a one-year contract employee. During that first year, he single-handedly designed the 1927 LaSalle.

His work on the LaSalle landed Earl a permanent position at General Motors. He was made director of GM's newly developed Art and Color Section. The position allowed Earl the freedom to advance his styling ideas without the outside influence of engineers and division managers who might question his artistic vision. Earl continued to design extravagant automobiles accentuated with chrome, fins, and sweeping curves throughout the 1930s.

Earl's designs defined the look of GM's product lines for a generation. As his commercial successes increased in number so did the size of his department. In 1937, Sloan rebranded the "art and color" section as the "styling" section and made Earl the department's vice president. It marked the first time in history that a styling department employee was promoted to vice president within a large automotive corporation.

The 1938 Buick Y-Job and World War II

It was during this time that Earl began development of the industry's first-ever concept automobile: the 1938 Buick Y-Job Concept. Built on the chassis of a 1937 Buick, Earl and his team designed a machine that fully realized his personal vision of what an automobile could be. They incorporated new technologies into the Y-Job not yet seen in automobiles from that era.

When finished, the Y-Job was a beautifully proportioned two-seater with a long, sweeping hood and rear decklid. It featured concealed headlights, flush door handles, electrically operated windows, and the first-ever power-retractable convertible top hidden by a metal deck assembly.

The introduction of the 1938 Buick Y-Job coincided with the start of World War II and was therefore never developed beyond its conceptual phase. The car nonetheless established a new standard for design at General Motors that continued to resonate both during and after the war. It also provided the world (and a generation of

Harley Earl was the first-ever vice president of styling for General Motors. In this role, Earl defined the look of GM's automobiles for a generation and created one of the most iconic sports cars of all time: the Chevy Corvette. (Photo Courtesy General Motors LLC)

Recognized as the automobile industry's earliest concept car, the 1938 Buick Y-Job was also Earl's personal vehicle until 1951. Years later, the car was restored by the Henry Ford Museum and returned to the GM Heritage Center, where it remains to this day. (Photo Courtesy General Motors LLC)

Harley Earl named his concept car the Y-Job because, in his words, the "Y" went "one step beyond" the "X" prefix that was used on experimental prototype cars being developed by General Motors in the late 1930s. (Photo Courtesy General Motors LLC)

young, would-be automotive consumers) with a glimpse of things to come.

During the war, most of Earl's design work focused on supporting the war effort overseas. In 1942, he established a camouflage research and training division within General Motors, which resulted in the creation of a 22-page document titled the "Camouflage Manual for General Motors Camouflage."

Additionally, Earl's graphic engineering team developed a pilot training manual in 1945 titled *Flight Thru Instruments*. Illustrated by GM's design department, the book was considered one of the best instructional publications of its day and a pinnacle of GM's contribution to the war effort.

By the late 1940s, Earl was eager to begin work on something new. His postwar endeavors had been focused on the development of production vehicles for General Motors, including the 1949–1950 Buick Roadmaster Riviera and Cadillac Coupe deVille. However, his personal

The 1951 Buick LeSabre Concept was the first post-World War II "Dream Car" (concept car) designed by Earl and built by General Motors. Like the Y-Job before it, Earl drove the LaSabre as his personal car after it finished its year-long tour with GM's traveling Motorama auto show. (Photo Courtesy General Motors LLC)

The look of the LeSabre was heavily influenced by Earl's desire to fuse modern aircraft design into the styling of the automobile. This car featured several design elements inspired by its namesake: the US Air Force's F-86 Sabre jet. (Photo Courtesy General Motors LLC)

Developed as a counterpart to the LeSabre, the XP-300 was engineered around GM's popular "long and low" design philosophy. The car was more than 16 feet long and stood just 39.1 inches tall. (Photo Courtesy Dan Vaughn, author/developer of ConceptCarz.com)

ambition was to return to developing experimental prototypes like his Buick Y-Job from a decade earlier.

Earl's first postwar concept "dream" cars were both two-seater automobiles. First was the 1951 Buick LeSabre, which contained several design elements inspired by aircraft from that era. Next came the Buick XP-300, which was developed as a counterpart to the LeSabre. Both cars established new design concepts, including a wraparound windshield, aircraft-inspired tail fins, and a "long and low" ground-hugging design philosophy.

While neither of these vehicles evolved beyond their conceptual phase, both traveled across the United States as part of GM's Motorama tour. Moreover, they provided Earl with much of the groundwork he needed to begin his next project: a small two-seat "sporty" car that he first envisioned while attending a race weekend at Watkins Glen.

Project Opel

In the late fall of 1951, Harley Earl began putting considerable thought into how he could manufacture a low-priced "sporty car" that would outsell the European sports cars that were dominating that portion of the automotive market. He envisioned a car that offered consumers more vehicle for their money while also being

One of GM's original press photographs shows the original 1953 Motorama Corvette Roadster. Like the production model that followed it, the concept model was painted Polo White with a Sportsman Red interior. (Photo Courtesy General Motors LLC)

While there is no question that Harley Earl advanced the use of fiberglass in commercial automotive production, Bill Tritt (and others like him) pioneered its use in cars such as the Alembic 1 more than a half-decade before the first Corvette was produced. (Photo Courtesy Geoff Hacker, author/owner of undiscoveredclassics.com)

easier to maintain. He wanted to design a sports car that could be serviced at the same GM dealership where it was purchased.

Earl developed his "sporty car" in secret. For years, he'd had access to a small workspace adjacent to GM's main body development studio. It afforded him the privacy to work on personal design projects until he was ready to present them. Earl knew that prematurely exposing one of his design ideas, even given his many commercial successes, could bring the idea to an untimely and final end.

Instead, Earl enlisted the assistance of his closest design associates. His handpicked design team included Vincent Kaptur Sr., the director of body engineering efforts at the styling studio, and Carl Peebles, the draftsman who helped transform many of Earl's design ideas into reality. He also enlisted designer Carl Renner, stylist Bill Bloch, and clay modeler Tony Balthasar.

Earl codenamed his secret project "Opel." He chose the name because Chevy's design team frequently performed work for the Opel corporation, a European division of General Motors. Earl knew that the name would help his project avoid attention, which was exactly what he wanted.

The initial design directives Earl presented to his team were somewhat vague. He emphasized the importance of designing a car that could be purchased for $1,850, which was approximately 15 percent less expensive than a 1951 British MG TD. Earl recognized that selling his car at this price point meant it would have to be designed around a mostly stock GM chassis. It was from these assumptions that the Opel's initial design studies evolved.

Earl Finds Inspiration: The Alembic I

Things changed when Earl discovered a concept car on display in the GM styling auditorium down the hall from his office. Known as the "Alembic I," this fiberglass-bodied automobile had been designed and built by Glasspar company owner Bill Tritt for Naugatuck Chemical, a division of the U.S. Rubber Company.

Earl found inspiration and a new enthusiasm for Project Opel in the bodylines of the Alembic I. He accelerated work on his two-seater sporty car with the assistance of some additional resources. Among them was Robert F. McLean, a young sports car enthusiast and California Institute of Technology (Cal Tech) graduate who held degrees in both engineering and industrial design.

Earl tasked McLean with developing a basic layout for the car. While the traditional automotive design practice of that era was to frame the car (both fore and aft) from the firewall, McLean elected to begin visualizing the car from the back forward. In so doing, he was able to position various elements of the car, from the seats to the engine, in the same fashion as the British roadsters that had inspired this project in the first place.

Project Opel Takes Shape

McLean's layout established two fundamental truths about Earl's new concept car. First, the car's basic proportioning resulted in a low center of gravity and nearly balanced (53-47) front-to-rear weight distribution, both of which were vital when building a successful sports car. Second, McLean's design showed that Project Opel required the development of a custom frame and chassis. Unfortunately, this also meant that Earl's original vision of producing a competitively priced sporty car was no longer certain.

Despite these realizations, Earl continued to look for ways to lessen production costs whenever possible. He visualized his sports car being widely accepted by people of all ages, especially among college students, if its specifications and pricing could be properly managed.

The rounded contour of the early Corvette's rear bumper/fascia (including the Project Opel prototype) was a carryover from an earlier design element wherein a spare tire housing (form follows function!) was intended to be installed. When the idea of a spare tire was dropped entirely, the exterior styling was retained. (Photo Courtesy General Motors LLC)

As the car came together, Earl was adamant that the project remain a secret from anyone outside his immediate circle of engineers and designers. Because of this, it is unclear which design elements were contributed by other members of Earl's team. Earl was solely responsible for the car's overall profile, its wraparound windshield, and its exposed headlight assemblies, and there is no question that the idea for the Project Opel concept originated with him. At the same time, it is worth noting that the Opel prototype was the result of many talented people, all of whom had worked covertly under Earl's direction.

More Than a Show Car?

A full-size clay model of the car was completed in April 1952. From it, a plaster model was cast and presented to seek design approval from corporate leadership. Still proceeding with a degree of caution, Earl initially approached Edward Cole, Chevrolet's recently appointed chief engineer, with the design. Cole had displayed more than a passing interest in sports cars while working as an engineer at Cadillac to the extent that he had assisted Briggs Cunningham with his 1950 Cadillac Le Mans racers.

Cole was elated with Earl's two-seater sports car design. He promised to give Earl whatever assistance was needed to get the design approved by GM's executives. He also agreed to support Earl's efforts to produce a working prototype.

Next, Earl approached GM President Harlow "Red" Curtice with his sports car concept. He took Curtice on a private walk-around tour of the plaster model. At that meeting, Earl enthusiastically explained that his new

Ed Cole (left) and Thomas Keating inspect the Corvette concept in the lobby of the Waldorf Astoria Hotel. The synergy of Cole, Keating, and Harley Earl all but guaranteed that Chevrolet's new sports car would be the hot topic of the 1953 Motorama Auto Show. (Photo Courtesy General Motors LLC)

car would not only be profitable for Chevrolet but also add some "much-needed sparkle" to Chevrolet's current family car image. Like Cole, Curtice loved what he saw. During that meeting, he suggested that the Opel might make a great addition to the coming year's Motorama show, which is exactly what Earl had hoped.

On June 2, 1952, Chevrolet Division General Manager Thomas H. Keating joined Earl, Curtice, and Cole for the formal unveiling of the car in GM's styling auditorium. Keating shared in Curtice's and Cole's enthusiasm for Earl's sports car. The go-ahead was given to develop a working prototype of Project Opel for the 1953 Motorama show. Even more significant, it was decided that Chevrolet's engineering staff should begin development of a working chassis so that provisional plans for a production version of the car could get underway.

At the completion of that meeting, which was arguably one of the most pivotal moments in the genesis of the Corvette, the "Project Opel" moniker was abandoned, and a formal engineering designation was assigned to the car.

The 1953 EX-122/EX-52

It is often acknowledged that the first Corvette produced in the fall of 1952 was given the designation "EX-122" by Chevrolet. However, there has been some disagreement among automotive historians as to the accuracy of this claim. Considerable research has been conducted over the years into the history of the first Corvettes, and there is increasing evidence that supports the belief that the EX-52 was the first Corvette ever produced.

The jury is still out as to which of these cars was first presented to the public at the Waldorf Astoria Motorama in January 1953. The following introduction to the EX-122/EX-52 is based on the information available at the time of this publication. Future historians may shed additional light on past events that determine once and for all which of these concept Corvettes was really the first example ever built.

On July 3, 1952, with the 1953 Motorama just seven months away, Chevrolet initiated a work order authorizing production of the first "Experimental Opel Car." Earl and Cole, recognizing the amount of work that needed to be completed to meet the production deadline, immediately began assigning work to members of Chevrolet's engineering team.

Maurice Olley

Maurice Olley, a well-respected engineer from England and acting head of Chevrolet's Research and Development department, was assigned the challenging task of developing the car's chassis and suspension. Olley immediately set his team to work on the project.

Karl Ludvigsen's book *Corvette: America's Star-Spangled Sports Car*, included the following presentation that Olley made to the Society of Automotive Engineers in 1954. It summarized the challenges this assignment presented to his team: "On June 2, 1952, Chevrolet engineers were shown a plaster model of a proposed car of 102-inch wheelbase, for which a chassis was required. The need was to produce a sports car using components of known reliability with adequate performance, a comfortable ride, and stable handling qualities in something less than 7 months before showing (at the 1953 Waldorf Astoria Hotel) and 12 months before production. There was not much time."

Olley's chassis for the would-be Corvette featured boxed side members and a central X-member, both of which were incorporated into the car's frame to ensure increased rigidity. The completed frame weighed just 213 pounds.

One of Maurice Olley's design drawings shows the configuration and placement of the 1953 Corvette's chassis and steering assemblies. (Photo Courtesy General Motors LLC)

A Hotchkiss drive replaced Chevy's more-conventional torque-tube driveshaft assembly, and the location of the rear leaf springs dictated the placement of the car's rear axle. The rear axle assembly was adapted from a stock Chevy axle. It was supported by four leaf springs, each of which measured 51 inches long and 2 inches wide.

The car's front suspension featured a parallel wishbone layout with 1-inch Delco tubular shock absorbers mounted inside coil springs. A Saginaw worm and sector steering box was developed that featured a shorter (faster) 16.0:1 steering ratio. The steering linkage was constructed of a two-part track rod assembly that was split near the center, where it was activated by a trailing idler arm. Because of engine placement, the idler arm required a unique design developed by Olley's engineering group.

Olley's team confirmed that McLean's initial design produced a front-to-rear weight bias of 53-47 percent. After adding passengers and a fully loaded rear trunk, it reached a near 50-50 balance. Because of this, Olley recognized that a faster, more responsive braking system would be necessary. He achieved this by increasing the bore diameter of the master cylinder to 1 inch, which improved the rear braking bias from 44 percent to 47 percent.

Powering the EX-122/EX-52

As Olley's team worked on developing the chassis and underpinnings, Ed Cole began developing the car's powertrain. He selected Chevrolet's freshly minted large displacement (235.5 ci) "Stovebolt Six" 6-cylinder engine. The new engine featured aluminum pistons (a first in the history of Chevrolet) and a redesigned bottom end that included steel-backed inserted rod bearings.

The stock engine operated at a compression ratio of 7.5:1 and produced just 115 brake hp and 204 ft-lbs of torque. Cole knew the engine output would need to be increased, so he set to work bolstering the horsepower and torque. Working closely with the rest of the powertrain team, Cole's efforts resulted in improvements to the engine's induction, timing, and exhaust systems. These changes included the introduction of mechanical lifters paired to a new, long-duration camshaft; cast-iron pistons; dual springs for each valve; and the installation of three horizontally positioned Carter "YH" sidedraft carburetors mounted to a special aluminum manifold. The changes resulted in an improved compression ratio of 8.0:1 and an improved engine output of 150 bhp at 4,200 rpm. Additionally, torque output increased to 223 ft-lbs at 2,400 rpm.

One of the more controversial decisions made during powertrain development was Cole's choice of a Powerglide 2-speed automatic as the car's sole transmission. He selected it for two reasons. First, both the engine and transmission were Powerglide components and were designed to mate flawlessly with each other. Second, the shifter assembly had to be floor mounted, as the linkages for a column shifter would interfere with the rear-most of the three Carter carburetors. The location of the Powerglide transmission linkages worked perfectly with this arrangement.

Glass Reinforced Plastic

While installing an automatic transmission in a sports car may have been considered contentious, the idea of building a production automobile exclusively out of fiberglass was unprecedented. General Motors had made extensive use of fiberglass, or more precisely glass reinforced plastic (GRP), on several of its display and experimental cars but never one intended for mass production.

Earl, recalling the Alembic I, insisted his car's body panels be manufactured out of GRP. Cole also petitioned for the use of fiberglass. He received GM's consent after he proposed the EX-122 could serve as a testbed for the

One of the 1953 Motorama prototype cars is driven by Zora Arkus-Duntov at the Milford Proving Grounds. Early road testing allowed General Motors the opportunity to fully evaluate the Corvette in advance of production later that same year. As seen here, Duntov pushed the car to its limits (and beyond!) to measure the durability of its suspension under extreme driving conditions. (Photo Courtesy General Motors LLC)

The "Corvette" moniker only appeared in two places on the original Corvette: on the front fascia and on the rear decklid. All other badging, including the hood emblem, the horn button, and the front fenders said "CHEVROLET." (Photo Courtesy Dan Vaughn, author/developer of ConceptCarz.com)

use of GRP technology in other production vehicles.

Earl appointed a styling team to aid in the development of the car's body panels. Plaster molds were taken from the clay styling model. These were used to produce the 46 separate fiberglass panels for the Motorama show car. These individual components were then bonded together to create eight major subassemblies: the floor pan, hood, front fenders and fascia assembly, front gravel pan, driver and passenger doors, trunk lid, top cover, and the rear fenders/rear gravel pan assembly.

Despite having a scheduled completion date of early October, final assembly of the Motorama show car was not finished until late December 1952.

Duplicate body panels were produced from the original plaster molds, and at least one other drivable prototype was assembled during the same period as the show car. The second example, officially designated as Chevrolet Test Car No. 856, was completed on January 15, 1953, and immediately shipped to the GM Proving Grounds in Milford, Michigan. While there, body engineers from GM's Fisher Body division subjected the car to rigorous testing to determine its durability and drivability prior to production. This second prototype became known as the "Fisher Test Car."

A Corvette by Any Other Name

General Motors recognized that its new sports car needed a name that conveyed an image of speed and power to potential buyers. With just weeks left before its unveiling, General Motors turned to its own employees for inspiration. The automaker hosted a company-wide contest to officially name the Project Opel car. More than 300 submissions were received, but it was a name submitted by Myron E. Scott that would forever resonate with future consumers and would leave an indelible mark on automotive history.

Scott, who had worked for Chevrolet since 1937 as an assistant director of public relations, submitted the name *Corvette* for consideration. The name had previously been linked to fast-strike ships called "Corvettes" that were used by the US Navy throughout World War II. Scott believed the military connection to the Corvette moniker might appeal to American men (and potential automobile consumers) who had served in the war. Interestingly, use of the Corvette name started a tradition of

The Original Corvette Emblem

The original Corvette hood emblem was designed by Chevrolet interior designer Robert Bartholomew for the 1953 Motorama concept car. The emblem featured a pair of crossed flags: a checkered flag on the right and the flag of the United States of America on the left. The name *Chevrolet* was printed in gold capital letters above the flags, and below them was the name *Corvette* in a stylized cursive script.

Upon seeing the emblem for the first time, GM management insisted it be replaced immediately. The styling team was informed that use of the US flag as part of a logo or emblem on any commercial product was both inappropriate and illegal.

With just four days left before the Corvette's premiere, its hood and steering wheel emblems were quickly redesigned and replaced. Although the gold lettering and checkered flag remained, the US flag was replaced with a red one featuring a gold-colored Chevy bowtie and a fleur-de-lis.

The original Motorama Corvette concept car hood emblem, featuring the crossed United States and checkered flags, is on display at the National Corvette Museum in Bowling Green, Kentucky.

Unlike many concept cars of that era, the Motorama Corvette featured a fully furnished (and functional) interior. Everything, down to the speedometer, the instrument gauges, and the AM radio, operated as expected. (Photo Courtesy Dan Vaughn, author/developer of ConceptCarz.com)

The Motorama Corvette was nearly identical to the 1953 production model. The only identifiable differentiator was the inverted arrow/spear on the car's pair of rub rails and the placement of the Chevrolet logo below said arrow. (Photo Courtesy Dan Vaughn, author/developer of ConceptCarz.com)

nautical terms being applied to other Corvette concepts for decades, including the Mako Shark and the Sting Ray.

The Corvette Is Unveiled to the World

GM's first Motorama of the year opened its doors to the public on January 17, 1953, in the lobby of the Waldorf Astoria Hotel in New York City. As spectators flooded

The EX-122/EX-52 Corvette prototype is on display at the 1953 GM Motorama in the lobby of the Waldorf Astoria Hotel in New York City. The car was so well received by the public that just days after its introduction management decided to move the car directly to production. (Photo Courtesy General Motors LLC)

the show, they were greeted by a beautiful two-seat roadster finished in a shimmering Polo White with a contrasting Sportsman Red interior. The car featured several subtle chrome accents, including its grille, its front and rear bumpers, as well as an inverted fin/rub rail with *Chevrolet* in raised script beneath it. The *Corvette* marquee was displayed in raised letters just above the front grille and across the rear decklid just above the license plate enclosure.

The Corvette was an instant and overwhelming success. Within days of its unveiling, Chevrolet received an onslaught of inquiries asking when the car would be available at local dealerships, how much it would cost, and so on. While Chevrolet's top brass had anticipated the car would be a success, the outpouring of support it received was so overwhelmingly positive that any doubts about moving from concept to production evaporated overnight. On June 30, 1953, just over six months after its introduction in New York City, Chevrolet began production of the Corvette in Flint, Michigan.

Cars of the 1954 Motorama

Still reveling in the overwhelmingly positive response that the Corvette concept car had received when introduced at the Motorama the previous year, Earl and his team of designers had set to work. They began envisioning other dream cars that would capture the attention of the American public just as the Corvette had. Naturally, they turned to the 1953 Corvette as the source of their inspiration.

Earl's team began scheduling brainstorming sessions, wherein the team developed new versions of his original two-door "sporty" car. In a matter of weeks, three new dream cars based on the Corvette were developed, and all were introduced at the 1954 Motorama in New York City.

The success of the 1953 Corvette led to the development of other concept vehicles for the 1954 Motorama, including (front to rear) the Corvette Hardtop, the Nomad, and the Corvair. (Photo Courtesy General Motors LLC)

The 1954 Corvette Hardtop

The 1954 Corvette Hardtop was most like its production counterpart save for two unique features. First, this Corvette included exterior door locks. Second (and far more remarkable), it was equipped with a fixed, rounded fiberglass hardtop mounted atop the car. While a hardtop

The 1954 Hardtop concept was built using a production Corvette with a custom-built, fixed-but-detachable hardtop. It was also equipped with roll-up windows, a glove box on the right kick panel, updated door panels, and custom waffle-pattern upholstery. Both the car and the hardtop were painted pale yellow prior to being unveiled as part of the 1954 Motorama during its stop in Miami, Florida. (Photo Courtesy General Motors LLC)

would not be offered as an option on the Corvette until 1956, the 1954 Hardtop gave American consumers a preview of things to come.

The 1954 Corvette Corvair

Where the Corvette Hardtop had been nearly identical to its production counterpart, the 1954 Corvette Corvair was a superbly reimagined interpretation of what a potential fastback Corvette coupe would look like—and the car was spectacular!

The Corvair concept included the same front end, fenders, doors, and rear quarter panel assemblies as a stock Corvette. However, it featured a completely reimagined windshield and roof line. Where the original Corvette utilized forward-sloping A-pillars that followed the contour of the front windshield, the Corvair had vertical windshield pillars that merged with the front of the fastback roofline before sweeping back dramatically toward the rear of the car.

One of the most interesting design elements on the Corvair was its cowled enclosure at the base of the rear decklid. Allegedly influenced by European design, the stylized assembly could best be compared (at least in terms of appearance) to the engine exhaust port found on military jets from that era. The cowled enclosure housed a bright metal plate that contained approximately 270 Chevy bowties etched onto its surface. Both the car's rear license plate and a pair of backup lights were mounted onto this plate.

The Corvair included a cockpit ventilation system comprised of three small, rectangular intake vents mounted one atop the other along the trailing edge of the front fenders. These vents allowed air to pass into the car's interior. Slatted exhaust vents mounted in the car's C-pillars opened and closed manually via a control lever inside the car. The car also had a pair of slotted chrome vents on its hood designed to exhaust heat away from the engine.

The Corvair's interior was significantly less dramatic than its showy exterior. Except for the innovative ventilation system (air-conditioning would not be offered in a Corvette until 1963), the majority of its interior remained unchanged from the 1953 donor Corvette used to create it.

This rendering of the 1954 Corvette Corvair by Harley Earl's design team showcases several design elements that were also being considered for future iterations of the Corvette. (Photo Courtesy General Motors LLC)

Like the 1953 Corvette before it, the 1954 Corvette Corvair featured a 102-inch wheelbase, a 2-speed Powerglide transmission, and a 235.5-ci 6-cylinder engine that produced 150 hp. (Photo Courtesy Dan Vaughn, author/developer of ConceptCarz.com)

This GM press photograph of the 1954 Corvette Corvair was taken during the Motorama national tour. Images of this type were designed to entice people to attend GM's extravagant automotive show. (Photo Courtesy General Motors LLC)

All the same, the 1954 Corvette Corvair was a stunning entrant at the 1954 Motorama. The favorable response it received once more caused GM's management to consider approving the car for production. Likewise, the Corvair's unique "jet engine" cowling was contemplated as a possible styling upgrade to the 1955 Corvette. Both decisions were later overturned because of the 1954 Corvette's poor sales numbers.

It is generally believed that the 1954 Corvair was destroyed by General Motors at the end of that season's Motorama tour.

The 1954 Corvette Nomad

The 1954 Corvette Nomad was the third and final entry from Harley Earl's design team for that year's Motorama in New York City. Like the Hardtop and the Corvair, the Corvette Nomad shared several of the 1953 Corvette's design and mechanical elements, including a 235-ci Blue Flame 6-cylinder engine and Powerglide automatic transmission.

Unlike the other concept vehicles, the Nomad was built on a stock 1953 Chevrolet 115-inch chassis. It also offered a more expansive interior with upholstery wrapped in blue and white leather as well as several unique design details, including a ribbed headliner and wraparound rear glass.

The Nomad was designed by Carl Renner in one of the GM styling special studios. The car, which evolved from a series of sketches by Renner, was a unique four-seater variant of the Corvette. It shared most of the same front- and rear-end hardware as its sporty counterpart. However, the Nomad's elongated chassis had doors and other elements that were akin to Chevrolet's large sedans.

That's not to say the car looked commonplace in any

As seen in this rendering by the GM design team, the 1954 Nomad Concept car demonstrated how the Corvette might be readily transformed into a more practical family vehicle. In this instance, it transformed into a beautiful sport station wagon. (Photo Courtesy General Motors LLC)

The Corvette Nomad is displayed in the grand ballroom of New York City's Waldorf Astoria Hotel during the 1954 GM Motorama. Of the three Corvette-inspired cars present, the Nomad was far and away the crowd favorite. (Photo Courtesy General Motors LLC)

way. In fact, the 1954 Corvette Nomad was a two-door, six-passenger sport wagon with a low profile and aggressive stance. It cleverly combined the streamlined styling of a sports car with the utility and versatility of a station wagon. It also showcased technologies that were cutting edge at the time, including an electronically operated rear window that automatically retracted when the tailgate was unlocked. That same window could also be remotely controlled through a button mounted on the dashboard.

In *Corvette: America's Star-Spangled Sports Car,* Ludvigsen quoted Clare "Mac" MacKichan, the chief designer of the Chevrolet studios, as saying, "We thought this would be a good double cross. Nobody would expect to see a wagon version of the Corvette."

MacKichan's words proved to be prophetic.

The Corvette Nomad was an overwhelming success when it was unveiled to the world on January 21, 1954, in the grand ballroom of the Waldorf Astoria Hotel. The car was far and away the crowd favorite of the three Corvette concepts introduced that year. The public's response to it was so overwhelmingly positive that on the second day of the New York Motorama, Harley Earl phoned MacKichan and stated that he wanted the team to start work on a production version of the Nomad immediately.

Much of GM's top brass believed that more Nomads would sell if its design was attached to the popular Bel Air chassis instead of the Corvette. Reluctantly, Renner worked many of his Corvette-inspired design elements into the production version of the Nomad, which was introduced in 1955.

It is believed that the 1954 Corvette Nomad, like the Corvair, was destroyed at the completion of that year's Motorama circuit. Although there are reports that allege that as many as five Corvette Nomad concept vehicles were produced, there is virtually no evidence that these cars are in existence today.

Cars of the 1955 Motorama

By 1955, GM's Motorama had become recognized across the United States as the most extravagant auto show of the year, and why not? The company, which now operated 160 manufacturing plants globally, could certainly afford it. Besides, the free-to-the-public shows attracted massive crowds, which was the best advertising money could buy.

Some attendees came for the dancing girls and the live music, but the show's biggest draw each year was the incredible concept "dream" cars that filled the showroom floor. In 1955, General Motors welcomed more than two

This GM press photograph of the Corvette Nomad concept vehicle was taken during the 1954 Motorama national tour. The Nomad's marketing was so well received by the public that would-be buyers clamored for a production model of the Nomad after seeing this "dream car" station wagon. (Photo Courtesy General Motors LLC)

million people through the doors over the course of the show's five-city tour. The company received more than a million dollars in new automobile orders because of it.

The 1955 LaSalle II XP-32 Sedan and XP-34 Roadster

GM's Cadillac division first introduced the LaSalle brand of automobiles in 1927. It was one of four GM marque brands (LaSalle, Marquette, Viking, and Pontiac) developed by former GM Chairman and CEO Alfred P. Sloan. Each of these brands was developed to fill perceived price gaps within the established GM product portfolio.

Sloan created the LaSalle brand as a companion marquee for Cadillac and marketed the LaSalle line of automobiles as the second-most prestigious brand that General Motors offered at that time. LaSalle automobiles were manufactured by General Motors until 1940.

In the mid-1950s, some GM executives decided to revisit the LaSalle moniker as a possible product marquee to expand GM's offerings. Harley Earl, who had been instrumental in the earliest successes of the LaSalle automobile in the late 1920s, embraced the idea and put his team to work on two different concepts, both of which carried the name "LaSalle II."

The larger of the LaSalle II concepts was a four-door, six-passenger, hardtop sedan with suicide-style doors (XP-32, Shop Order 2217). It featured a curved windshield (similar to the one used on the 1955 Chevy Biscayne) that wrapped above and behind the driver's field of vision. The sedan's overall length was just 180.2 inches with an overall height of 69.5 inches and a wheelbase of 108 inches. This gave the car a uniquely sporty appearance, despite having an open, spacious interior. For comparison, the 2020 mid-engine Corvette has an overall length of 182.3 inches and a wheelbase of 107.2 inches.

The second LaSalle II was a small, two-passenger roadster (XP-34, Shop Order 2220). Notably shorter than the sedan, it featured a prominent front end with a pair of flared fenders as well as a highly stylized rear end that included partially open rear wheels just ahead

Although this incredible-looking concept car never made it to production, the 1955 LaSalle II Roadster included many prominent design elements, such as the body side coves that were "introduced" on the 1956 Corvette. (Photo Courtesy General Motors LLC)

The appearance of both the LaSalle II Sedan (pictured here at the 1955 Motorama in New York City) and the Roadster models led some automotive enthusiasts to speculate whether General Motors intended to resurrect the brand. (Photo Courtesy General Motors LLC)

Believed to have been destroyed at the conclusion of the 1955 Motorama, the LaSalle II roadster was recovered and restored by Joe Bortz and is now part of the Bortz Auto Collection. (Photo Courtesy Dan Vaughn, author/developer of ConceptCarz.com)

of two chrome bumperettes that housed the car's only taillights. The roadster measured 151.7 inches in overall length with a wheelbase of 99.9 inches. It was considerably more compact too, measuring just 42.8 inches tall.

Both cars shared the same ground clearance of 5.1 inches. Additionally, both vehicles rode on a set of 13-inch, turbine-style wheels that featured specially integrated brake drums cast into the center section of each wheel.

Neither of the LaSalle II show cars were divisional specific. Instead, the cars were given the LaSalle II moniker as an homage to Harley Earl and his original 1927 LaSalle. Ironically, it was Carl Renner (and not Earl) who was responsible for most of the LaSalle II's styling. Renner, who served as the assistant chief designer in GM's body development studio, introduced several unique design elements on the LaSalle II roadster. The concave side coves sculpted into the front fender and door assemblies became a prominent part of the restyled 1956 Corvette.

The 1955 LaSalle II dream cars also featured elements that were inspired by the canceled 1941 LaSalle, including six prominent front grille openings framed by a pair of Dagmar-style bullet guards that were integrated into the car's front bumper. "LaS" emblems, which became a LaSalle tradition during the division's final years of business in the late 1930s, were also featured prominently on the hood of each car.

Both cars were finished in Pearlescent White paint with contrasting blue (LeSabre Blue for the sedan, Bahama Blue for the roadster) body side coves.

Both cars were introduced at the 1955 Motorama fitted with compact, lightweight, aluminum V-6 engines. Although these engines were incomplete and nonfunctional when displayed, the finished units would have produced approximately 150 hp and featured aluminum heads and blocks, a fuel-injection system, and dual overhead camshafts. As it was, the displayed engines were little more than aluminum castings without any internal components installed.

Another unique design element of the LaSalle II was Renner's placement of the exhaust. The sedan featured a conventional exhaust system that exited through a port carefully cut into the trailing lower edge of the rear quarter panel. The roadster's exhaust system, including the car's muffler and exhaust pipes, were concealed behind the rocker sills and exited through an opening at the rear of the sill plate just ahead of the car's rear wheels.

The LaSalle II sedan and roadster had a significant and lasting impact on the future look of Harley Earl's original "sporty" car. In addition to introducing body side coves, the roadster's unique exhaust system undeniably inspired the next generation of designers to begin mounting side pipes (exposed this time) on future iterations of the Corvette.

The 1955 Biscayne (XP-37)

While not designed to be a showpiece depicting the potential evolution of the Corvette, it is worth noting that this elegant four-passenger, four-door dream car included a number of new design elements that eventually found their way into future iterations of Chevrolet's two-seater sports car.

The Chevy Biscayne is shown in this preconstruction drawing. Full-size renderings of this type were created to give designers a better means of communicating vehicle proportion. They were also used to seek preliminary design approval without the added cost and time of developing a clay model or full-scale mockup. (Photo Courtesy General Motors LLC)

Carl Renner

Carl Renner was an integral part of Harley Earl's "dream team" and played a significant role in the creation and development of the first Chevrolet Corvette.

Renner was born in Nuremburg, Germany, in 1923. His family moved to Detroit, Michigan, when he was just 4 years old. Growing up, Renner dreamed of working as an animator. He moved from Detroit to Los Angeles to pursue a career at Walt Disney Studios shortly after his 17th birthday.

In 1943, Renner landed a position as an animator at Walt Disney Studios. He quickly discovered that animation was not the creative outlet he had envisioned. Renner returned to Detroit and headed to GM styling with a portfolio full of sketches depicting his unique automotive designs. GM's management was impressed with his work and hired Renner as a junior designer for its orientation studio in 1945.

After World War II, General Motors resumed production of commercial automobiles. Many of Renner's design elements appeared on these new models. Management took notice of his work and promoted him to be a senior designer in 1946. He was also transferred to the Chevrolet design studio, where he was introduced to Harley Earl.

From 1950 to 1955, Renner played an active role in designing many of Chevrolet's production vehicles. As part of Earl's "ninth floor" crew at the body development studio, Renner became an integral part of the team responsible for the development of the original Motorama Corvette. The grille of the Project Opel concept was based on Renner's renderings.

In 1954, he was promoted to assistant chief designer in the body development studio. There, he led the development of the 1954 Corvette Nomad roofline as well as its deluxe steering wheel, grille, recessed hood, the "notch belt" fender line, parking lights, bumper guards, and side trim. He is credited with the introduction of the Corvette side cove in 1956 and the Corvette ducktail rear end in 1961.

Renner passed away on January 22, 2001. He was inducted into the Corvette Hall of Fame at the National Corvette Museum in Bowling Green, Kentucky, in 2007.

Carl Renner (left) has often been described as GM design's unsung hero. Although Renner helped design many of Chevrolet's vehicles throughout the 1940s and 1950s, there is almost no information available (including in his own notes) that identifies his individual contributions to the original Motorama Corvette. (Photo Courtesy General Motors LLC)

Renner (left, standing) remained a part of the Corvette's design group even after Earl's retirement in 1958. He is pictured, along with a young Larry Shinoda, next to an early full-scale design drawing of the second-generation Corvette convertible. (Photo Courtesy General Motors LLC)

Creating dream cars such as the Chevy Biscayne gave engineers a venue to showcase the latest automotive technologies and gave stylists a platform to gauge customer response to new advances in automotive design. In turn, the feedback received from consumers often influenced the development of future production vehicles, including the Corvette. (Photo Courtesy General Motors LLC)

The interior of the Chevy Biscayne featured a dropped floor that provided occupants with increased legroom and headroom. The car's thin-profile front bucket seats were designed to pivot outward, allowing both the driver and passenger easier entry into and out of the car. (Photo Courtesy Dan Vaughn, author/developer of ConceptCarz.com)

The sleek-looking Chevrolet Biscayne sedan was introduced in the lobby of the Waldorf Astoria Hotel on January 20, 1955, as a centerpiece of that year's Motorama. A highly stylized and futuristic-looking automobile finished in Atlantic Green throughout, the Biscayne was conceived and developed by Harley Earl and his team as "an exploration in elegance." It was introduced as a "true hardtop sport sedan" and wowed showgoers from the moment it was unveiled.

The Biscayne concept included a panoramic "Stratospheric" wraparound windshield that cascaded up and over the driver before blending with the roofline. From there, the roof panel swept back along a pair of chrome-plated side rails to a pair of triangular C-pillars. These same pillars also framed the car's rear window. A pair of B-pillars appeared as a fixture between the car's front and rear doors. In reality, they weren't pillars at all but rather the frame and guide track for the backdoor windows. Because the Biscayne lacked actual B-pillars, its front and rear doors instead latched to anchors on the car's rocker panels.

Although it shared the same 115-inch wheelbase as

many of Chevrolet's 1955 production models, the Biscayne's roofline was lowered a full 10 inches to give the car an aggressive, streamlined appearance. Even with its diminished roofline, the Biscayne's passengers still had plenty of headroom thanks to the car's unique perimeter frame, which allowed for the placement of the floor panels along the lower, inner edge of the chassis. The added space gave the cockpit an open, airy feeling.

Like the Corvette, the Biscayne's body panels were composed entirely of reinforced fiberglass. This enabled Earl and his designers to create beautifully sculptured bodylines that were far more dramatic than anything previously seen on cars from that era.

The Biscayne's front end contained many of the car's most interesting features. Its grille consisted of nine vertical slats finished with chrome accents framed by two chrome-trimmed coves on the front of each fender. The placement of conventional headlights in the front fascia was abandoned in favor of integrated lamp assemblies as a feature of the car's hood. Each headlight included a long fairing that tapered back along the length of the hood. Each of these ended just ahead of a functional inlet that was designed to allow cooling air into the car's interior.

A pair of signature coves were sculpted into the sides of the car. Each cove started at a point along the leading edge of the front doors and traversed the length of the car before wrapping around the trailing edges of the quarter panels. From there, the coves turned and framed the corners of the rear fascia, creating a recessed housing for the car's taillight assemblies. Although the placement of the body side coves was inverted (meaning they became more prominent toward the rear of the car), their inclusion on the Biscayne was a precursor to the body side coves that appeared the following year on the 1956 Corvette. Similarly, the rear taillamp assemblies and the slim chrome rear bumpers were ultimately integrated into the design of the second-generation Stingray.

The interior of the Biscayne featured thin shell front seats that pivoted outward toward their respective driver or passenger doors. They were engineered to create easier access when entering or exiting the vehicle. The swiveling seats were one of the only unique design elements introduced in the car's otherwise conventional interior.

Interestingly, most of the interior components installed in the Biscayne were "appearance-only" items. When presented at the Motorama, the car lacked side windows. The power window switches were not wired to anything. The same was true of the instrument panels. In fact, apart from a few solenoids and motors that had been installed to operate the car's doors while on display, the Biscayne had virtually no electrical systems to speak of when it was first introduced.

Although considerable attention had been put into the car's exterior aesthetics, the 1955 Biscayne's real purpose was to showcase Chevrolet's new 265-ci Turbo-Fire V-8 engine. The engine, which had been developed by Ed Cole and his engineering team, evolved from the drafting table to a viable powerplant in just four months' time. It was rated at 215 hp and featured a high-lift cam, a 4-barrel carburetor, and enough chrome to make it shine like a jewel beneath the car's hood.

Motorama Dream Cars (the Survivors)

At the completion of the 1955 Motorama national tour, the Biscayne (along with several other concept vehicles) was supposed to be transported to Warhoops Used Auto & Truck Parts in Sterling, Michigan, to be scrapped and destroyed. Instead, General Motors stored the Biscayne in one of its warehouses for several years. When the car, along with the LaSalle II roadster, was shipped to Warhoops for demolition in December 1959, both cars were spared from the crusher and secretly preserved by Warhoops owner, Harry Warholak Sr.

Today, the 1955 Chevrolet Biscayne, the LaSalle II sedan, and the LaSalle II roadster are the only surviving concept cars from GM's famed Motorama extravaganzas. All three cars were purchased from Warhoops junkyard in the late 1980s by car collector Joe Bortz. Bortz then spent the next several years restoring each of the iconic concept vehicles to their original show car condition. They are now part of the Bortz Auto Collection in Highland Park, Illinois.

Joe Bortz stands with the original 1955 Chevy Biscayne concept car at Warhoops Used Auto & Truck Parts in Sterling, Michigan. Bortz restored the car to its original show car condition after learning the Biscayne had survived the unfortunate fate of so many other Motorama show cars. Today, the Biscayne is a treasured part of the Bortz Auto Collection in Highland Park, Illinois. (Photo Courtesy Bortz Auto Collection)

CHAPTER 2

FROM SHOW CAR TO SPORTS CAR

I thought it wasn't a good car yet, but if they're going to do something, this looked good.
—Zora Arkus-Duntov
(on the 1953 Motorama Corvette)

No one would argue that Harley Earl, the original "Father of the Corvette," and his design studio changed the world when the Project Opel prototype was unveiled in January 1953. There is also no question that Zora Arkus-Duntov saved Earl's sporty car and transformed it into an American icon.

Zora Arkus-Duntov spent more than 20 years working as an automotive engineer for General Motors, including several years as Corvette's chief engineer. His extensive contributions to the Corvette and high-performance engine programs vastly improved consumer opinion of GM performance and racing divisions. Like Harley Earl, Duntov is often referred to as "the Father of the Corvette." (Photo Courtesy General Motors LLC)

Zora Arkus-Duntov

Zachary (Zora) Yakovlovich Arkus was the eldest son of wealthy, Russian-born Jewish parents Yakov "Jacques" Arkus and Rachel Kogan. The couple met in 1908 while pursuing their studies at university in Brussels, Belgium. Following a whirlwind courtship, they married in 1909. On December 25 of that same year, Rachel gave birth to Zora at St. Giles District Hospital. The couple graduated the following spring and returned home to St. Petersburg, Russia. Zora was less than a year old.

Once the family was situated in St. Petersburg, both Yakov and Rachel eventually found work within the Russian government. Because of their professional and political obligations, one of Zora's parents was frequently absent from the family home. It caused a significant strain on both their marriage and Zora's childhood. By the age of 11, Zora was running wild on the streets of St. Petersburg, causing trouble by instigating fights or accepting dangerous dares from friends and schoolmates.

On February 11, 1917, Zora's mother gave birth to his brother Yura. The brothers formed a strong bond early on, and Zora assumed the responsibility of caretaker and protector of his younger sibling. The close friendship that formed between the two boys lasted the rest of their lives.

A month after Yura's birth, the Russian monarchy was abolished, giving rise to political discord and eventual civil war. The Russian Revolution (as it is known today) had a profound impact on all of Russia, including its privileged upper class. Food, which had once been available in abundance, was now strictly rationed. Bread was in such short supply that it was often defended at gunpoint.

At 15 years old, Zora (shown here in his early teens) designed and constructed one of the first examples of a snowmobile/personal watercraft. He built the vehicle from a pair of retired aircraft fuselages and two 6-cylinder aircraft engines. This was the first recorded attempt by Zora to build a vehicle of his own design. (Photo Courtesy General Motors LLC)

Duntov (far right) had his first encounter with racing at the controls of his 350-cc German Diamant motorcycle. He loved the feeling of control that piloting the bike gave him, especially when driving it at high speeds. Duntov's passion for his motorcycle led him to begin racing it in open-class events at the Avus racetrack near Berlin. (Photo Courtesy General Motors LLC)

During the Russian Revolution, Zora's father, Yakov, found work as a mining engineer. The new job required him to leave home for weeks at a time, forcing Rachel and the boys to fend for themselves. Simultaneously, Rachel's work within a constantly shifting government consumed much of her time. Feeling overwhelmed and immensely lonely during Yakov's long absences, Rachel began seeking male companionship elsewhere. Yakov and Rachel eventually divorced.

In time, Rachel began a new relationship with an electrical engineer named Josef Duntov. Due to the harsh economic conditions that still existed for the family, Yakov was forced to remain part of a household that now included Rachel's new husband. Although Zora disliked Josef initially, he and Yura gradually developed an admiration for their stepfather. As a sign of respect toward their father and stepfather, the boys took the hyphenated last name of Arkus-Duntov.

Elfi Wolff met Duntov while studying dance in Berlin, Germany. By 1939, she relocated to Paris, France, with her family. She found work as a dancer there with the world-famous Follies Bergere, where she performed cabaret-style dance reviews across France. (Photo Courtesy General Motors LLC)

Duntov in Germany and Elfi Wolff

The entire Arkus-Duntov family moved to Germany in 1927 after Josef was transferred to Berlin by the Russian government. Zora enrolled at the University of Darmstadt as an electrical engineering major. His decision to pursue electrical, not mechanical, engineering was doubtless done out of deference for his stepfather. While in Berlin, Zora made two major discoveries that defined the rest of his life.

First, he found part-time employment at a Berlin motorcycle shop. The position afforded him the opportunity to pursue his lifelong passion for motorcycles. His first bike, a 350-cc German Diamant, enabled him to explore the streets of Berlin and the assortment of racetracks that surrounded the city. It wasn't long before Zora began competing in lower-level road racing.

Second, 20-year-old Zora Arkus-Duntov met 14-year-old dance protégé Elfriede "Elfi" Wolff via a chance encounter at a local Berlin café. Elfi was captivated

Recognizing that he needed a race car to pursue his racing ambitions, Duntov purchased this derelict 1922 Type 30 Bugatti from a friend in Berlin and restored it to good working order. He raced his Bugatti throughout his years in college. Additionally, he and Elfi (pictured together here) spent many of their early days together in it touring the German countryside. (Photo Courtesy General Motors LLC)

After attending the Grand Prix in Monte Carlo, Duntov decided he should build a race car of his own design. He called it "the Arkus." The car was plagued with problems from the start. However, the Arkus taught Duntov how to build a roadworthy race car, and the value of having proper financial backers when attempting to build one. (Photo Courtesy General Motors LLC)

by Duntov's good looks and piercing blue eyes. Duntov found himself likewise attracted to Elfi. Their unlikely meeting blossomed into a whirlwind romance. Unfortunately, fate had other plans for the new couple. Elfi's success as a dancer in Berlin presented her an opportunity to tour Europe for most of the 1930s. Love, it seemed, would have to wait.

Driven by his growing passion for racing and inspired by the continual advances being made in automotive technologies, Duntov left Darmstadt and his pursuit of electrical engineering behind. Instead, he enrolled as a mechanical engineering major at Charlottenburg Technical University in 1930. He continued to race recreationally throughout his college career, although he never advanced beyond the low-level racing tiers where he had first started competing.

Duntov graduated from Charlottenburg University in 1934 with his degree in mechanical engineering. After graduation, he began writing technical essays that described potential automotive technologies for the racetrack. His topics included the benefits of four-wheel drive and the advantages of building mid-engine sports cars. Duntov's writing was well received by the German automotive community. Several of his essays were later published in the German magazine *Auto Motor und Sport*.

World War II

Recognizing the economic and political declines taking place in Berlin, as well as the rise of anti-Semitism throughout Germany, Duntov and his family relocated

Yura and Zora (top left) and Elfi Wolff (bottom right) are pictured with (unidentified) family and friends after successfully escaping Nazi-occupied Paris for New York City at the height of World War II. (Photo Courtesy General Motors LLC)

to Paris in 1938. Soon after his arrival, Duntov was reunited with Elfi Wolff. She and her family had settled in Paris after Elfi received an invitation to join the popular French dance troupe Folies Bergère. The couple was married on February 11, 1939, just seven months before World War II began.

Following the outbreak of war across Europe, Yura and Duntov enlisted in the Armée de l'Air (the French Air Force). The brothers were stationed together in

Merignac, France. There, they served (though briefly) in a unit that supported an attachment of Potez bombers. France surrendered to Germany in June 1940, less than a year after the brothers enlisted.

Upon France's surrender, Duntov obtained exit visas for his entire family from the Spanish consulate in Marseilles. The family fled Paris for Lisbon, Portugal, where they found passage aboard the *Nyassa*, a refugee ship bound for Hoboken, New Jersey. After approximately 10 days at sea, the Arkus-Duntov family arrived in the United States. They were processed through Ellis Island and granted US citizenship on December 4, 1940.

After taking up residence in New York City, Duntov and his brother opened the Ardun Mechanical war munitions company in 1941. The fledgling company soon landed several lucrative government contracts to produce ship propeller shafts, bomb cones, and distributor valves, the last of which controlled the pitch of airplane propellers. Over the next four years, Ardun Mechanical grew to employ nearly 300 people.

Following the war, Ardun Mechanical became the Ardun Engine Company of New York. The company shifted its focus from munitions to high-performance automobiles. It was during this time that Duntov developed the Ardun overhead valve (OHV) cylinder head conversion kit for the Ford flathead V-8. The Adrun OHV conversion is still used in street rods today.

Duntov Discovers the Chevrolet Corvette

It is often said that fate is simply a matter of being in the right place at the right time. This certainly proved to be true for Zora Arkus-Duntov when he attended GM's Motorama in January 1953.

Duntov had already been seeking employment with Ford, Chrysler, and General Motors prior to his fateful visit to the Waldorf Astoria Hotel. He had been enticed by the almost limitless resources that the large automotive companies could provide to an ambitious engineer such as himself. The Ford Motor Company had been of particular interest to Duntov initially, due mostly to his previous affiliation with the Ford flathead V-8 engine.

Everything changed for Duntov the moment he laid eyes upon Chevrolet's brand-new, two-seater sports car. The Corvette's sleek fiberglass body with its low stance and understated-yet-refined swept-back design was one of the most beautiful automobiles he had ever seen. It literally stopped him in his tracks.

However, it did not take long for Duntov to realize that the Motorama Corvette was more sparkle than substance. He knew that a sports car equipped with an underpowered 6-cylinder engine and a 2-speed automatic transmission would not satisfy the demands of potential consumers interested in purchasing a performance-driven automobile.

Still, of all the cars introduced at that year's Motorama, Duntov believed that the Corvette was the one most likely to surpass its status as a "turntable queen" and become a viable production vehicle. Unable to get it out of his mind, Duntov refocused his professional aspirations on General Motors. He drafted a series of letters to Maurice Olley, whom he had previously corresponded with regarding a potential appointment with General Motors.

In his first letter dated January 28, 1953, Duntov complimented the work that General Motors had put into the Corvette: "I went to the Motorama and found the Chevrolet sports car breathtaking [sic]. I think this is the

Duntov moved to London and joined Allard Motor Company Ltd. in 1948 after selling his stake in the Ardun Motor Company. For the next four years, Duntov worked with owner Sydney Allard to manufacture and race hand-built British sports cars powered by Ford V-8 engines. His time with Allard provided Duntov with beneficial mechanical engineering experience without the added burden of managing his own business. (Photo Courtesy General Motors LLC)

Ed Cole

Ed Cole may not have played a leading role in the creation of the Corvette, but its continued existence today is the direct result of Cole's support of the original Motorama dream car during his time as Chevrolet's chief engineer and his approval of the first Corvette racing program while serving as Chevrolet's general manager.

Cole lived by the motto "Kick the hell out of the status quo!" He believed–as Harley Earl and Duntov did–that cars should be more than a reliable means of transportation. They should go fast and be exciting. When he was introduced to the Corvette, he knew it had the potential to be both.

Cole spent his entire career working for General Motors. He started with the company as a co-op student at the General Motors Institute (known today as Kettering University) in Flint, Michigan. After graduation, Cole joined General Motors as an engineer and began searching for opportunities to advance his career. His ambitions caught the attention of Thomas Keating, Chevrolet's general manager. Keating took a special interest in Cole and requested his assignment as Chevrolet's chief engineer in May 1952.

Cole's first major task as chief engineer was to develop a new engine platform that could supersede the Stovebolt Six, which was offered in most Chevrolet automobiles. Cole's engineering division spent the next several years developing a lightweight V-8 engine that became Chevy's gold standard for decades to come. To this day, the small-block Chevy V-8 reigns supreme as one of America's most successful and widely produced engine platforms.

During this era, Cole took a special interest in the creative visions of Harley Earl, Zora Arkus-Duntov, and Bill Mitchell. When Cole was promoted to Chevrolet general manager in 1956, he used his influence to keep the Corvette program alive by supporting first Duntov's and later Bill Mitchell's desires to transform the car from a well-intentioned beauty queen into a legitimate race car.

Over the course of his career, Cole directed the development of the Chevy Corvair, which helped Chevrolet break into the compact car market. The early success of the rear-engine, rear-wheel-drive Corvair made Ed Cole a household name in the automotive community, especially after he appeared on the cover of *Time* magazine on October 5, 1959. He was promoted to vice president of the GM car and truck group in 1961, to executive vice president in 1965, and finally to the president of General Motors in 1967.

Under Cole's management, General Motors became a global leader in safety research. He was one of the first presidents of a major automobile corporation to order the reduction of engine compression ratios based on emerging legislation that mandated stricter emission regulations. Cole drafted a declaration in 1972 that required the installation of catalytic converters in every new GM automobile by the 1975 model year.

Ed Cole retired from General Motors in 1974. After his retirement, he became the chairman and CEO of Checker Motor Corporation. On May 2, 1977, Cole was tragically killed while piloting his private twin-engine airplane near Kalamazoo, Michigan. That same year, he was inducted into the Automotive Hall of Fame.

On August 1, 1998, Ed Cole was inducted posthumously into the National Corvette Museum Hall of Fame.

Even though Ed Cole had no direct involvement in the Corvette's design, he recognized its potential from the moment he laid eyes on it. Cole's motto was "Kick the hell out of the status quo." After seeing the Corvette, he threw the status quo out the window and used his influence to ensure Harley Earl's sports car was produced. (Photo Courtesy General Motors LLC)

Ed Cole is seated at the wheel of the street-legal version of the Corvette SR-2 concept. This car, which had been designed and built at the request of Harlow Curtice, exemplified the look that Ed Cole envisioned for all future GM automobiles, most especially the Corvette. (Photo Courtesy General Motors LLC)

turning point from which European [sic] body designers can look for inspiration from Detroit."

In a second letter dated March 17, 1953, Duntov wrote to Olley again with the hopes of securing an interview with the company. In that letter, he told Olley that he would gladly travel from New York to Detroit "under my own steam" if an interview could be arranged. Olley responded to Duntov the following week, inviting him to Detroit at GM's expense. The ensuing interview went so well that Olley had his secretary mail an official employment application to Duntov on March 30.

General Motors

On Friday, May 1, 1953, Duntov joined General Motors as an assistant staff engineer. From the start, his aspirations were focused on advancing his own engineering visions and helping General Motors realize the full potential of the Corvette. This type of bravado was normally frowned upon in the bureaucratic culture of a large corporation like General Motors. Fortunately for Duntov, he reported to Maurice Olley who, in turn, reported to Ed Cole. Like Duntov, Cole was a nonconformist. He believed that strong engineering minds were paramount to GM's long-term success.

Despite existing geopolitical tensions between the Soviet Union and the United States, Cole hired Duntov because he was certain the Russian-born engineer had the pedigree to transform the Corvette into a real sports car. More than that, Cole was familiar with Duntov's work on the Ford flathead. He was confident Duntov could find ways to improve performance output from the new lightweight V-8 engines that Cole's engineering division had been developing.

In September 1953, Duntov was invited to speak at a Society of Automotive Engineers (SAE) gathering in Lansing, Michigan. Although Duntov's official role within General Motors was engineering support of its truck programs, his passion for the Corvette along with his well-established perspective on sports cars and how they fit within the American transportation industry made him an ideal presenter for the event.

During his presentation, Duntov discussed the potential for Corvette's long-term future in the United States. He believed the Corvette would eventually achieve commercial success with American consumers because it "provides the means to ascertain his (the driver's) individuality to himself and everybody around." He described it as "an experiment in ambitious engineering or as a visionary move that (would) open new markets and make our lives freer," as stated in *Zora Arkus-Duntov: The Legend Behind Corvette* by Jerry Burton.

Duntov's success on the SAE circuit proved that he was not only a talented engineer but also a capable speaker who could hold sway over public opinion.

"Thoughts Pertaining to Youth, Hot Rodders and Chevrolet"

Just six months into his career at General Motors, Duntov drafted the memo "Thoughts Pertaining to Youth, Hot Rodders and Chevrolet." In it, he described the challenges Chevrolet had been experiencing in the automotive marketplace. He also outlined a list of changes that needed to be made to revitalize the organization for future generations of consumers. First published on December 16, 1953, the memo is remembered as one of the most important documents ever written by Duntov in his long career at General Motors.

Duntov began his memo with the assertion that hot rodding was a rapidly growing subculture within the automotive world and that the majority of hot rodders were Ford owners. He explained that most hot rod magazines were packed cover to cover with images of and articles about custom-built Ford automobiles. Print media saturation, it seemed, held considerable sway over consumer influence.

Although Chevrolet lacked credibility within the hot-rodding community, Duntov argued that installing Chevy's new V-8 engine into a Corvette would quickly improve that demographic's perception of the car (and by association, the company). He believed it was just a matter of time before hot rodders started racing the Corvette, so long as they could also modify it to their own specifications.

Duntov concluded that Chevrolet should develop a performance parts program. It could provide higher-performance parts for Chevy's V-8 engine: more radical camshafts, manifolds, pistons, and the like. Additionally, it could offer hardware to fortify the chassis, including improved brake hardware and more capable suspension components.

The "Thoughts Pertaining to Youth, Hot Rodders and Chevrolet" memo elevated Cole's professional opinion of Duntov. He used his influence to develop the very performance parts program Duntov had so brilliantly outlined. He also made certain Duntov's talents were channeled into Chevrolet's engine program.

While the opportunity to be part of Chevrolet's research and development team was a momentous turning point in his career, Duntov still yearned to be part of the Corvette design and development group. That opportunity came less than a year later when Duntov penned his next memo and changed the course of the Corvette forever.

Corvette in Trouble

Duntov's initial memo carried a warning within its commentary that was becoming increasingly evident in the Corvette's sales numbers: lackluster performance equated to lackluster sales. It was true that Chevrolet manufactured more than 10 times as many Corvettes in 1954 as it had in 1953, but nearly a third of them sat unsold at Chevrolet dealerships by year's end. The problem was obvious: the Corvette looked good in the showroom but performed poorly on the road and at the track.

On October 15, 1954, following an announcement made by an anonymous GM executive that indicated the Corvette was "finished," Duntov drafted a memo to Ed Cole and Maurice Olley to try and save his beloved sports car. He stated that the Corvette in its current form "did not have value for the money." He reasoned that a consumer's desire to purchase a car was based upon two things: practical values and emotional appeal. Since the Corvette lacked practical value (it could only accommodate two passengers with limited luggage space), it needed to provide greater emotional appeal. If the Corvette was to succeed as a sports car, he concluded, it needed to perform like a race car.

Duntov predicted that the 1955 Corvette, now equipped with a V-8 engine, would change consumer perception of the car. He also hinted that Ford's new Thunderbird, which was being marketed as a rival to the Corvette, would be a major embarrassment to General Motors if it succeeded where the Corvette had not. Duntov concluded this memo by proposing that Chevrolet "reimagine" the Corvette through the development of a team with the singular focus of continued advancement of the car as a serious performance vehicle.

"I am convinced," wrote Duntov, "that a group with a concentrated objective will not only stand a chance to achieve the desired result, but devise ways and means to make the operation profitable in a direct business sense."

Duntov's memo was the catalyst that saved the Corvette program from being terminated. Chevrolet was not about to let Ford beat them at their own game. It also established Zora Arkus-Duntov as the "go-to" resource for anything Corvette related. Although Ed Cole remained the final authority on all decisions made within Chevrolet's engineering department, Duntov became the final authority on the Corvette . . . at least for now.

The 1954 EX87 "Test Mule"

The EX87 was not developed as a Corvette concept car in the conventional sense. Instead, it is recognized as one of the early concept cars because of a notable engine modification it received that revolutionized the Corvette's engine program forever.

Zora Arkus-Duntov is in the cockpit of the EX87 Corvette. Even before he was assigned to the Corvette program, Duntov realized that Chevrolet's new sports car needed to perform well on the racetrack if it was ever going to be taken seriously by consumers. (Photo Courtesy General Motors LLC)

The EX87 started life as a 1954 Corvette "test mule," which had been set up to evaluate an experimental 283-ci V-8 engine being developed under the guidance and direction of Ed Cole. The car's "EX87" designation had been assigned to the Corvette by Chevrolet to track the "mule" throughout the engine's testing cycle.

Just as Duntov is known as the "Father of the Corvette," Elfi is known as its "First Lady." Elfi frequently traveled with Duntov to racetracks and road courses all over the country. During Duntov's test runs at Pikes Peak, she watched for oncoming traffic while sitting in a Corvette strategically parked farther up the mountain. (Photo Courtesy General Motors LLC)

Zora Arkus-Duntov saw the EX87 prototype as an opportunity to publicly demonstrate the Corvette's potential as a high-performance vehicle. He proved that a Corvette equipped with Cole's newly developed V-8 engine could handle the rigors of racing to the top of Pikes Peak. Now, he wanted to prove that a production Corvette equipped with the same engine could reach a top speed of 150 mph. Cole loved the idea and immediately gave consent for Duntov to proceed with his plan.

A second tracking number (5951) was allocated to the EX87 before it was reassigned to Duntov's engineering division in the fall of 1955. Duntov set to work on the car at once. First, he added an underpan to reduce drag. Next, he replaced the car's factory windshield with a small, curved plexiglass windscreen and enclosed the passenger's side of the cockpit with a fiberglass tonneau cover. Finally, he fabricated a headrest with a trailing tailfin designed to increase the car's stability at high speeds.

Setting Records in the Mule

Duntov began making trial runs in the car at GM's new Technical Center in Warren, Michigan. Despite his improvements to the car's aerodynamics, it still lacked the power to achieve speeds even close to 150 mph.

Duntov turned his attention to the car's engine. He estimated it would need to produce approximately 30 more horsepower than the 283-ci engine could deliver. Drawing on past experience, Duntov increased the engine's displacement to 307 ci. He also designed a new camshaft that added the horsepower he needed by improving positive acceleration.

Duntov presented his camshaft design to Cole's engineering team for review. Initially, the cam was criticized as being "unorthodox" when compared to other camshafts already being used in the V-8 engine. Duntov's camshaft had longer inlet and exhaust opening durations and less valve lift than its counterparts, both of which led Cole's engineers to question its viability.

Unwilling to wait for their final approval to produce a sample camshaft, Duntov loaded the EX87/5951 Corvette onto a trailer and transported the car to GM's Mesa Proving Grounds to begin testing the car with its fortified V-8 engine. Upon further review, Duntov's camshaft was approved for production. A sample unit was manufactured and shipped to Mesa.

Just as Duntov had predicted, the custom camshaft brought the EX87's engine to life. On December 20, 1955, Duntov piloted the Corvette to a top speed of 163 mph at 6,300 rpm in the arid Arizona air. Duntov felt confident that the engine, with its newly minted "Duntov Cam," would be good enough to achieve the 150-mph goal during its test run on the sandy beaches of Daytona.

A 1956 Corvette (No. 6901) was used for the record-breaking test run at Daytona. The EX87's engine, transmission, and rear axle, as well as its tachometer and instruments, were all removed and reinstalled in the second Corvette chassis. In January 1956, running wide open on the sandy beaches of Daytona, Zora Arkus-Duntov clocked a two-way average speed of 150.583 mph in the flying mile.

Duntov's work on the EX87 and his subsequent successes in Mesa and Daytona Beach began to change

Duntov pilots the EX87 at the GM Proving Grounds in Mesa, Arizona. While not a concept car in the strictest sense of the word, the custom-built 1954 Corvette "test mule" became the first Corvette prototype/concept for future racers, including the SR-2 and the SS models. (Photo Courtesy General Motors LLC)

Duntov pilots the modified 1956 Corvette (No. 6901) at Daytona in late December 1955. This car was equipped with most of the EX87's original underpinnings, including the fortified V-8 engine, which enabled the EX87 to hit 163 mph in the dry air of Arizona. (Photo Courtesy General Motors LLC)

the way car enthusiasts around the world looked at the Corvette. It was from these humble beginnings that the Corvette's reputation as a serious sports car started to take root.

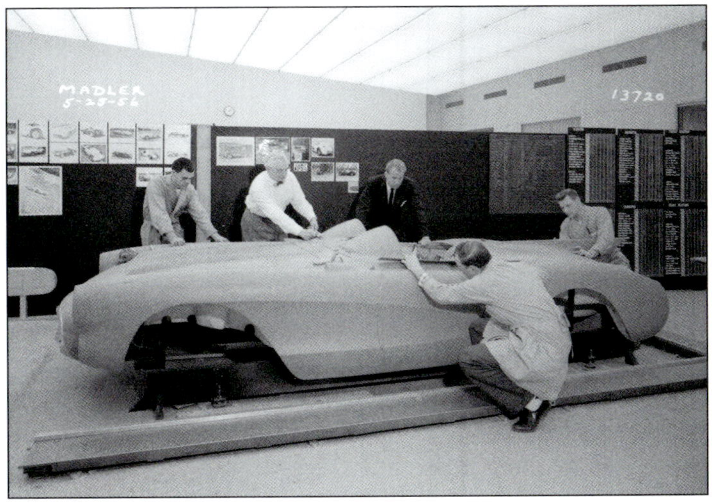

The look of the SR-2 Corvette was styled by GM designer Dave Wheeler (pictured in the suit) and a team of clay modelers between May and June 1956. Once the model was complete, the design elements captured in clay were reproduced on the body of the 1956 Corvette donor car (VIN 2522). Earl's original SR-2 called for the smaller spoiler seen on this model. (Photo Courtesy General Motors LLC)

From the Turntable to the Racetrack

Despite being a major attraction for automotive consumers across the United States, General Motors elected to discontinue its annual Motorama show after 1956, although two additional shows were later hosted in 1958 and 1961. Instead, the budget previously allocated for these auto show extravaganzas was funneled into Chevrolet's research division. The intent was to develop the Corvette into a purpose-built race car that could win at events such as Le Mans and Sebring.

Even as he neared retirement, Harley Earl felt strongly that the Corvette's legacy was still very much his to protect. He recognized that the car's continued success relied heavily on the talents and foresight of men such as Zora Arkus-Duntov and Ed Cole, both of whom had proven they shared Earl's vision of what the Corvette could become. Armed with this certainty, Earl's final act in the evolution of the Corvette proved to be a fundamental part of its long-term success.

The 1956 Corvette SR-2 Sebring Racer

The 1956 Corvette SR-2 Sebring Racer was one of the last Corvette concepts developed under the tutelage of Harley Earl. The SR-2 was a respected race car in its own right, and it was the precursor of the Corvette SS, a purpose-built racer envisioned by Earl and fully realized by Zora Arkus-Duntov. Both the SR-2 and the Corvette SS catapulted the first-generation Corvette onto the world automotive racing stage (at least briefly) as a respected contender in the sport.

The original SR-2 was commissioned by Harley Earl for his son Jerry. Much like his father, Jerome "Jerry" Earl discovered a passion for cars and for auto racing early in life. When he announced his intention to compete at Sebring during the 1956 racing season, in a Ferrari 250 MM no less, the elder Earl stepped in and instead

Although stories vary, it has been said that the SR-2 was developed by Harley Earl for his son Jerry after GM executives learned of the younger Earl's desire to race a Ferrari at Sebring. At GM's insistence, Harley allegedly bribed his son out of driving the Italian race car by promising to build him his very own Corvette racer. (Photo Courtesy Dan Vaughn, author/developer of ConceptCarz.com)

The dashboard of the SR-2 racer was reworked to include a centrally mounted tachometer and several analog gauges in the driver's direct line of sight. The additional gauges were overlaid on the existing dashboard assemblies. Likewise, the factory windshield was removed and two small windscreens were put in its place. (Photo Courtesy Dan Vaughn, author/developer of ConceptCarz.com)

appointed GM automobile designer Robert Cumberford to design a Corvette race car.

The first SR-2 was developed atop the chassis of a 1954 production model Corvette (No. 2522), which Earl pulled off the St. Louis assembly line. The car was then shipped to the GM design center in Warren, Michigan, along with shop order No. 90090, which stated the car was to receive "racing modifications and cosmetic additions."

The car featured an extended front end with a more aggressive-looking grille framed by a pair of driving/foglights and sculpted fiberglass fairings in place of the factory headlights. Its original hood was removed and replaced with a custom unit that included a pair of raised ridges and a large, central vent.

Farther back, two small racing windscreens replaced the factory windshield, a pair of functional air scoops were incorporated into the rear section of the body side coves, and a centrally located, low-hung tailfin was mounted atop the rear deck assembly. The car was finished in metallic blue paint with bright aluminum accentuating the body side coves.

A 265-ci V-8 with dual 4-barrel carburetors provided power to the SR-2 Corvette. Like the EX87 before it, the SR-2's engine was fitted with a Duntov camshaft to bolster horsepower. The engine was then mated to a 3-speed manual transmission. The SR-2 benefited from the installation of heavy-duty suspension components previously evaluated by expert driver John Fitch during testing of his original SR racers at Sebring in March 1956. The car was equipped with four-wheel drum brakes with "Cerametallic" (ceramic-metallic) brake linings and Halibrand mag wheels.

At the Racetrack

Earl's SR-2 Corvette race car was completed and ready for testing by mid-June 1956. It was registered with the Sports Car Club of America (SCCA) later that same month and was officially designated SCCA Car No. 144. The car was then shipped to Elkhart Lake, Wisconsin, where it made its inaugural run on June 24 at the June Sprints at Road America.

Jerry Earl was the first to drive the car at Road America, although only briefly. Unaccustomed to the power and handling of the SR-2, Earl lost control of the car during his first practice session and spun out uncontrollably. Fortunately, neither he nor the car sustained any damage.

Dr. Dick Thompson, a dentist and professional driver who had caught the attention of Zora Arkus-Duntov while racing his production Corvette in SCCA sanctioned events, stepped in to pilot the SR-2 racer at Road America. Even with his considerable experience behind the wheel, Thompson struggled to pilot the car around the track. He acknowledged that the car showed enormous potential, but he also noted that it felt excessively heavy and lacked the necessary braking power to handle the rigors of the racecourse.

Jerry Earl is seated in the cockpit of the SR-2 Corvette race car. Despite a mishap at Road America that forced him to retire early from his first race in the new car, Jerry piloted the SR-2 at various SCCA races throughout the 1956 and 1957 race seasons. (Photo Courtesy Richard Earl, automotive historian, and grandson of Harley Earl)

Thompson ended up finishing in 16th place overall.

Despite Thompson's criticisms of its weight and braking limitations, the SR-2 Corvette continued to compete at select SCCA events throughout the remainder of the 1956 and 1957 racing seasons, most often with Jerry Earl behind the wheel. Earl achieved a career-best fifth-place finish in the SR-2 at the SCCA Milwaukee Regionals. Stock car driver Buck Baker piloted the SR-2 to a second-place finish at the 1957 Daytona Speed Weeks in the flying mile, achieving an average top speed of 152.86 mph.

Nicknamed the "Flying Dentist," Dr. Richard Thompson served as Chevrolet's unofficial test driver throughout the late 1950s and early 1960s. Thompson's success behind the wheel of cars like the SR-2 and the Corvette SS helped transform the brand into a well-respected sports car. (Photo Courtesy General Motors LLC)

The Bill Mitchell SR-2

A second example of the SR-2 racer was built for Bill Mitchell in the fall of 1956. Mitchell, who worked as director of design under Harley Earl, had also been an avid fan of sports car racing. Although he was still two years away from replacing Earl as GM's vice president of design, he had already garnered enough clout within General Motors to order the construction of a second SR-2. He even took the liberty of changing the original design to his personal specifications.

Mitchell's SR-2 differed from the one built for Jerry Earl in several ways. The most notable outward difference

Bill Mitchell stands beside his SR-2 Corvette race car at the GM Tech Center. The second of three cars to wear the SR-2 moniker, it was designed by and built specifically for Bill Mitchell in the fall of 1956. Mitchell raced his SR-2 at venues including Daytona, Sebring, and Road America. It also made frequent appearances at auto shows across the United States. (Photo Courtesy General Motors LLC)

The original 1956 Corvette SR-2 survived a six-year road racing career without a single crash. It was operated briefly as a drag racer before becoming part of several collections over the next 30 years. In 2015, collector Irwin Kroiz acquired and restored the SR-2, debuting it at the 2018 Amelia Island Concours d'Elegance, where it won Best in Class–Race Cars (1946–1957). (Photo Courtesy Dan Vaughn, author/developer of ConceptCarz.com)

The engine built by Smokey Yunick featured an as-yet unreleased Rochester fuel-injection system. The Rochester company worked with Yunick and allowed him to install its fuel injection system on the 283-ci engine he'd built for Mitchell's SR-2. This program paved the way for the installation of Rochester fuel injection on production Corvettes. (Photo Courtesy Dan Vaughn, author/developer of ConceptCarz.com)

A GM press photo shows race driver Betty Skelton behind the wheel of Bill Mitchell's SR-2 Corvette. Mitchell's SR-2 included a larger, more dramatic rear fin trailing off the headrest. It also featured a single-passenger cockpit with a glass cover that closed over its occupant like the canopy of a World War II–era fighter plane. (Photo Courtesy General Motors LLC)

was that the car featured a taller tailfin, reminiscent of the one installed by Duntov on the EX87. Also like the EX87, the new spoiler integrated into a streamlined nacelle that surrounded the driver's headrest. Its placement behind the cockpit required the rear decklid to be rehinged to open backward. The car also received additional ducting to improve brake cooling during harsh driving conditions. It was finished in red with white striping.

Mitchell Makes It Faster

Bill Mitchell hired Henry "Smokey" Yunick, a well-respected NASCAR mechanic, to improve engine output in his SR-2 and to reduce its overall weight. Mitchell didn't want a car that just showed up on race day, he wanted one that could dominate the field and be first to the checkered flag. Mitchell's SR-2 was to be an all-out race car.

The donor Corvette's original 283-ci engine was bored and stroked to a 336-ci displacement. Like the powerplant in the first SR-2, the engine received the high-lift Duntov Cam. A new Rochester fuel-injection system was also added, along with advanced Packard Electric solid-core stainless-steel, high-tension ignition wires and a higher-voltage ignition coil.

A ram-air scoop was installed along the driver-side inner fender well. It delivered cooling air to the engine from an opening in the front grille. Finally, an optional 48-gallon fuel tank was installed for long-distance racing.

Most of the car's weight reduction was accomplished through the installation of thinner body panels and modifications made to the cockpit. Some of its panels were so thin that the fiberglass matting could be seen when viewed at certain angles.

In the cockpit, the factory Corvette seats were replaced with smaller, lighter bucket seats designed by Porsche. All nonessential hardware was removed from the car's interior, and fiberglass components replaced their heavier steel counterparts. Even the interior door panels were swapped out for fiberglass panels. When complete, the Mitchell SR-2 weighed just 2,200 pounds, which was approximately 700 pounds lighter than Earl's original example!

In hindsight, Mitchell's improvements to the original SR-2 were both obvious and necessary to the car's future successes at the racetrack. Recognizing the advantages of Mitchell's design, Earl had the original SR-2 similarly modified during the winter of 1956. It received a taller tailfin and many of the same weight-saving changes to its cockpit.

In February 1957, Mitchell took his SR-2 to Daytona Beach Speedweek. To make the car as aerodynamic as possible, he had it fitted with a fully enclosed canopy, full Moon-disc wheel covers, and semi-enclosed rear wheels. During that event, the Mitchell Corvette SR-2 was piloted by Buck Baker. It reached a top speed of 93.047 mph in the standing mile and 152.886 mph in the flying mile.

Bill Mitchell's SR-2 Corvette was at the inaugural Amelia Island Concours d'Elegance. The car, which is now owned by retired Chevrolet Development Engineer Bill Tower, received the Earl B. Hadlow award at that event. The car remains part of Tower's private collection. (Photo Courtesy Dan Vaughn, author/developer of ConceptCarz.com)

The third and final Corvette SR-2 was built for Harlow Curtice. The car came equipped with a stainless-steel removable top, fuel injection (one of the first Corvettes ever to be so equipped), and a 4-speed synchronized manual transmission. (Photo Courtesy General Motors LLC)

Harlow Curtice was the president of General Motors from 1953 to 1958. He was responsible for the revitalization of General Motors during the early 1950s. Under his regime, the corporation became the first ever to earn one billion dollars in a single year. He was also responsible for the inclusion of Harley Earl's original Corvette concept car in the 1953 Motorama at the Waldorf Astoria Hotel. (Photo Courtesy General Motors LLC)

Mitchell's racer also competed in the 12 Hours of Sebring that year. It was piloted by drivers Paul O'Shea and Pete Lovely. Despite being plagued with excessive pit stops, the SR-2 took the checkered flag, coming in seventh in class (S5.0) and sixteenth overall. This victory proved beyond a doubt that the Corvette was a capable race car.

A third example of the SR-2 was built for GM president Harlow Curtice. It was a common practice in those days for high-ranking executives at General Motors to drive custom-designed/custom-built automobiles. Curtice had favored the styling of the original SR-2, so he ordered a stock 1956 Corvette to be modified at the GM Technical Center to look like Earl's race car.

Curtice's SR-2 was built to be driven on the open road and lacked the underpinnings of its race car counterparts. Instead, it came equipped with all of GM's latest factory offerings, including a heater, an AM Signal-Seeking radio, a parking brake alarm, courtesy lights, windshield washers,

Harlow Curtice's SR-2 came equipped with a smaller fin like the original fin installed by Harley Earl on his son's racer (before the Earl SR-2 was modified in the winter of 1956). Although the finished car was presented to Curtice for his personal use, the Curtice SR-2 spent much of its first year on the auto show circuit. (Photo Courtesy General Motors LLC)

Betty Skelton

Betty Skelton set 17 aviation and race car records over the course of her amazing career. While many of these records still stand today, she is best remembered for changing the way women were perceived in the fields of aviation, motorsports, and business. (Photo Courtesy General Motors LLC)

Betty Skelton pilots a Chevrolet Corvette convertible down the sands of Daytona Beach. She set three women's land speed records at the Daytona Beach Road Course, including a top speed record of 156.99 mph in a 1956 Corvette. (Photo Courtesy General Motors LLC)

Known as the "First Lady of Firsts," Betty Skelton was a commercial and aerobatic pilot, a radio personality, a professional racer and test car driver, an astronaut trainee, a spokesperson for Chevrolet, a real estate agent, and a published author.

She was born on June 28, 1926. From the time she was a toddler, Skelton had a fascination with the airplanes that flew over her Pensacola, Florida, home. At age 8, she began reading books about aviation and hitching rides with pilots at the local municipal airport. There, she befriended Kenneth Wright, a Navy ensign, who began instructing her how to fly his Taylorcraft airplane. She was just 12 years old.

Skelton earned her private pilot's license at age 16 and immediately qualified for the Women Airforce Service Pilots (WASP) program. The minimum age for the program was 18½, so she had no choice but to wait to join. Unfortunately, the program was discontinued four months before she reached the eligible age. Never deterred, she sought employment with Eastern Airlines, as a clerk at first, while she worked to earn her commercial pilot license. She became a certified flight instructor at age 19 and joined the Civil Air Patrol shortly thereafter.

Skelton's father organized an amateur airshow in 1945 as a fundraiser for the local Jaycees. He approached Skelton about performing in the show. Having never done aerobatics, she borrowed a Fairchild PT-19 and taught herself how to loop and roll the plane.

In just two weeks' time, she became proficient at basic aerobatic maneuvers. She purchased a 1929 Great Lakes 2T-1A Sport Trainer biplane and started her first career as a professional aerobatic pilot. During this time, she piloted airplanes, blimps, gliders, helicopters, and jets. She was the US Female Aerobatics Champion in 1948, 1949, and 1950.

Betty joined the Campbell-Ewald advertising company in 1956 and represented General Motors as its first woman technical narrator at major auto shows, on television, and in print media. She became the official spokesperson for Chevrolet, which allowed her to continue working closely with the Corvette for much of her career. (Photo Courtesy General Motors LLC)

In February 1954, Skelton was invited to drive the pace car at Daytona during Speed Week. She piloted a Dodge sedan across Daytona beach to a speed of 105.88 mph, setting a new women's stock-car speed record. Skelton had discovered what she wanted to do next in her career.

During the next two years, Skelton became the first woman to receive an Automobile Association of America auto race driver's license, the first female test driver in the automobile industry, the first woman to drive a jetcar over 300 mph at the Bonneville Salt Flats, and the first to break Cannonball Baker's 40-year record for the fastest Transcontinental Auto Race, driving from New York to Los Angeles in 56 hours and 58 minutes.

Skelton became an advertising executive with Campbell-Ewald in 1956 and began working with General Motors on its TV and print ads. General Motors hired her to become the first female technical narrator at Motorama and other major auto shows. Skelton frequently attended and participated in events where the Corvette was being showcased. During one such event, she set the woman's land speed record of 145.044 mph behind the wheel of a Corvette.

Skelton worked side by side with Harley Earl, Zora Arkus-Duntov, and Bill Mitchell. She piloted many of the Corvette concepts developed by Chevrolet, including the EX87 and Bill Mitchell's SR-2. Harley Earl and Bill Mitchell designed a special translucent gold Corvette for her, which she drove as the official pace car of the 1956 Daytona 500. Shortly thereafter, Skelton became the official spokesperson for Chevrolet.

Skelton helped launch the publication *Corvette Quarterly* and served as its editor for several years. In 1959, she was invited by NASA to undergo the same physical and psychological testing as the first seven Mercury astronauts. Although women weren't launched into space until 1983, Skelton was the first woman to qualify for the astronaut program. The other astronauts, whom became known as the "Mercury 7," even gave her the nickname "7½."

Skelton married Hollywood television director/producer and navy veteran Donald A. Frankman in 1965. In 1969, she became vice president of Campbell-Ewald's new women's marketing and advertising division. She retired from the agency in 1976. The couple moved to Winter Haven, Florida, that same year. In 1977, she started work as a real estate agent and published her book *Little Stinker*, which was named after her original 1929 biplane.

Her first husband passed away in 2001. That same year, she was inducted into the National Corvette Museum's Hall of Fame in the racing category.

At age 79, Betty Skelton married Dr. Allan Erde, a retired naval surgeon. The couple spent their remaining years together at a retirement community in Florida. While most residents relied on golf carts to get around, Betty was frequently seen driving her bright red C5 Corvette convertible. In 2008, Betty was quoted as saying, "I just like to go fast. I enjoy it. I really do."

Betty Skelton passed away on August 31, 2011.

whitewall tires, power windows, and a power-operated folding top. It also featured Daytona wire wheels instead of the Halibrand knock-off wheels used on the race cars.

The car's exterior was modified to look like the other SR-2 Corvettes. It received an extended nose and a reimagined hood with futuristic-looking louvers and chrome supports (a precursor of the hood installed on the 1958 Corvette). It also had anodized aluminum side coves with custom air scoops similar to those installed on the racers, although these scoops were strictly cosmetic. On the rear decklid, a special "shark fin" spoiler finished the look. The car was painted a custom-mixed Blue Metallic specially chosen by Curtice (the same color he preferred on all his personal automobiles).

A 283-ci V-8 engine with fuel injection was installed under the custom hood. It was paired to a T-10 BorgWarner 4-speed transmission. Curtice's SR-2 was the only "production" Corvette built in 1956 equipped with either fuel injection or the special T-10 transmission, although both options were offered in later model years.

Harlow Curtice drove his SR-2 for several years. After Curtice's passing in 1962, the car changed hands several times among prominent Flint business owners before being purchased by Corvette Collector and Specialist Richard Fortier in the early 1980s. It is believed that the car remains in the family's private collection to this day.

The 1957 XP-64 Corvette SS

Earl's early aspirations to create the Corvette SS originated from lessons he'd learned while racing the SR-2. Although public opinion of the Corvette had improved

The XP-64 was the first purpose-built Corvette race car in the history of the brand. The car was inspired by both the Jaguar D-Type and the Mercedes-Benz 300 SL race cars. Its body was constructed of lightweight magnesium (in place of fiberglass) to help reduce the car's overall weight. (Photo Courtesy Kolecki Photography)

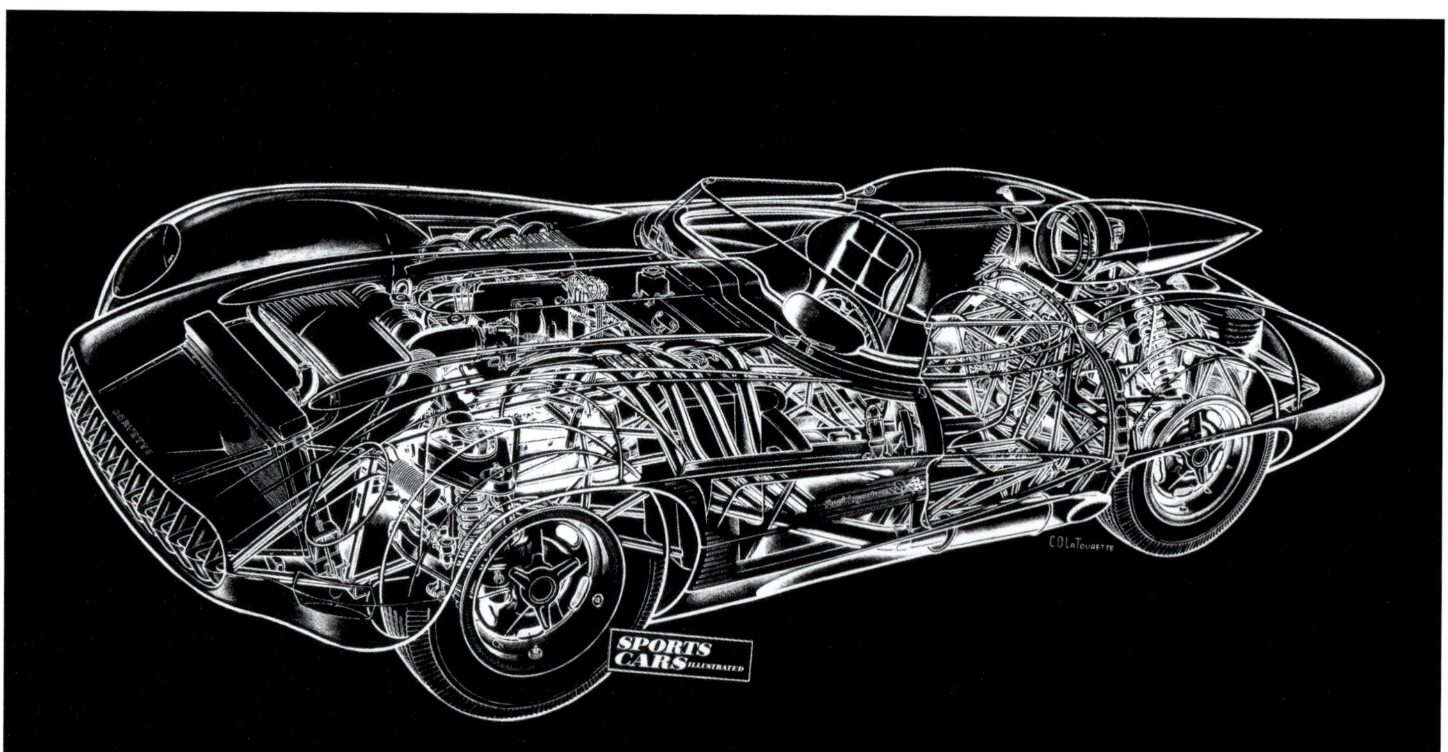

This black-and-white cutaway rendering of the XP-64 Corvette SS race car depicts the placement of the car's 315-hp 283-ci fuel-injected V-8 engine as well as its front-wheel independent suspension. Also shown are the car's coilover shock absorbers at all four wheels. (Photo Courtesy General Motors LLC)

Designers are hard at work adding details to the nearly completed clay model of the XP-64 Corvette SS in the Chevrolet styling studio. The clay model was assembled under the direction of the studio's chief designer, Clare "Mac" MacKichan (pictured left). Prior to working on the Corvette SS, Mac was also responsible for designing elements of the original EX-122 prototype as well as the 1954 Motorama Corvette-themed concept cars. (Photo Courtesy General Motors LLC)

through its successes at the track, Earl knew the SR-2 would never be competitive against the purpose-built race cars being manufactured by companies like Ferrari, Maserati, and Porsche.

Ed Cole and Zora Arkus-Duntov had similar opinions about the SR-2 after seeing it race at Sebring in 1956. They understood that building a legitimate Corvette race car would elevate consumer opinion of its production counterpart. Unfortunately, Cole's recent appointment as Chevrolet's general manager forced him to shift his attention to more pressing issues within the company. A purpose-built Corvette race car would have to wait.

Harley Earl Manipulates the Situation

Earl saw Cole's attention being pulled in different directions. If the momentum to develop a genuine race program was lost, Earl was certain Corvette's recent successes in the showroom would suffer. With his mandatory retirement from General Motors on the horizon, Earl knew he had to act quickly if he hoped to get his Corvette race car funded and built. Fortunately, he knew exactly what needed to be done.

Earl "acquired" a Jaguar D-Type race car from business owner and Indy car driver Jack Ensley. Ensley, along with 1955 Indy winner Bob Sweikert, had driven the D-Type to a third-place finish at Sebring in 1956. After the race, they'd inadvertently destroyed the Jaguar's engine while over-revving it during a spirited victory lap.

This all fit perfectly into Earl's plan. He had the Jaguar, minus its engine, delivered to GM's styling department. Upon its arrival, Earl publicly announced his intention to have the car fitted with a Chevrolet engine and to rework its body to resemble an "experimental Corvette." Said "Corvette" would then be registered to compete at Sebring the following year.

It did not take long for Cole to learn of Earl's intentions. He contacted Duntov while Duntov was vacationing in New York City to give him the news. Duntov objected to Earl's plans at once, citing several engineering problems that would make such an unusual transformation exceptionally difficult to perform. He quickly sketched several drawings and drafted a persuasive proposal outlining the design and construction of a new Corvette race car. He presented the proposal to Ed Cole and GM's top brass, where it was promptly approved.

Earl's bluff had worked. In truth, he had only borrowed Ensley's Jaguar and made enough "noise" to motivate Duntov and get things moving. The D-Type was

This early GM press photo shows the completed Corvette SS race car. Of particular interest are the buckled leather straps securing the front hood and rear cover. Straps of this sort helped prevent the stock hood latch assemblies from popping open from body flex during hard cornering. (Photo Courtesy General Motors LLC)

returned to its former owner. Ironically, Ensley successfully installed a fuel-injected Chevy V-8 in the D-Type shortly after it was returned to him.

Designing the Corvette SS

Work began on a clay mockup of Duntov's design in July 1956. It was developed in the Chevrolet styling studio under the direction of Clare MacKichan. The model featured a 90-inch wheelbase and highly rounded contours influenced by the bodylines of the Jaguar D-Type. It was presented to Ed Cole and Chevrolet's top brass later that same month. Dubbed Chevrolet's "1957 Sebring car," the model was approved for production as presented.

By mid-September, after learning that Jaguar had scored another victory at Le Mans, a new order was issued to the design team. According to *Corvette: America's Star-Spangled Sports Car*, the order was: "The XP-64 will be a competition racing car with special frame, suspension, engine, drivetrain, and body."

This unprecedented directive meant that General Motors was preparing to "declare war" against the likes of Jaguar and Ferrari. The automaker intended the XP-64 to dominate against all competitors at the racetrack: first at Sebring in March 1957 and later that same year at Le Mans.

Development of the Corvette SS was fully underway by October under the constant supervision and direction of Duntov. With just six months until Sebring, the challenges of building a completely new race car were monumental. Despite this, Duntov recognized the opportunity this car represented, and he worked tirelessly to meet the rigorous development schedule placed before him.

At the Heart of the Beast

The XP-64 received the same 283-ci V-8 engine used in all production Corvettes that year, although its output was increased to 307 hp (versus 275 hp from the stock engine). It featured brand-new Rochester fuel injection, custom-cast aluminum cylinder heads, and Duntov's longer-duration camshaft. The engine was also equipped with a tubular steel exhaust system that added nearly 20 brake hp while simultaneously reducing the car's overall weight.

Other weight-saving measures were also incorporated into the car. Custom aluminum assemblies were developed for the XP-64's clutch housing, transmission case, and radiator core (all of which would eventually be integrated into the production Corvette). Special close-ratio gears of 1.22, 1.54, and 1.87 were integrated into the 4-speed transmission's aluminum housing.

Inspired by Mercedes-Benz?

The Corvette SS needed a chassis that was both rigid and lightweight, but Duntov lacked the time to properly engineer one from scratch. Instead, he obtained the frame of a Mercedes-Benz 300SL and used it as the foundation for the new car's chassis. From it, he developed a tubular space frame design. Much of the SS chassis mirrored the German design, although smaller tubes were added to accommodate the XP-64's engine and suspension components. Additional tubular components were also added to increase stiffness. The completed chassis was fabricated entirely out of chrome-moly steel tubing and weighed just 180 pounds.

Duntov oversaw the development of a custom front suspension designed to give the Corvette SS a higher resistance to roll over. The car used nonparallel wishbones hand fabricated from sheet metal with fitted ball joints on the outer ends. The wishbone frame pivots were made of rubber bushings (instead of steel-to-steel bushings). A small-diameter anti-roll bar tied the lower wishbone assemblies together. The modified suspension placed the car's roll center just 3.5 inches above ground level.

A curved, one-piece de Dion tubular suspension was installed behind the car's rear differential. Four tubular trailing arms were also installed, all of which were mounted to the frame via rubber bushings. The upper arms were angled outward slightly and fitted with ball joints that mated with the top of each rear hub assembly. The lower trailing arms were also fitted with ball joints that were secured to the underside of the de Dion assembly.

Zora Arkus-Duntov is seated at the controls of the 1957 XP-64 Corvette SS race car. The car was originally constructed with a plastic canopy per 1957 Fédération Internationale de l'Automobile (FIA) regulations, but it was removed prior to the race at Sebring. (Photo Courtesy General Motors LLC)

John Fitch and Zora Arkus-Duntov inspect the rear assemblies of the XP-64 Corvette SS prior to its inaugural run at Sebring in March 1957. Notice the spare tire strapped to the car? The FIA included a rule that each team had to carry a spare tire onboard their race car, and it had to be used for the first tire change of the race. (Photo Courtesy General Motors LLC)

The grille of the Corvette SS resembles the grille from the 1957 production model, save for the number of teeth in each grille. A production 1957 Corvette has 13 teeth, whereas the Corvette SS has 15. The difference in the number of teeth was due to the larger diameter of the front air opening on the race car.

Duntov believed that maintaining familiar elements of the production Corvette in the SS race car was paramount to establishing brand recognition with spectators. He had the styling studio work body side coves into the dramatic lines of the Corvette SS body. While these coves are significantly smaller than those on the production model, they still created the desired result.

Time limitations forced Duntov to turn to a competitor for brake hardware. The Corvette SS was fitted with brake shoes, cylinders, shoe pivots, and retractors from a 1956 Chrysler. Front brake cooling was provided by ducts mounted along both sides of the car's front grille. Special grilles were also installed along the tail end of the car's body to push cooling air toward the rear brake assemblies.

Building the XP-64's Body

Perhaps the most impressive aspect of the XP-64's development was the evolution of the car's body. Its final design was drawn by Clare MacKichan under the guidance of Harley Earl. Both men knew the car needed to resemble the production Corvette, but it also needed to be streamlined to limit drag and eliminate lift. Its rapid transformation from paper drawing to final product required close coordination between GM's styling staff and Chevrolet's engineering department.

The body included two massive assemblies that could be opened for easy access to the chassis beneath. The front bonnet opened on pivot hinges toward the front of the car to reveal the engine and front suspension assemblies. The back cover similarly opened toward the rear of the car to expose the transmission, rear differential, and suspension, the latter of which could be quickly adjusted or replaced based on driving conditions.

The XP-64's overall aesthetic was unmistakably Corvette but with more than a bit of European race car flare built in. Its front end included a grille like the street-going model (though with 15 teeth instead of 13) and body side coves reminiscent of the ones that had been introduced on the 1956 Corvette. However, the largely exaggerated front fenders, the abbreviated doors, and the wedge-shaped rear end produced a side profile that was far more dramatic than its production counterpart. A bullet-shaped headrest concealed a solitary roll bar designed to protect the driver in the event of a rollover.

No Time for Testing

Chevrolet's original build order called for the construction of four Corvette SS race cars. Because of the high production and development costs and an extremely

Duntov and his engineering staff inspect the Corvette SS Test Mule prior to rolling it out onto the Sebring racetrack. Although the Test Mule was, at best, a close approximation of the actual SS race car, it enabled the team to identify deficiencies in several of the race car's vital systems. (Photo Courtesy General Motors LLC)

The Corvette SS Test Mule was rolled onto the Sebring racetrack prior to testing. Unlike the actual race car body (which is built out of magnesium), the Corvette SS Test Mule was constructed of fiberglass. As a result, none of the Mule's drivers experienced the searing heat that was felt by John Fitch and Piero Tauffi during the race. (Photo Courtesy General Motors LLC)

Duntov (seated in car) helped sway public opinion of the Corvette through his dedication to its racing program. The Corvette SS was the first purpose-built race car model. Prior to the AMA ban in the summer of 1957, it was one of the most widely anticipated and sought-out race cars by enthusiasts and critics alike. (Photo Courtesy General Motors LLC)

limited time schedule, the original order was rescinded. A new order was placed to complete development of a single race car.

Despite this, Duntov cobbled together a Corvette SS Test Mule from duplicate parts that had been fabricated for the race car as well as an earlier "mocked up" chassis that had been discarded by the development team. He needed the mule to test/verify the performance of various systems before they were incorporated into the actual race car. He was also apprehensive that the racer's compressed development schedule would prevent much of that testing from taking place.

Duntov's concerns were justified. With the Sebring race now just weeks away and the actual Corvette SS still being tweaked for its inaugural run at the event, the Mule (as it was known) became an integral part of the SS's test program. Early runs in the Mule identified deficits in the cooling and braking systems, which allowed corresponding changes to be made on the other car. At another practice session, the custom aluminum cylinder heads were damaged due to overheating and were replaced by stock iron heads.

In addition to identifying deficiencies, the Mule also proved the Corvette SS was a force to be reckoned with on the racetrack. During the final Friday practice session at Sebring, Duntov invited drivers Juan Manuel Fangio and Stirling Moss, arguably two of the greatest racing drivers in the history of the sport, to put the Mule through its paces.

Fangio succeeded in running a lap time of 3:27.2, which was more than 2 seconds faster than his previous track record of 3:29.7 set in a Ferrari a year earlier. It also ended up being one of the fastest lap times of any driver at Sebring throughout the 1957 season.

Trouble at Sebring

Final touches were still being made to the car as it was being transported to Sebring in early March. The completed Corvette SS had a dry weight of approximately

John Fitch is behind the wheel of the Corvette SS on its inaugural (and only) run at Sebring Raceway on March 23, 1957. Unfortunately, the car was retired from the race during its 23rd lap after experiencing engine and suspension issues. (Photo Courtesy General Motors LLC)

Despite an early and disappointing retirement at Sebring, the Corvette SS proved it could compete against Jaguar, Maserati, Porsche, and Ferrari. This picture of John Fitch (left), Duntov (middle), and Elfi Arkus-Duntov was taken shortly after the race. It includes the following inscription: "To Duntov and Elfi, With fond memories of a fascinating occasion. Love John Fitch." (Photo Courtesy General Motors LLC)

1,850 pounds. To Duntov's delight, the car was about 100 pounds lighter than the Jaguar D-Type. It was decidedly light enough to compete in the long-distance endurance race. Last-minute wind tunnel testing also proved the car had a low coefficient of drag about equal to the Jaguar.

Unfortunately, race day at Sebring resulted in heartbreak for all involved with the Corvette SS program. It began with that morning's practice laps. American driver John Fitch and his Italian copilot Piero Tauffi both complained of unbearable heat inside the cockpit. The car's magnesium body conducted heat from its mufflers, which were mounted just below the door sills. This design deficiency was missed in the Mule because its body had been fabricated mostly out of fiberglass. Working in earnest to resolve the issue, Chevrolet mechanics cut away portions of the magnesium body to allow the cockpit to "breathe."

Matters got worse after the race started. Fitch ran the first two laps without incident. In fact, his performance against the Ferraris and Maseratis captured the attention of spectators around the track. After those first two laps, the Corvette SS literally began to fall apart.

First, the right front tire developed flat spots that caused significant vibration inside the car. Second, a bad coil connection forced Fitch to limp the car back to the pits with a dead engine. The team lost a quarter-hour trying to troubleshoot the issue before replacing the coil with a new one. The car was retired for good during its 23rd lap when the rear suspension buckled, causing the back fenders to collapse onto its tires.

Even given these setbacks, Ed Cole was sufficiently impressed with the car's performance at Sebring. He approved assembling a three-car team for the 24 Hours of Le Mans. The Corvette SS had pulled away from the D-Type Jaguars in the straightaways and had accelerated faster than many of the Ferraris. Yes, the potential was there, and Cole wanted to see it fully realized with a victory at Le Mans.

Sadly, it was never meant to be.

The AMA Racing Ban

Feeling rundown after his enormous effort to get the Corvette SS ready for the 12 Hours of Sebring, Duntov elected to remain in Florida for a few days to enjoy some well-deserved time off. During this time, he received a phone call informing him that the Automobile Manufacturers Association (AMA) was getting ready to implement a ban on manufacturer-backed racing programs.

The AMA coalition, which included General Motors, Ford, and Chrysler, had started hosting discussions about the ban after a horrific race day accident during the 1955 running of the 24 Hours of Le Mans that claimed the lives of 83 spectators and injured 180 more. Although the AMA ban would not officially go into effect until June 6, 1957, General Motors immediately canceled all factory-sponsored race programs.

The Corvette SS program was suddenly and permanently terminated. Although the race car was scheduled to be destroyed, Duntov persuaded General Motors to instead put it into storage, where it remained for several years. At Duntov's urging, the car was donated to the Indianapolis Motor Speedway in 1967. It remains part of the Speedway's collection of historic race cars to this day.

The 1957 Corvette Super Sport Show Car

The 1957 Corvette Super Sport Concept was the first car built by Chevrolet to carry the "Super Sport" moniker. It was developed by GM styling in the late fall of 1956 at a

The Chevrolet Corvette Super Sport concept/show car was built by Chevrolet as a potential production counterpart of the popular SS Corvette race car. It featured design elements similar to those introduced on the SR-2 Corvettes. It was first displayed at the Waldorf Astoria Auto Show in December 1956 as a potential 1957 model year offering. (Photo Courtesy General Motors LLC)

The interior of the 1957 Corvette Super Sport received several unique appointments, including a centrally mounted tachometer ahead of the speedometer and a redesigned gauge cluster finished in brushed aluminum. The conventional windshield was also replaced with a pair of smaller windscreens. (Photo Courtesy Dan Vaughn, author/developer of ConceptCarz.com)

cost of more than $18,000 (or approximately $169,900 in 2021). The car, which started as a 1956 Corvette (VIN E56S001589), was reworked to incorporate the same engine and some of the same styling cues as the 1957 Corvette SS Race Car. It debuted at the 42nd Annual New York Auto Show on December 8, 1956.

Ed Cole created shop order No. 90181 after observing the overwhelmingly positive response Earl's original SR-2 had received at race events across the country. Order No. 90181 called for the development of a more competitive production Corvette. Given that the car's creation (and eventual introduction) coincided with the introduction of the Corvette SS race car, Cole named it the Corvette Super Sport.

The 1957 Super Sport started as a stock 1956 Corvette. It spent its first year as a show car in the lobby of the GM building before being repurposed for Cole's project. The 1956 Corvette was issued an altered VIN (E57S101001) to reclassify it as a 1957 model. It was then sent to GM's styling department.

The 1957 Corvette Super Sport received a fresh 283-ci, 283-hp V-8 engine with all-new Ramjet fuel

An early color photograph of the Corvette Super Sport shows one of the car's more interesting features: the addition of air scoops mounted in the rear section of the driver and passenger body side coves. These scoops, first introduced on the Corvette SR-2, were nonfunctional and were added to convey a greater sense of power and speed. (Photo Courtesy General Motors LLC)

The Corvette Super Sport is displayed in the lobby of the Waldorf Astoria Hotel in New York City in December 1956. (Photo Courtesy General Motors LLC)

Today, the 1957 Corvette Super Sport is privately owned by John and Gina Baldwin of Malabar, Florida. The car was presented at the Amelia Island Concours d'Elegance car show in March 2017. (Photo Courtesy Dan Vaughn, author/developer of ConceptCarz.com)

injection paired to a close-ratio 3-speed manual transmission (a 4-speed manual transmission was introduced in all other 1957 Corvettes equipped with fuel injection). A polished injection plenum was installed, and the rest of the engine was wrapped in chrome. The car was also equipped with a limited-slip differential, metallic brake linings, finned brake drums, special heavier-duty springs, and specially placed air ducts for the brakes.

To give the Super Sport its distinctive look, the car's original windshield, door glass, and windshield wipers were removed. A pair of rounded windscreens, similar to those introduced on the SR-2 and SS racers, was installed in front of the driver and passenger seats. Custom inserts were developed to enclose the window openings at the top of each door.

The exterior was finished in special Pearlescent White paint with blue striping that ran the length of the car. Each of the body side coves was detailed in brushed aluminum, and each received an air scoop that appeared to feed air to the rear brakes (though it is generally believed that these scoops were nonfunctional). Special taillamp assemblies were also fabricated into the rear fenders. The car sat on US Royal thin-line whitewall XP-140 experimental tires. Each tire had the Corvette crossed flags emblem branded into its sidewalls.

Inside the cockpit, the seats were covered in leather (a first for Corvette) that had been dyed blue (another Corvette first) to match the exterior stripes. The car's floor panels were reworked and layered with plywood and anodized aluminum to create custom footrests for both the driver and the passenger. Both the instrument panel and the center console were redesigned, as were the door panels and the driveline tunnel cover. A tachometer was mounted to the steering column and a console-mounted clipboard was installed for use during rally racing. It was also the first Corvette interior to feature cupholders.

After its debut in New York City, the Super Sport Corvette continued to travel the auto show circuit, which included a stop at the Chicago Auto Show in January 1957. The car was also showcased at the 1957 Sports Car Club of America (SCCA) in Detroit, Michigan, and on the June cover of *Speed Age* magazine. It was eventually returned to General Motors before being shipped to Dick Doane Chevrolet in Dundee, Illinois.

Per an article published at Hemmings.com in March 2017, the 1957 Corvette Super Sport was eventually sold to Ralph Pool's Albuquerque Auto Sales, where it resided briefly before being purchased by a private owner. Said private owner drove the car well into the 1960s before crashing the car into a telephone pole during an illegal street race. The ensuing damage made it undrivable, and so the car sat for several decades. It was eventually relegated to a local junkyard before being purchased by Bill Hovey, a resident of Albuquerque.

John and Gina Baldwin of Malabar, Florida, purchased the car from Hovey in 1996 and began the process of restoring it. In March 2017, the fully restored Corvette SS was reintroduced to the world at the historic Amelia Island Concours d'Elegance in Amelia Island, Florida.

The 1957 Q-Corvette

In early 1957, GM's engineering division started work on a new passenger car design, which used a rear-mounted transmission and transaxle assembly. Codenamed simply "Q" by the engineering team, the car's split powertrain was meant to reduce its front-to-rear weight bias and to improve overall handling. When Zora Arkus-Duntov learned of the Q-car's unique transmission placement, he began exploring a similar arrangement for the Corvette.

Meanwhile, Bill Mitchell started developing a new look for the Corvette. His current vision for the next-generation model was heavily influenced by the Italian-built Abarth race cars he'd seen at the 1957 Turin Motor Show. Each Abarth racer featured a sleek, wedge-shaped design accentuated by a sharp edge running around its perimeter. Upon Mitchell's return to the design studio, he shared photos of the Abarth with many of the department's key designers, including Tony Lapine, Chuck Pohlmann, Pete Brock, and Bob Veryzer. Afterward, he challenged each of them to create their own unique design based on the Italian race car.

Duntov outlined the basic layout of a new chassis with a rear-mounted transmission and transaxle. Because of his work on the original Corvette, Bob McLean was brought onto the project by Duntov to manage the confluence of his chassis and Mitchell's new Corvette body. By the end of 1957, the two departments, under McLean's direction, developed a highly stylized clay model that became known as the Q-Corvette concept.

The Q-Corvette was more compact than the first-generation Corvette. The removal of the bulky transmission housing from the rear of the engine allowed the car to ride on a wheelbase of just 94 inches with a rear track width of 53 inches (the 1953–1962 Corvette's wheelbase and rear track width were 102 inches and 58 to 60 inches, depending on year). Additionally, the Q-Corvette sat at just 46 inches tall, approximately 6 inches shorter than the height of any first-generation Corvette. Despite this reduction in length, width, and height, the car reportedly allowed for a more spacious cockpit.

Unfortunately, development of the Q-Corvette never evolved past the clay model stage. The economic recession of 1958 was expected to impact automobile manufacturers, so GM's executives canceled most of the Q-series development programs. Had the car made it to production, it would have featured a fuel-injected 283-ci V-8 engine built extensively out of aluminum. It would have also used a dry-sump oil system, independent rear suspension, and coilover shock absorbers at all four wheels.

While development of the Q-Corvette ended before a genuine prototype was produced, it still had a lasting impact on future Corvettes. Its outward aesthetic directly influenced the look of the second-generation Stingray, and its unique rear-mounted transmission was integrated—successfully this time—into both the prototype and production versions of the fifth-generation Corvette in 1997.

The 1957 Q-Corvette may never have moved past the clay model stage, but many of its mechanical underpinnings, most especially its rear-mounted transmission, served as the foundation for improving the fifth-generation Corvette's front-to-rear weight bias. When building the C5, General Motors adopted and successfully implemented the same setup on the production car. (Photo Courtesy General Motors LLC)

Because of its rear-mounted transmission, the Q-Corvette had a more spacious cockpit than the 1957 production model, despite being shorter in length and height. It also featured a permanent arch behind the cockpit and removable roof panels (both of which would eventually be introduced on the 1968 Corvette Stingray). (Photo Courtesy General Motors LLC)

The 1957 Q-Corvette has been attributed with introducing many of the styling elements seen on both the 1959 Sting Ray Racer and the second-generation Corvette, including recessed headlights, a strong character line, and distinct fender bulges that gave the car a more aerodynamic appearance. (Photo Courtesy General Motors LLC)

CHAPTER 3

SHARKS AND STINGRAYS

That's the fun of a sports car. There's so damned much you can do with it to make it exciting.
—Bill Mitchell

By the late 1950s, Harley Earl and Zora Arkus-Duntov had helped advance the Corvette's reputation as both a credible sports car and racer. Unfortunately, Earl was facing mandatory retirement from General Motors, which meant that GM's styling department (the division that oversaw the Corvette) was going to require new leadership. For Earl, this meant that his successor would direct the future of his beloved sports car. So, by leveraging the weight and breadth of his authority within General Motors, it was Earl who chose the next vice president of styling.

William L. "Bill" Mitchell

Bill Mitchell was the son of a Buick dealership owner and automobile enthusiast from the small town of Greenville, Pennsylvania. From an early age, Bill exhibited a talent and passion for drawing. However, it was at his father's dealership that he first developed an interest in automobiles, especially those of the "sporty" variety. Although cars of that sort were far and few between in those days, Bill took a particular interest in the occasional Stutz Bearcat or Mercer Type 35R

The 1961 Mako Shark (aka Mako Shark I) concept was the brainchild of GM Vice President of Styling Bill Mitchell. Brilliantly designed by Larry Shinoda, the "Shark" (along with Mitchell's Sting Ray racer) defined the look of the second-generation Corvette Sting Ray. It remains one of the most iconic-looking Corvettes in the history of the brand. (Photo Courtesy GM Media)

Bill Mitchell was GM's second vice president of design and styling. After replacing Harley Earl, Mitchell transformed the Corvette by creating a series of radical concept cars, including the Sting Ray Racer, the Mako Shark, and the Manta Ray. Under his tutelage, Chevrolet developed one of the most successful Corvettes in the history of the brand: the 1963 Split-Window Coupe. (Photo Courtesy General Motors LLC)

Raceabout that came into the dealership on trade. His father frequently customized these cars and souped them up for his own enjoyment. By the time he was 10 years old, Bill knew he wanted to race cars and drive fast.

On July 2, 1927, Bill's 15th birthday, he started down the path that eventually united him with the Chevrolet Corvette and automotive history. Bill landed his first real job as an office boy in the art department of the Barron Collier agency in New York City. Working part time at first, he spent each summer at the agency throughout his high school career. After graduating from high school, he accepted a full-time position there as an illustrator.

From 1931 to 1932, Mitchell attended night classes at the Art Students League of New York to improve his skills as an artist. Much of the art he created there was inspired by the automobiles he'd observed in various dealership showrooms while walking up and down 57th Street on his lunch breaks. Of particular interest were the European exotics displayed by Hispano-Suiza, Rolls-Royce, and Mercedes-Benz.

A young Bill Mitchell worked as a graphic designer. His artistic talents, combined with his passion for fast cars, helped catapult his career into high gear when a friend of Harley Earl's took notice of Mitchell's automobile designs and presented his work to GM's vice president of design. (Photo Courtesy General Motors LLC)

His talent as a graphic artist caught the attention of his employers at Barron Collier. It wasn't long before they commissioned young Bill Mitchell to design the first-ever Morris Garages (MG) print ad for publication in American automobile media. During this time, Mitchell also developed a close association with Sam and Miles Collier, Barron Collier's sons.

Bill Mitchell Goes Racing

Sam and Miles introduced Mitchell to European-style road racing, a venue the brothers had been promoting in the United States for years. The trio raced whenever they could, using the roads around the family's Pocantico Hills Estate as their first racetrack.

The brothers' avid enthusiasm for the sport eventually led them to establish the Automobile Racing Club of America (ARCA) in 1933. They hired Mitchell to design the club's first logo and much of its badging. Just over a decade later, the Automobile Racing Club of America became more famously known as the Sports Car Club of America (SCCA).

Mitchell's involvement with ARCA afforded him many opportunities to experience road racing first-hand. Time spent behind the wheel fostered an unbridled enthusiasm for the sport within him. It also left him wondering why American automobile manufacturers had never bothered to produce and market a sports car of their own. This question motivated Mitchell to begin sketching sports cars similar to those he observed almost daily at the racetrack . . . that is, when he wasn't behind the wheel pushing those same cars to their mechanical limits.

In the summer of 1935, some of Mitchell's sketches caught the attention of Walter Carey, an insurance executive and friend of Harley Earl. Carey was impressed by what he saw. He asked Mitchell if he had ever considered a career in automotive design. When Mitchell replied that he'd seriously considered it, Carey insisted on sending some of Mitchell's work to Harley Earl. Earl responded via letter a short time later and asked Mitchell to sketch some original automobiles of his own design.

Mitchell spent the rest of the summer creating a series of unique chalk and charcoal sketches. He mailed his newly created portfolio to Harley Earl that October. In early December, Mitchell received an invitation to come to Detroit and meet with Earl at General Motors. During that meeting, he was offered a position with Earl's Art and Color Section.

Bill Mitchell joined General Motors on December 15, 1935.

General Motors and the 60 Special

During his first year at General Motors, Mitchell showed immense promise and was promoted to chief designer of the Cadillac studio. His first assignment in this new role was to design the 1938 Cadillac 60 Special. Initially intended to be distributed as a LaSalle, the 60 Special was instead developed as the first "youth image" Cadillac of its kind. The car presented Mitchell with a variety of interesting challenges, such as incorporating a steeply raked windshield, four front-hinged convertible-style doors, and a coupe-like trunk into his final design.

Bill Mitchell poses next to a vintage Pontiac inside the GM design studios. Despite his ongoing commitments to Cadillac's studio, Mitchell visited GM's other department studios to help broaden his personal ideas about design. (Photo Courtesy General Motors LLC)

The brass at General Motors loved everything about Mitchell's brilliant addition to the Cadillac lineup. For Mitchell, however, designing large, family-style automobiles lacked the excitement of the race cars he'd left behind in New York. He soon found himself longing to do something different with his career.

Mitchell requested a leave of absence from General Motors with the intent of temporarily joining the Mercedes-Benz company. Mercedes had become the world leader in sport and race car engineering. It had developed the W154 racer and was now using it to compete against the Auto Union at race events across Europe. Mitchell very much wanted to be a part of it. General Motors said no.

The denial of his request forced Mitchell to follow the European racing series through foreign journals and automobile magazines. He occasionally came across an article talking about the exploits of the Collier brothers or a high-profile race being sponsored by the Automobile Racing Club of America. These stories only added to his feelings of frustration and isolation. He yearned to share his enthusiasm for sports car racing with other members of the Detroit automobile community, but most failed to see its attraction, except for Harley Earl.

Bill Mitchell and Harley Earl

Earl and Mitchell toured the shops of several independent coach builders while on a business trip to the West Coast in the summer of 1941. Their exploits included a stop in a shop owned by Tommy Lee, the son of Earl's former employer. The cars they observed while visiting these shops redefined and stretched Mitchell's understanding of automobile design. They weren't limited by the numerous design constraints of larger commercial automobile manufacturers. Moreover, many of the West Coast shops were building automobiles with the express purpose of racing them!

Mitchell returned to Detroit more downtrodden than before. Enthusiasts and independent businesses on both coasts were advancing the sport of auto racing. More than that, they were successfully fabricating—and selling!—some of the first American-made sports cars and doing so without the backing of a large corporation like General Motors. Meanwhile in Detroit, none of the major manufacturers had shown even a passing interest in developing anything that remotely resembled a sports car.

Bill Mitchell is behind the wheel of a Mercedes-Benz W125. This Grand Prix racer was the type of car that he, along with the Collier brothers, dreamed of driving in the early days of ARCA (SCCA). Recognizing his affinity for its cars, Mercedes-Benz permitted him to pilot the priceless antique race car around its Stuttgart test track in 1958. (Photo Courtesy General Motors LLC)

Despite his personal frustrations, Mitchell continued to rise in rank and file within the GM styling department. He worked diligently to distinguish himself in the eyes of Harley Earl, Harlow Curtice, and Semon "Bunkie" Knudsen. At the start of World War II, Earl helped Mitchell earn a commission with the navy. He produced several navy training manuals throughout the war, including one on how to fly military aircraft solely by their instruments.

Bill Mitchell returned to work in Cadillac's design department at the end of the war. He ran the department for the remainder of the 1940s and oversaw the division's product designs. His 60 Special model was transformed a total of five times, with each generation of the popular Cadillac showcasing another facet of Mitchell's amazing design prowess. It also laid the groundwork for his involvement on other GM projects, including the 1949 Cadillac Coupe DeVille. Despite his many successes, Mitchell still longed to work on something fast and sporty.

From late 1949 to early 1953, Mitchell left General Motors to help Earl launch an independent design company. The Harley Earl Corporation was meant to be a collaborative venture between Earl, Mitchell, and Earl's two sons for the express purpose of building and marketing cars of their own design without any corporate interference. While Mitchell did most of the heavy lifting early on, from building a respected client base to negotiating some potentially lucrative opportunities, both he and Earl soon discovered that the younger Earls lacked their father's talents. Both men eventually conceded that the business would be less lucrative than the opportunities afforded them by General Motors.

Earl brought Bill Mitchell back to General Motors in 1953 as his director of styling. He needed Mitchell to assist in managing the design programs for Chevrolet's 1955 lineup so that he could maintain his focus on other projects, including the Chevy Corvette. Earl also recognized that he needed to begin grooming a successor who shared his intuition for automotive design. Bill Mitchell had the goods. Additionally, Earl appreciated their common passion for automobile racing. He knew that the Corvette would only succeed if the people guiding its future could demonstrate its potential on a racetrack.

So it was that Bill Mitchell, the designer with a lifelong passion for designing and driving fast cars, became one of the automotive innovators striving to steer the Corvette toward its still-uncertain future.

Bill Mitchell Succeeds Harley Earl

Harley Earl retired from General Motors on December 1, 1958. He had reached GM's then-mandatory retirement age of 65 and left the corporation after overseeing

Harley Earl retired from General Motors at the mandatory retirement age of 65. He passed away at the age of 75 in West Palm Beach, Florida, on April 10, 1969. In addition to being the father of the Corvette, he is also widely considered to be the father of modern automotive design, a distinction that still resonates true among today's automobile designers. (Photo Courtesy Richard Earl, automotive historian, and grandson of Harley Earl)

GM's portrait of Bill Mitchell was taken around the time of his promotion to vice president of styling in December 1958. (Photo Courtesy General Motors LLC)

the final designs of the corporation's 1959 model lineup. It came as little surprise to most within the GM styling department when 46-year-old Bill Mitchell was named as Harley Earl's successor.

Not everyone agreed with Mitchell's appointment as vice president of styling. For one thing, he had a reputation of having an overbearing personality and a massively over-inflated ego. For another, there were a multitude of other stylists who believed they were better qualified for the position and with more years of experience. Regardless, Bill Mitchell had been handpicked by Harley Earl. Given that Earl had been the first and only vice president of styling since the inception of the department decades earlier, there was nobody within General Motors who was going to question his decision on the matter.

Just the same, Mitchell recognized the importance of establishing his own identity within the styling department. He knew that a break between Earl's long-standing design motifs and his own was paramount if he ever hoped to successfully usher in a new era of automotive styling within General Motors. He needed to develop a car that would transcend anything that had come before it; something that was utterly new and irrefutably his.

The 1959 Sting Ray Racer XP-87

The AMA ban was still in full effect when Bill Mitchell succeeded Harley Earl as vice president of styling. Although a factory-backed race program was currently considered taboo by General Motors, Mitchell knew that offering consumers a high-performance sports car that they could race would have a positive impact on the company's sales numbers. He also realized he could advance the reputation of the Corvette at the racetrack if he did so without the consent, cooperation, or participation of Chevrolet/General Motors. His success would also silence the naysayers who questioned his promotion in the first place.

Bill Mitchell stands next to the XP-87 Sting Ray concept after its transformation from racer to show car during the winter of 1960. (Photo Courtesy General Motors LLC)

In 1958, Bill Mitchell negotiated an interesting deal with Ed Cole to obtain the original Corvette SS Test Mule chassis fabricated by Zora Arkus-Duntov a year earlier. He purchased the chassis from Chevrolet for one dollar against the wishes of Duntov, who realized his participation in the Corvette's continued development would be restricted because of the AMA ban. Despite Duntov's efforts to prevent the purchase, Mitchell acquired the chassis with the strict understanding that the car would in no way be associated with either Chevrolet or Corvette. He agreed to the terms and started revamping the car for his private use.

Mitchell's first order of business for the car was a new body. After the Mule had completed testing at Sebring, it had been shipped back to Detroit, cleaned up, and refurbished for use at the 1957 24 Hours of Le Mans. Once the AMA ban had gone into effect, work on the chassis immediately stopped and orders were given that it should be destroyed. Instead, it had been quietly stowed away in one of GM styling's warehouses before it could be fitted with a new SS body.

Shinoda Designs Mitchell's XP-87

Mitchell hired GM stylist Larry Shinoda to adapt elements of the short-lived Q-Corvette into a body for his newly acquired chassis. Working under Mitchell, Shinoda created a highly stylized design that incorporated the Q-Corvette's low, wide grille and wedge-shaped profile. It also included similar, though less prominent, fender flares above its squared-off front and rear wheel openings.

Elsewhere, Shinoda incorporated entirely new elements into his design. These included a long, tapered bulge in the car's hood to accommodate fuel injection. He also replaced the enclosed cockpit with a front windscreen and incorporated an integrated headrest/roll bar assembly behind the driver's seat like the one used on the Corvette SS.

The exterior of the XP-87 Sting Ray was originally painted bright red per Bill Mitchell's specifications. Mitchell's favorite color was red, and he had many of his personal cars painted accordingly, including his Corvette SR-2 race car (not pictured). (Photo Courtesy General Motors LLC)

A fiberglass body based on Shinoda's designs was fabricated by hand during the winter of 1958. Ducts were added behind the front grille to feed air into the fuel injection and front brakes while additional flush duct inlets were placed in the rear deck assembly to provide cooling air to the rear brakes.

The car's high beltline created a clean division between the body's relatively flat top and rounded bottom halves. Chrome exhaust pipes passed through and out the front fenders (behind the front wheels) before turning back and running along the car's rocker panels. The body was finished in a bright, glossy red paint.

Mitchell named his rebodied SS race car the "Sting Ray." He felt the name added an aura of fierceness to the car. Its sleek, modern lines and low, aggressive stance exuded an image of speed and agility, much like an actual stingray moving through tropical ocean waters. The choice of name was also inspired by Mitchell's passion for deep-sea fishing.

Getting Around the AMA Ban

The finished Sting Ray was Mitchell's personal property. He had privately paid for Larry Shinoda's after-hours design work and for the extracurricular efforts made by the styling shop to fabricate a new body. Now he had to fund the car's mechanical preparation for use at the racetrack.

This was the reason Mitchell elected to repurpose so much of the original Mule's chassis and powerplant. The Sting Ray had a 280-hp 283-ci V-8 engine, which was nearly identical to the one used in the 1957 Corvette SS. Experimental aluminum cylinder heads and a repurposed 1957 Rochester fuel injection system had been successfully mounted to the Sting Ray's engine. They helped produce a high 11.0:1 compression ratio.

A prototype Harrison aluminum radiator and oil cooling system was introduced in the Sting Ray. Considerable attention was given to improving the heat dissipation issue at the front of the car. About a third of the air exiting the radiator vented out of the engine compartment through special outlets in the car's hood. The rest was routed through vents near the exhaust pipe openings in the front fenders.

The Sting Ray's cockpit was a reimagining of the earlier SS interior with a couple of exceptions. The new cockpit featured a deep-dish, three-spoke steering wheel

Although the current badges on the XP-87 Sting Ray include the word "Corvette," this wasn't always the case. Bill Mitchell privately funded the Sting Ray build and could not legally use the Corvette name. It was only after General Motors elected to use his race car as a design concept for its second-generation production model that the Corvette name was added to the "Sting Ray" emblems. (Photo Courtesy Dan Vaughn, author/developer of ConceptCarz.com)

and a simplified dashboard panel, the latter of which had a more conventional layout compared to the SS's wildly conceptualized design.

Bill Mitchell's new race car was sparsely badged with custom "Sting Ray" emblems and nameplates. It made no reference to the Corvette or Chevrolet monikers. Despite this, GM management still had concerns about Mitchell operating the car at sanctioned events for fear of public backlash. They argued the Sting Ray might be seen as a covert attempt by GM to circumvent their consensual participation in the AMA racing ban. To help alleviate these concerns, Mitchell drafted an official statement that declared his intent to register and operate the car at all race events strictly and solely as his personal vehicle. Only then was he given permission to proceed.

The Sting Ray Racer Makes Waves at the Track

The Sting Ray's first track appearance was in the President's Cup at Marlboro Raceway on April 18, 1959. Mitchell recruited Dr. Dick Thompson to pilot the car. Zora Arkus-Duntov also attended the event. He wanted to see how well the Sting Ray would perform once it got up to speed. He feared it would encounter the same struggles his original Corvette SS had. His fears were well-founded.

The Sting Ray's first and only test drive happened the day of the race. Thompson piloted the car out onto the twisting road course and started putting it through its paces. He soon discovered the car's inverted airfoil design created front-end lift at speeds over 100 mph, which caused the car to begin drifting all over the track. He also found the car's split-system brakes to be unpredictable. They frequently locked up throughout the practice session.

Thompson brought the car back to the pits for an impromptu shakedown. He had a pair of grilles removed from the hood to reduce lift. Unfortunately, there was nowhere near enough time to address the braking issues before the start of the race.

The Sting Ray took an early lead after the green flag dropped but was quickly passed by a Lister-Corvette. Thompson reclaimed the front spot when that same Corvette retired a short while later. Throughout the race, Thompson struggled to maintain control. The Sting Ray's nose lifted erratically, causing the car to drift into other competitors. The brakes seized and caused similar issues. At one point late in the race, Thompson felt the front end slide out from beneath him, causing him to lose half a lap.

Thompson finished in fourth place behind two Porsche RSKs and a Lister-Jaguar. Despite experiencing mechanical and handling difficulties throughout the event, Dick Thompson successfully piloted the Sting Ray to its first checkered flag. Unfortunately for Thompson, his erratic, overly aggressive driving resulted in a three-month suspension of his SCCA license. Even so, his performance at Marlboro proved the Sting Ray was a viable race car. More importantly, it was one of the most recognized cars from that race, which was exactly what Bill Mitchell had planned from the start.

Bill Mitchell (left) and Dr. Dick Thompson (right) discuss various performance aspects of the Sting Ray racer during one of its shakedown sessions. Thompson's first bout with the Sting Ray in April 1959 resulted in a three-month suspension of his SCCA license. However, his masterful handling of Mitchell's race car radically improved public opinion of the Corvette brand. (Photo Courtesy General Motors LLC)

Bill Mitchell's XP-87 improved public opinion of the Chevy Corvette as a serious race car almost overnight. The irony is in the fact that the Sting Ray Racer was privately funded and built by Mitchell with no support from Chevrolet. (Photo Courtesy General Motors LLC)

After Marlboro, Mitchell enlisted Dean Bedford from Corvette Engineering, Ed Zalucki from Duntov's engineering staff, and Kenny Eschebach, a mechanic from GM's styling/special vehicles division to rework the Sting Ray race car. He rented a small shop in Roseville, Michigan, and paid the team overtime rates to work evenings and weekends.

Dr. Dick Thompson (left), racing legend George Constantine (middle), and Bill Mitchell are pictured at the 6th Annual International Bahamas Speed Weeks in June 1959. Out of the 66 race entrants, Constantine's No. 49 Aston Martin DBR2/420 ended up winning the Nassau Trophy Road Race while Thompson piloted the Sting Ray to a very respectable third-in-class and 11th-place overall finish. (Photo Courtesy Dave Friedman)

In an interview in the October 1977 publication of *Car Classics* magazine, Bill Mitchell said, "My agreement was that I'd keep it off the Tech Center property and spend my own money to run it. It cost me quite a bit, too. I financed it all out of my own pocket. I couldn't afford to do it that way today. But it pleased me to no end to go up against Cunningham and those boys with the faster cars and take any of them."

The Sting Ray competed in multiple events throughout the remainder of the 1959 race season, although not without incident. It suffered more braking and lifting issues at Elkhart Lake with driver John Fitch behind the wheel, which resulted in the car's early retirement from the event.

At the infamous Meadowdale track near Chicago, Illinois, Dick Thompson experienced sudden brake fade while entering a sharp embankment and rolled the car. During its second run at Elkhart Lake in August 1959, the car performed well until brake issues caused Thompson to retire the car yet again.

Mitchell's Sting Ray Racer Gets an Overhaul

After its second showing at Elkhart Lake, the Sting Ray received a major overhaul. The car's complex double-booster braking system was replaced by a single Hydrovac power assist assembly that had been modified to allow for brake pedal pressure adjustments. Due to time and budget limitations, the drum brake system remained, although the metallic braking surfaces were welded to their linings. The car also received a stiffer set of springs, which Duntov first produced for the 1957 Corvette SS racer.

A new body was fabricated for the Sting Ray Racer in October–November 1959. Its panels were constructed of layered fiberglass silk, which made them lighter and more durable than those used on the first body. Each panel was also reinforced with balsa wood and bonded in place with heat-treated aluminum brackets. The fully assembled body was approximately 75 pounds lighter than its predecessor. It sported a stunning new metallic silver paint job with matching silver interior.

The revamped Sting Ray Racer made its debut at Marlboro Raceway on April 16, 1960. Piloted once more by Dr. Dick Thompson, the car performed

Between 1959 and 1960, both the mechanicals and the body of the Sting Ray were completely reworked. Mitchell and his team used fiberglass silk, balsa wood, and heat-treated aluminum brackets to build a lighter, though no less rigid, body. The car was finished in a stunning metallic silver paint with matching silver interior. (Photo Courtesy Dan Vaughn, author/developer of ConceptCarz.com)

The interior of the Sting Ray Racer lacked the chrome and flourish of the race cars previously built during Harley Earl's regime. Instead, Mitchell tended to favor straight, clean lines, and he took a minimalist approach that favored function over excessive and unnecessary flourish. (Photo Courtesy Dan Vaughn, author/developer of ConceptCarz.com)

The reworked Corvette Sting Ray was unveiled on April 16, 1960, as a participant in the President's Cup National Races at Marlboro Raceway. (Photo Courtesy Tom Bigelow)

exceptionally well. It placed first in the C-Modified class and third overall behind two RSK Porsches.

Two weeks later, Thompson and the Sting Ray finished first in class again and second overall at the Virginia International Raceway. Two weeks after that, they earned a third-straight class victory in the Cumberland National Sports Car Races in Wiley Ford, West Virginia. By the end of the season, Thompson had earned nearly three times as many points as the next team in his class. He and the Sting Ray Racer were declared the SCCA's C-Modified National Champions of 1960.

The Sting Ray's entire race career lasted from April 1959 to October 1960. Thompson's championship season had garnered volumes of positive press and publicity for Mitchell's race car. More importantly, at least to Bill Mitchell, it had given him credibility among the naysayers within General Motors who had questioned his promotion two years earlier.

The Sting Ray Racer was converted into a show car at the end of the 1960 race season. GM's styling staff installed a flush-fitting tonneau cover over the passenger's area and a wraparound canopy on the driver's side. The car also received a fresh paint job as well as "Corvette" and "Fuel Injection" emblems. The Corvette Sting Ray Concept was unveiled at the Chicago car show in February 1961.

The lighter, nimbler Corvette Sting Ray dominates the field during the 1960 running of the President's Cup at Marlboro Raceway. Thanks in large part to Dr. Dick Thompson's talent behind the wheel, the Sting Ray would lead most of the race and finish first-in-class and third overall. That race would be the first of several back-to-back podium finishes for both Thompson and the car. (Photo Courtesy Tom Bigelow)

The 1959 XP-87 Corvette Sting Ray is on display at the 2018 Amelia Island Concours d'Elegance. The car is a testament to Bill Mitchell's skill as both an automobile designer and a businessman. His intentional marketing of the Sting Ray as a race car and a show car improved public opinion of the Corvette and laid the groundwork for the creation of the 1963 split-window coupe. (Photo Courtesy Dan Vaughn, author/developer of ConceptCarz.com)

Dick Thompson pilots Mitchell's Corvette Sting Ray in the USAC Road Racing Championship at Laguna Seca on October 23, 1960. This race marked the car's final appearance in a sanctioned track event. It finished 10th in class and 18th overall. (Photo Courtesy Dave Friedman)

After only a brief time on the automotive show circuit, Bill Mitchell had the Sting Ray fitted with a passenger-side windscreen, a speedometer, and a rear license-plate mount. It became the vehicle he drove back and forth to work anytime the weather was decent.

Both as a race car and a concept car, the Sting Ray received enormous amounts of praise from the public, the automotive press, and even GM's top brass. It convinced Mitchell that a production version of the car was an obvious choice for a next-generation Corvette. He contacted Larry Shinoda, in his official capacity as vice president of design this time, and tasked him with designing a production version of the Sting Ray Racer. Shinoda's efforts evolved into the second-generation Corvette Sting Ray.

Larry Shinoda

Larry Shinoda was one of the most influential Corvette designers in the history of the brand. Working under the direction of Bill Mitchell and Harry Haga, Shinoda designed the second-generation Sting Ray and developed the "Coke bottle" look of the third-generation Corvette. (Photo Courtesy General Motors LLC)

Lawrence Kiyoshi (Larry) Shinoda was a respected automotive designer whose work gave rise to two of the most celebrated American-made sports cars of all time: the 1963 Corvette Sting Ray and the 1970 Boss 302 Mustang.

Larry was born on March 25, 1930, in Los Angeles, California, to Japanese-born parents. Even as a young boy, he showed an aptitude for drawing machines and automobiles. Although Larry was an inattentive student in most other subjects, his artistic talents were quickly recognized and encouraged by his grade school instructors.

During World War II, Larry and his family (along with thousands of other Japanese Americans) were interned under U.S. Executive Order 9066 at a war relocation camp in Manzanar, California. Despite facing many hardships in the camps, Larry continued to develop his artistic and engineering talents using broken pencils and scraps of discarded paper to sketch his designs. He even designed and built a set of reclining-back armchairs from a set of old crates.

A young Shinoda tinkers with his 1929 Roadster, the* No. 69 Chopsticks Special IV. *He raced the* Special *and won his class at the first NHRA Nationals, which were held in Great Bend, Kansas, in 1955. (Photo Courtesy General Motors LLC)

After being released in the spring of 1944, Larry moved briefly to Grand Junction, Colorado, to work on his family's farm. He returned to Los Angeles a few years later, and he began building and racing hot rods. His combined passion for racing and art led him to enroll at the Art Center College of Design to pursue an education in automotive design.

Shinoda found the college environment suffocating. He felt his coursework was too varied and lacked content relevant to his own future. His struggling grades and lack of focus caught the attention of the college administration. He was asked to leave but not before befriending a product design teacher who encouraged

Shinoda's love for racing made him an obvious choice to design the Corvette Sting Ray Racer. Aside from the "Pontiac" badging on its front fenders (possibly done to deter rumors that he was designing Mitchell's race car as an extracurricular activity), there is no mistaking the signature look of the Sting Ray–including its flared fenders and prominent side pipes–in Shinoda's design. (Photo Courtesy General Motors LLC)

Shinoda to present some of his work to the Ford Motor Company.

The design team at Ford was impressed with Shinoda's work and hired him shortly thereafter. Over the next 18 months, Shinoda moved from Ford to Packard to the crew of the John Zink Special at the 1956 Indianapolis 500, where he designed the body of the team's Watson-Offenhauser race car. The car won the Indy 500 that year and instantly made Larry Shinoda a sought-after commodity in the automotive design world.

General Motors hired Shinoda as a senior designer with just 18 months of design experience. He went to work in the Chevrolet design studio. His design proposal for the 1959 Chevy caught the attention of upper management, including Bill Mitchell. A chance drag race between Shinoda and Mitchell a few days later convinced the soon-to-be vice president of design to seek out this young designer and racer for the Corvette development program.

During his time in this role, Shinoda designed the Sting Ray Racer, the Mako Shark I & II, and the legendary 1963 Corvette Sting Ray split-window coupe. Although there has been some disagreement about who created the initial design profile of the second-generation Corvette, there is no question Shinoda formalized and streamlined the final design.

Additionally, his Mako Shark II served as the foundation for the third-generation Corvette, which arrived on the scene in 1968. By then, Shinoda had followed former Chevy General Manager Bunkie Knudsen to the Ford Motor Company. There, Shinoda designed the 1970 Boss 302 Mustang, which is still considered to be one of the most desirable Mustangs of all time.

After leaving Ford, Shinoda began his own design studio in Livonia, Michigan. He worked as a consultant with Ford, General Motors, and the Chrysler Corporation. He helped design the Jeep Grand Cherokee, Roger Penske's race trailers, and even elements of the Goodyear blimp. Shinoda continued consulting on the Corvette, developing his own aftermarket body treatment for the fourth-generation model. He also designed the logo for the National Corvette Museum in Bowling Green, Kentucky.

Shinoda developed significant kidney problems in 1996. Despite this, he continued to work tirelessly as a design consultant. He became the subject of a massive fundraising effort to help pay for his kidney transplant. Tragically, Shinoda passed away of heart failure before the transplant could be scheduled. He died in his home in Bloomfield Hills, Michigan, on November 13, 1997.

Larry Shinoda was inducted into the Corvette Hall of Fame in 1998.

The 1958 XP-700 "Phantom" Corvette

The XP-700 Corvette was conceived by Bill Mitchell and built in the summer of 1958 to serve as one of his personal vehicles. Its design contained several unique elements that Mitchell had already been developing for General Motors, including a new ducktail back end that made its first commercial appearance on the 1961 Corvette. The XP-700's design also broke with the traditional "toothy" look of Earl's original Corvette in favor of a car that was markedly sleeker in appearance.

Bill Mitchell designed the XP-700 Corvette to showcase design cues he'd been developing for other GM automobiles. It was one of his first efforts to give the production Corvette a sportier, more streamlined appearance. (Photo Courtesy General Motors LLC)

The 1958 XP-700 "Phantom" Corvette used many regular Corvette parts, including the frame, chassis, and engine. It was the "Grand Prix" flourishes–a longer, low-hung snout; large air scoops; and wire wheels (with racing hubs)–that gave the car its one-of-a-kind appearance. (Photo Courtesy General Motors LLC)

When introduced in 1958, the first iteration of the XP-700 included a broader-but-shorter snout and included "Corvette" badging on its nose just above the elliptical grille. (Photo Courtesy General Motors LLC)

The XP-700 Corvette underwent a transformation in the fall of 1959 from Mitchell's daily driver to GM show car. It received revised front and rear ends, an enclosed cockpit, a silver paint job, and new badging on its nose that now read "Phantom" instead of "Corvette." (Photo Courtesy General Motors LLC)

Bill liked to drive the cars he designed. He believed the benefit of building fully functional concept vehicles vastly outweighed the creation of static models like those showcased at GM's Motoramas in the early 1950s. He made it a division policy that all "dream" and concept cars built by the styling studio should be fully operational whenever possible. Further, these cars were to be driven on the open road to gauge public opinion.

Much of the mid-section of the XP-700 was built from a standard 1958 Corvette, including its frame, its 283-ci fuel-injected engine and powertrain, and several of its mid- and rear-section body panels. Mitchell also used chassis components from GM's abandoned "Q" series passenger cars, as well as body parts from the Grand Prix racers of that era.

One of the most notable "Q" elements introduced on the XP-700s was the high, elongated nose with its narrow oval air inlet. This elliptical inlet included a chrome ring that served as the car's front bumper. Framed within this chrome bumper ring was a mesh grille and a larger version of the production Corvette's traditional crossed-flags emblem.

The XP-700's "double-bubble" canopy became a popular design element on several of Mitchell's future concept vehicles. While it never appeared on a production Corvette (due in part to the fastback shape of the second-generation model), versions of the bubble canopy continued to appear on GM's concept vehicles (and others) throughout the mid-1960s.

An assortment of stylized openings framed the front nose and fed air into the radiator, the front brakes, and the engine. A recessed air scoop protruded downward from below/behind the front grille. Surrounding this was a pair of smaller air intakes mounted to either side of the front fascia directly below the car's headlights. Farther back, a pair of cowl scoops sat atop each fender in front of the windshield.

Bill Mitchell loved the look and sound of side pipes and frequently included them in his designs. The XP-700 was no exception. The car's rocker panels were eliminated to accommodate a twin side pipe exhaust system paired to elongated mufflers mounted on each side of the car. Header pipes exited the engine compartment through an opening in the bottom of each fender and ended in a tailpipe that jutted from the mufflers in a small, outturned flourish just ahead of the rear wheels. Above this, a pair of double-slotted air intakes were incorporated into the quarter panels that provided cooling air to the rear brakes.

The rear of the XP-700 was short and sleek. Its "ducktail" rear end started with a break line at the rear wheels that extended gradually downward toward the rear of the car. From there, it rounded the corner and formed a dramatic straight edge that intersected the car's cascading rear decklid from the top and its rounded fascia and chrome bumpers from the bottom. The normally concealed fuel filler neck and gas cap found near the top of the rear fender on a production model Corvette was replaced by a fully exposed gas cap assembly in approximately the same location.

The XP-700's interior was essentially the same as the production model Corvette, although it had specially designed metallic floor grates and a custom steering wheel with three hollow spokes that were devoid of the traditional "lightning holes" design.

Bill Mitchell had the XP-700 finished in his favorite colors: red with silver side coves. The coves, which were framed in chrome trim, were further accentuated by a set of triple louvers that were also painted silver. The car rode on a pair of thin-line whitewall tires paired with a set of Dayton knock-off wire wheels. The XP-700 served as one of Mitchell's personal vehicles from 1958 through the autumn of 1959.

In October 1959, the XP-700 Corvette was overhauled and updated so it could serve as GM's centerpiece at stops along the 1960 auto show circuit. The car's original ducktail design underwent a complete transformation to conceal it since that same feature was about to be unveiled on the 1961 Corvette. Its engine bay was dressed in chrome coverings and black-crackle-finished trim.

The open-air cockpit was enclosed with a dramatic "double-bubble" hardtop. It was made of transparent plastic lined with a thin film of vacuum-deposited aluminum that had been designed to deflect sunlight and regulate cabin temperature. A "periscope" rearview mirror was installed, and it enabled the driver to see what was going on behind the car (much like a backup camera provides us with improved rear visibility today). An experimental manual overdrive unit and a dash-mounted chronometer were also installed. The entire car was repainted Metallic Silver.

The refreshed Corvette XP-700 made its public debut at the 4th Annual International Automobile Show in New York City. It traveled the show circuit across the United States throughout the remainder of the year. At the conclusion of its year-long tour, the XP-700 Corvette essentially vanished.

There isn't much information available that explains what happened to the XP-700 after 1960. One of the most common theories is that the car was transformed by Bill Mitchell and the styling studio into the XP-755 (the first Mako Shark). This theory is supported by a memo on record from General Motors dated March 28, 1981, which simply states this: "plans made to use components from XP-700 for XP-755." While this is hardly substantial evidence, it remains the most plausible explanation of the XP-700's mysterious disappearance.

The 1960 XP-720

The GM styling department began work on a new secret project in the fall of 1959. The project, code-numbered XP-720, was to be a "from-scratch" production Corvette design based on the Sting Ray race car. Like Harley Earl before him, Bill Mitchell elected to develop this project without the knowledge, or the probable interference, of GM's upper management. Instead, he and multiple members of his styling department met in the same windowless basement studio where they'd constructed the Sting Ray Racer.

Mitchell's desire for secrecy was tempered by his need to base the design around an established chassis. Fortunately for Mitchell, Duntov had already begun development of a new substructure for the XP-720 based on design parameters he first outlined in a letter to GM Chief Engineer Harry Barr in December 1957. In *Corvette: America's Star-Spangled Sports Car,* Karl Ludvigsen included this section of the letter: "We can attempt to arrive at the general concept of the car on the basis of our experience and in relationship to the present Corvette. We would like to have better driver and passenger accommodations,

An early version of the XP-720 Corvette concept based on Bill Mitchell's Sting Ray Racer was presented to GM's management team in October 1959 for preliminary design approval. (Photo Courtesy General Motors LLC)

A refined version of the XP-720 Corvette concept car was developed by Larry Shinoda. While some of its design elements (most notably the grille-mounted headlights) were eventually relocated elsewhere, there is no mistaking its relationship to the second-generation Corvette. (Photo Courtesy General Motors LLC)

better luggage space, better ride, better handling, and higher performance."

While he had yet to construct a complete chassis, Duntov's design notes and prescribed dimensions allowed Mitchell's styling team to construct the first of two clay mockups of the XP-720 Corvette prototype. The model, which was based on a closed-top version of Mitchell's Sting Ray Racer, received a positive reaction from GM's top brass. To Mitchell's surprise, the initial design was approved for further development with virtually no other comment from anyone.

Serious work on the XP-720 prototype began in January 1960. While Duntov oversaw construction of a new chassis based on elements borrowed from both the 1957 Q-Corvette and Mitchell's 1959 Sting Ray Racer, Larry Shinoda began work on a second full-size clay model of the car. This second model detailed modifications to the earlier design while also promoting various styling elements, many of which eventually were incorporated into the next-generation Corvette.

Shinoda completed the new model on April 4, 1960. It was presented to GM management while parked next to a 1960 Corvette. The second XP-720 concept sat lower and looked far more aerodynamic than its first-generation counterpart. While certain provisional details on the clay mockup were still subject to change before a final production prototype was completed, the XP-720 Corvette concept was enthusiastically approved, effectively giving birth to the second-generation Corvette Sting Ray coupe.

The 1961 XP-796: The Four-Seat Corvette Sting Ray 2+2

By 1961, most of the design details of the XP-720 had been finalized and aerodynamics testing began in the GALCIT wind tunnel at the California Institute of Technology. During this phase of the car's development, Ed Cole began pushing for the addition of a four-passenger version of the new Corvette. Cole believed that adding a backseat to the second-generation model would make it more competitive in the marketplace against cars like the Ford Thunderbird. He also knew that the sizable cost of re-tooling the manufacturing plant to build a new Corvette would be more palatable if a broader array of automobiles could be manufactured at the plant.

Duntov and Mitchell hated the idea. They argued that a four-passenger Corvette would devalue the brand in the eyes of consumers who had come to consider it a serious sports car. Unfortunately for both men, Cole's directive was not open to debate. In August 1961, the

Ed Cole directed Larry Shinoda to develop a four-seat option of the soon-to-be second-generation Corvette Sting Ray. As seen in this full-sized clay model, both the car's roofline and the doors were lengthened by approximately 10 inches to accommodate the additional seating. (Photo Courtesy General Motors LLC)

The four-seat XP-796 Corvette was developed to be a competitor of the new four-seat Thunderbird. Ford had transformed the Thunderbird from its original two-seat configuration for the 1958 model year. Fortunately for the Corvette, GM executives put a quick-and-final end to the four-door XP-796 in October 1962. (Photo Courtesy General Motors LLC)

styling section started lining out a 2+2 (four-seater) version of the second-generation coupe.

Chevrolet Division General Manager Bunkie Knudsen also opposed the creation of a 2+2 Corvette. He considered the car useless. Despite this, he had no choice but to support the program since the directive had already come down from above. To help guide the four-seat Corvette's development, he approached Bill Mitchell and GM styling with the suggestion that they purchase a 2+2 Ferrari for reference. The following excerpt from his private journal, which was published in the December 2007 issue of *Corvette Fever*, explains: "Went to styling; cleared up four-passenger Corvette; told them to buy a 2+2 Ferrari. Mitchell feels this has correct dimensions. I told Mitchell I'd go along with him on dimensions, but I did not want a different front end from the Corvette. He agreed."

The coupe needed to be "stretched" in several areas to achieve the required dimensions: the car's overall length was increased by approximately 10 inches, the doors were lengthened to accommodate access to the rear seats, and the roof line was raised and lengthened to provide adequate headroom for the car's back seat passengers.

Larry Shinoda managed the construction of the four-seater Corvette, although he did so begrudgingly. Afterall, he had created the original Sting Ray design and spent countless hours finessing each section of the two-seat coupe. Now, he and his team had intentionally mutilated his finely proportioned design in favor of additional seating.

Nonetheless, Shinoda's team completed construction of the four-seat Sting Ray in January 1962. The car was presented to GM upper management parked next to a 1962 Ford Thunderbird. Although initial reactions were mixed, several of the GM executives present at the car's unveiling wanted to inspect the car's interior, especially its back seats. GM chairman Jack Gordon allegedly got stuck in the back seat when one of the front seatback latches "accidentally" locked. The front seats had to be unbolted from the floor and removed before Gordon could exit the car.

After this inspection, GM Vice President Bud Goodman contacted Knudsen to ask his opinion of the gangly looking 2+2 Corvette. During that discussion, Knudsen advised that building a 2+2 Corvette was "the wrong thing to do." The project was subsequently canceled, and the single existing prototype sent to the crusher.

Little else is known about the XP-796 2+2 Corvette. The type of engine installed is unknown, although the car wore "Fuel Injection" badges on its front fenders. Additionally, there is no record of the car's drivability, handling, or performance capabilities.

The 1961 XP-755 Mako Shark (I)

The Mako Shark Corvette was developed under the direction of Bill Mitchell to fill a perceived gap between the creation of the XP-720 concept car in 1961 and the launch of the second-generation Sting Ray, which was scheduled to begin production in 1963. Simply put, Mitchell did not want to wait two years to drive the new Corvette. Instead, he greenlighted a project to build a concept car that would showcase many of the next-generation Corvette's major design elements.

Mitchell's latest car was assigned project number XP-755 by General Motors, and design responsibilities were again assigned to Larry Shinoda. Shinoda's early sketches of the XP-755 were largely based on his XP-720 concept, save for the addition of the same "double-bubble" canopy that had been introduced on the XP-700. Although his drawings met Mitchell's design criteria (namely, develop a new concept car based on the XP-720's styling), Mitchell thought Shinoda's current

The XP-755 Mako Shark (or "Mako Shark I" as it is known today) began life with a "double-bubble" canopy top. Stylized canopies of this sort were a popular design element in the 1960s. The canopy enclosure was eventually updated and replaced with a retractable/removable soft top. (Photo Courtesy General Motors LLC)

Many of the Mako Shark elements from its paint scheme to its profile were inspired by an actual mako shark that Bill Mitchell caught while deep-sea fishing during the Christmas holiday. He was so impressed with the shark's speed and dexterity that it became his source of inspiration for the new car. (Photo Courtesy General Motors LLC)

Bill Mitchell had special badging created that featured the likeness of a short-fin mako shark. This unique badging motif continued with the Mako Shark II before being replaced by first a Manta Ray and then a Sting Ray, the last of which was featured prominently on the front fenders on both the seventh- and eighth-generation Corvettes. (Photo Courtesy General Motors LLC)

Automotive designer Anatole "Tony" Lapine revises a full-size rendering of the 1961 Mako Shark in GM's design studio. During his career with General Motors, Lapine worked closely with Larry Shinoda on several of the Corvette concepts, including the XP-87 and the CERV I & II. (Photo Courtesy General Motors LLC)

The full-size clay styling model of the Mako Shark included the car's dramatic double bubble canopy. It was also one of the first Corvettes to feature side pipes, a feature that showed up on many of Bill Mitchell's future designs. (Photo Courtesy General Motors LLC)

concept looked a bit too much like the earlier car.

Mitchell found additional inspiration for the body lines of the XP-755 while on a deep-sea fishing trip off the coast of Bimini in the Bahamas. He had hooked and successfully reeled in a short-fin mako shark. As he watched it aggressively twist, turn, and roll in the water, Mitchell realized the shark provided the perfect motif for the look—and future name—of his new Corvette.

Shinoda Shapes the Future

Upon his return to the design studio in early January, Mitchell re-engaged Shinoda on the XP-755 project. By April 1961, a clay model of the newly imagined Mako Shark was finished and approved by Mitchell. Construction of a fiberglass body began immediately thereafter.

The Shark's body was built to mate with the chassis of a 1961 Corvette. It featured a streamlined, pointed

The design of the Mako Shark was the "missing link" between the aging first-generation Corvette first introduced by Harley Earl in 1953 and the second-generation Sting Ray designed by Larry Shinoda and Bill Mitchell a decade later. (Photo Courtesy General Motors LLC)

Given the overwhelmingly positive public response to Shinoda's/Mitchell's styling choices for the Sting Ray Racer and the Mako Shark, there was no question that the second-generation Corvette would be based upon both of these amazing machines. (Photo Courtesy General Motors LLC)

snout with concealed headlights that had been mounted behind the corner sections of the grille. The grille itself extended the length of the front fascia and looked like the mouth of a shark. The "shark" aesthetic extended to the gill-like cornering lights mounted below the fenders just ahead of the front wheels.

The car's back end consisted of a short, upturned tail with three round taillights and twin chrome bumperettes. The rear decklid contained a cleverly concealed set of turn signals/emergency taillights that reflected off a pair of mirrored surfaces mounted inside two color-matched panels. Activating the turn signal switch on the steering column caused the respective turn signal panel to open and begin flashing. During harsh braking conditions, both panels would open and serve as a third pair of brake lights.

The cockpit of the 1961 Mako Shark was remarkably advanced in both design and function when compared to the first-generation Corvette. It used a variety of electronic controls, an angled wraparound secondary gauge cluster, and introduced the side-by-side placement of the speedometer/tachometer, which became the traditional configuration beginning with the 1963 Sting Ray. (Photo Courtesy General Motors LLC)

The upper two-thirds of the Mako Shark was painted a deep, iridescent blue that gradually transitioned to an off-white around the lower third of the car. Chrome accents, including a special "Mako Shark" logo and graphic, were installed on the front fenders just above the chromed exhaust headers. Like nearly all of Bill Mitchell's personal cars, the Mako Shark included chrome side pipes and bright aluminum mufflers tucked up alongside the car's rocker panels. They loosely resembled a shark's pectoral fins from a distance.

The XP-720's double-bubble canopy was reimagined for the Shark. This version included a prismatic periscope to provide the driver a better view out the back. The Shark's interior was a mix of old and new. The original concept featured the same instrument panel as the 1961 Corvette but had custom-built bucket seats and a personalized steering wheel that had been gifted to Bill Mitchell by Enzo Ferrari.

A supercharged 327-ci Chevy V-8 engine sat beneath the Mako Shark's massive hood. The engine had been hand built by Leonard McLay (Harley Earl's personal mechanic) from an engine that he developed for Earl's Le Sabre dream car a decade earlier. It featured a custom-fitted blower mounted to a manifold made of 2-inch plate aluminum. Four side-draft carburetors, mounted in pairs on either side of the engine, fed the blower while a high-pressure fuel pump fed gasoline directly into the manifold during wide-open-throttle situations.

Showcasing the "Shark"

The XP-755 Mako Shark made its unofficial debut on June 18, 1961, at the Road America race in Elkhart Lake, Wisconsin. Spectators stared in awe as it navigated the road course prior to the start of the race. The Shark wouldn't make another appearance until its official unveiling at the New York Auto Show in April 1962.

Bill Mitchell and GM's marketing departments hinted to the automotive press that the Mako Shark foreshadowed many of the design elements that would appear on the 1963 Corvette. In truth, the Shark was a stylized version of the fully developed second-generation Sting Ray.

In the years that followed its unveiling, the XP-755 Mako Shark underwent an assortment of mechanical and cosmetic changes. Several different engines, including a 427-ci Mark IV, were installed beneath its hood. Its front end received a set of chromed bumperettes, and a circular emblem was installed on the center of the grille. The cockpit was fitted with a new and more refined instrument panel, while lower and wider seats were installed to accommodate taller drivers who might otherwise hit their heads on the car's canopy.

The Mako Shark made its small-screen debut on October 27, 1961. During an episode of the popular television show *Route 66*, the car made a brief-but-significant cameo while being driven by actress Janice Rule. While the series was known for featuring cars provided by General Motors, this episode marked the first time that a concept vehicle was introduced in this fashion.

Today, the 1961 Mako Shark resides at the GM Heritage Center in Sterling Heights, Michigan.

The current engine in the Mako Shark is a production 1969 Chevrolet 427-ci ZL1 V-8. It uses all-aluminum block, heads, and intake manifold. Equipped with a single, 4-barrel carburetor, the ZL1 is said to produce approximately 425 hp. It is considered one of the rarest, and most coveted, Corvette engines of all time. (Photo Courtesy General Motors LLC)

The Mako Shark is now preserved as part of the General Motors Heritage Center collection in Sterling Heights, Michigan. General Motors will occasionally showcase the car at select Corvette and collector car shows across the United States. The Mako Shark will also make an occasional appearance, often as part of a larger exhibit, at the National Corvette Museum. (Photo Courtesy General Motors LLC)

CHAPTER 4

SWEPT BACK AND STREAMLINED

If you go by a school and the kids don't whistle, back to the drawing board.
—Harley Earl

The launch of the Split-Window Sting Ray coupe and convertible in 1963 bolstered public opinion of the Corvette almost overnight. America's sports car was finally on par with many of the finest GT automobiles that European manufacturers had to offer. The Sting Ray was fast, handled well, and was one of the best-looking automobiles commercially available in the United States.

Despite all of this, Bill Mitchell believed that the Corvette needed to continue evolving and quickly if it was going to maintain its relevance and prestige in the eyes of the American public. He wanted to find someone who could take everything that was good about the second-generation Sting Ray and make it even better. It was chiefly for this reason that Bill Mitchell appointed seasoned GM studio designer and automotive enthusiast Henry Haga as the chief of design for Chevrolet's Studio No. 3, the newly created studio home of the Corvette!

Designing the Wedge Corvette

Haga began development of a new body design for the Corvette in the summer of 1963. Over the next several months, he and the Chevy Studio Three team advanced the design from a series of sketches into a full-size clay model, which they dubbed the "Wedge Corvette" concept. The model depicted an extremely refined, streamlined restyling of the second-generation Corvette. It was devoid of body side coves, hood scoops, or any other detail that might detract from its swept-back airfoil appearance.

The nose of the Wedge Corvette featured leading-edge air inlets inspired by military aircraft of the period. A split-window windshield also added to the aircraft aesthetic, although this element served a functional purpose as well. Exposed rectangular exhaust side outlets were added just ahead of the rear wheel openings to give the car a hint of muscle. The rear end featured narrow,

The 1963 Wedge Corvette concept was a sleek, front engine design study developed and built by the GM styling department under the direction of Henry Haga. (Photo Courtesy GM Media)

Henry Haga

Like so many other automotive designers, Henry Haga grew up drawing automobiles. He joined General Motors in 1953 after graduating with a degree in industrial design from the ArtCenter College of Design in Pasadena, California. During his early years with General Motors, Haga was afforded many opportunities to advance his design career, first at Chevrolet, then at Cadillac, Buick, and Oldsmobile. By the time he returned to Chevrolet in 1962, he was recognized as a "master of proportion" among his peers, and one of the leading designers within General Motors.

Haga had always aspired to work on the Corvette, so when Bill Mitchell promoted him to lead the Chevy Studio Three in 1963, it was a dream come true. According to the National Corvette Museum, Haga said, "It was a fresh studio with a new product name, the Sting Ray, and a whole set of new responsibilities for me. The Corvette meant the epitome of design and performance in the GM line. Another exciting part of it was that I was given a company car with the appointment, and of course, it was a Corvette."

His passion for sports cars, most especially the Corvette, led Henry to develop a strong working relationship and fast friendship with Zora Arkus-Duntov. Their fortuitous meeting and eventual partnership proved beneficial to the Corvette's future.

Henry "Hank" Haga was the chief of Chevy's Two/Three Studio from 1963 to 1974. In addition to leading the efforts to "productionize" the Mako Shark II into the third-generation Corvette, he also helped develop several of the mid-engine Corvette concepts, including the XP-882, the Reynolds Aluminum Corvette, and the Aerovette/Four-Rotor Corvette. (Photo Courtesy GM Media)

rectangular taillights mounted just below its insert rear bumper. Halibrand-style wide-rim wheels with polished inserts completed the car's look.

The car's most dramatic feature was its upward-and-outward swinging driver and passenger doors. Each door opened in a gull-wing fashion along the split-windshield centerline pillar. This idea, which had previously been introduced on the Q-Corvette six years prior, worked perfectly with the rest of the design and provided occupants greater ease when entering or exiting the vehicle.

Unfortunately, the Wedge Corvette Concept was deemed a bit too radical for its time and never moved past the clay modeling stage. Even so, there is little doubt that Haga's model directly influenced many of the Corvette designs that emerged over the next 20 years.

An early model of the 1963 Wedge Corvette is at the General Motors Technical Center in Warren, Michigan. Full-size prototype models of this sort were frequently showcased next to production automobiles to evaluate differences in length, width, and height. (Photo Courtesy GM Media)

There is a notable absence of ducts, grilles, and other features on the hood/body of the 1963 Wedge concept. Henry Haga wanted to produce an extremely refined automobile that was devoid of any elements that might detract from its aerodynamic appearance. (Photo Courtesy GM Media)

Described as having a "bit of flying saucer look to it" by Larry Shinoda, the Wedge Corvette concept was seriously considered as a possible facelift to the second-generation's current styling or a potential candidate for the third-generation Corvette, complete with a new chassis and powerplant. (Photo Courtesy GM Media)

Zora Arkus-Duntov was in favor of Haga's front-engine Wedge Corvette design proposal, but Bill Mitchell hated it. He was so bothered by its appearance that he called it a "fat pig" and proceeded to kick the model with enough force to cause most of its back end to fall off. (Photo Courtesy GM Media)

The 1964 XP-833 Pontiac Banshee: The "Almost" Corvette Concept

The "Banshee" was a concept car envisioned and developed by Pontiac Chief Engineer and Division Head John Zachery DeLorean. Although DeLorean claimed at its introduction that he'd developed the Banshee as a potential competitor to the Ford Mustang, history has since proved that the Banshee came into being because DeLorean wanted to build a sports car of his own design that could then be distributed by Pontiac.

DeLorean started development of the Pontiac Banshee in early 1964. He even gave it the official GM project designation "XP-833" (the XP standing for Experimental Pontiac) despite his near certainty that General Motors would not approve the project. Even in its early stages of development, DeLorean believed (and perhaps intended) that the Banshee could be a direct competitor of the Corvette.

The XP-833 was designed and built by Pontiac's director of Advanced Engineering, William "Bill" Collins under the direction supervision of DeLorean and Pontiac General Manager Elliott M. "Pete" Estes. Over the next several months, Collins and his team developed two fully operational prototypes: a soft-top roadster and a coupe with a removable hard top.

"In Advanced Engineering, we did all the packaging on the 1964–65 XP-833 Banshee," Bill recalled in an article written by Thomas A. DeMauro in the October 2014 issue of *Hemmings Classic Cars*, "which included engineering the basic chassis design and people layout, etc. Then it went to GM Advanced Design, and I worked with that studio chief directly."

Both the coupe and the convertible were constructed of fiberglass panels fastened to steel substructures. A modified A-Body (Pontiac) steel perimeter box frame with a custom-fitted rear anti-roll bar served as the foundation

The Pontiac Banshee was conceived by Pontiac Chief Engineer John Z. DeLorean as a lighter, simpler, and less expensive sports car than the Chevy Corvette. In some respects, it was a return to the boulevard cruiser first envisioned by Harley Earl when he introduced the Project Opel car in 1952. (Photo Courtesy Bortz Auto Collection)

DeLorean claimed that the XP-833 was designed to be a direct competitor to the Ford Mustang. This profile study of the Banshee convertible and the Mustang (in silhouette) proves otherwise. (Photo Courtesy GM Media)

This full-scale model of the Pontiac Banshee looks remarkably like the third-generation Corvette from the front. There have been many claims made over the years suggesting that the Banshee was the genesis of the third-generation Corvette's final body styling. (Photo Courtesy GM Media)

Ironically, the rear of the Pontiac Banshee looked more like a mid-1970s Camaro and/or Trans Am back end. It seems likely that the Banshee inspired design elements on GM F-Body cars during this time. (Photo Courtesy GM Media)

of each chassis. Flat steel floor pans were then welded into the frames. Each frame was also fitted with coil spring double A-arm suspension up front and a 10-bolt live solid axle with a pair of coil springs in the rear.

The coupe featured a fastback roof. It was finished in silver paint with chrome accents and a red interior. Surprisingly, Collins placed a 230-ci overhead camshaft inline 6-cylinder engine with a single-barrel carburetor beneath the coupe's hood. The engine produced a paltry 155 hp. It was paired to a BorgWarner T-10 4-speed manual transmission.

The Banshee roadster was markedly more robust. Finished in white paint with a black interior, it was initially fitted with a 326-ci small-block V-8 engine and the same BorgWarner T-10 4-speed manual transmission.

Both XP-833 cars were smaller than the second-generation Corvette. They sat on a short, 90-inch wheelbase (the then-current Corvette's wheelbase was 98 inches). The cars were also lighter, with curb weights of just 2,300 pounds (coupe) and 2,615 pounds (versus the Corvette's curb weight of 3,170 pounds).

DeLorean, Collins, and the design team presented the XP-833 Banshee to GM's top executives in late 1964. DeLorean pitched his car as Pontiac's answer to Ford's popular pony car, going so far as to claim the coupe was fitted with an entry-level powertrain comparable to that found in a Mustang. DeLorean hoped this marketing approach would draw attention away from the car's undeniable similarities to the Corvette. GM Chairman James Roche didn't buy it. The project's funding and all subsequent requests for approval to proceed with further development were immediately and irrevocably denied.

Interestingly, the Pontiac Banshee concept looked remarkably like the third-generation Corvette that debuted four years later. It has been reported that Bill Mitchell drafted a memo in September 1965 directing his styling staff to update the XP-833's exterior clay model and interior bucks to more closely represent a two-passenger Chevrolet coupe. There are also claims that Larry Shinoda drew inspiration from the Banshee while he developed the Mako Shark II. However, it can also be argued that John DeLorean may well have drawn his own inspiration from Shinoda's 1962 Corvair Monza GT (and SS) models (See chapter 5).

Today, the Banshee roadster is a treasured part of the Bortz Auto Collection in Highland Park, Illinois. The coupe was part of the private collection of Lenny Napoli until his passing in 2008. At the time of this publication, the roadster is for sale at Napoli Kia in Milford, Connecticut, with an asking price of $750,000!

The 1965 XP-830: Mako Shark II

The development of the Mako Shark II coincided with the beginning of the sports and muscle car craze of the mid-1960s. Ford had already introduced its immensely popular 1964½ Ford Mustang and started development of its Le Mans–winning GT40 race car. Plymouth was developing several Hemi-equipped muscle cars that delivered massive horsepower on a budget. Even General Motors had joined in on the action with its introduction of the Oldsmobile 4-4-2 and the Pontiac GTO, to say nothing of its soon-to-be Chevy Camaro and Pontiac Firebird models. American automobile manufacturers, it seemed, had finally embraced the idea of building cars whose sole purpose was to go fast.

Bill Mitchell knew that the continued evolution of the Corvette would require the creation of a new concept model that would be every bit as exciting and attention-grabbing as the original Corvette Sting Ray race car. He also understood the fickle nature of sports car enthusiasts. While the second-generation Corvette's total unit sales continued to break each previous year's record,

In this GM publicity photo, Bill Mitchell poses with the Mako Shark II prior to its public unveiling at the Paris Auto Show in October 1965. (Photo Courtesy GM Media)

The 1965 GM X-15 was a concept car designed by Bill Mitchell based on Lance Reventlow's Scarab racer. Mitchell's X-15 concept was built on the same chassis and featured a spec'd Chevrolet Formula 1 engine. The car includes many of Bill Mitchell's favorite design elements, including an elongated snout and side exhaust pipes. (Photo Courtesy GM Media)

he knew that trend would eventually end. The public would expect something fresh and innovative. Mitchell wanted to make sure that General Motors was poised to give it to them.

Development of the Mako Shark II really started with the design for a single-seat, open-wheeled car that GM codenamed the "X-15" (an homage to the hypersonic, rocket-powered X-15 jet aircraft built in the late 1950s by the National Aeronautics and Space Administration [NASA]). This radically proportioned prototype was the furthest thing from a Corvette, but its creation demonstrated that the only limitation in automotive design was the imagination of the designer.

John DeLorean

While he's probably best remembered for designing the car made famous by Michael J. Fox in *Back to the Future*, John Zachary DeLorean had a remarkable career in the automotive industry long before Doc Brown ever built a time machine out of a DeLorean.

Born in Detroit, Michigan, on January 6, 1925, John DeLorean grew up surrounded by the automobile industry. He went to Cass Technical High School, where he studied electronics. His outstanding academic performance earned him a scholarship to the Lawrence Institute of Technology (known today as the Lawrence Technical University), where he studied industrial engineering.

DeLorean was drafted into the Army in 1943 after the US entered World War II. He served for three years before being honorably discharged. Upon returning home, he found work as a draftsman to help support his family during a period of economic difficulty. Then, he returned to Lawrence to finish his degree. He graduated in 1948 with a Bachelor of Science degree in industrial engineering.

After graduation, DeLorean found employment with Chrysler. He attended the Chrysler Institute of Engineering, which allowed him to further his education while gaining real-world experience as an automotive engineer. He graduated from the Chrysler Institute with his master's degree in automotive engineering.

DeLorean left Chrysler in 1953 after being offered a lucrative position at the Packard Motor Company. He gained the attention of his new employer after making significant improvements to their Ultramatic automatic transmission. Despite Packard's financial struggles in an evolving post–World War II automotive market, DeLorean climbed the engineering ranks to become the company's head of research and development.

DeLorean Joins GM

Packard merged with Studebaker in 1954. As DeLorean considered relocating to Studebaker's headquarters in Indiana, he was approached by Oliver K. Kelley, GM's vice president of engineering. Kelley presented DeLorean with an attractive offer to join any of GM's five major divisions. DeLorean accepted a position at Pontiac as its assistant chief engineer.

DeLorean was incredibly successful at Pontiac. He developed (and patented) dozens of innovations, including a rear-mounted transaxle, the "rope drive" flexible driveshaft, and an independent rear suspension. He was promoted to chief engineer in 1961. Shortly thereafter, DeLorean conceptualized, engineered, and successfully marketed the 1964 Pontiac GTO. He also oversaw the development of the Pontiac Firebird and the Pontiac Grand Prix. He became known as a corporate maverick, and his celebrity afforded him the luxury to travel the world while promoting the Pontiac brand.

On February 15, 1969, John DeLorean became general manager of Chevrolet. His brash, rebellious nature and his liberal, jet-setting lifestyle clashed with many of GM's more conservative executives. Even so, his strong business acumen helped guide Chevrolet through

Despite being a single-seat, open-wheel, open-cockpit, road-going race car, the X-15 contained design elements that directly influenced and eventually made their way into the Mako Shark II. (Photo Courtesy GM Media)

Shinoda Leads the Design of the Mako Shark II

In the fall of 1964, Bill Mitchell handpicked a team of stylists to begin designing the Mako Shark II. The team was led by Larry Shinoda and included other respected GM designers, including Kenny Eschebach, Art Carpenter, David Hollis, James "Jim" Barron, and Henry Haga.

During their initial meeting, Mitchell referenced the X-15 prototype and challenged Shinoda to incorporate styling elements from that car into the new Corvette concept vehicle. Mitchell also listed other design characteristics he wanted incorporated into the car: a coupe body with a narrow center section, prominent

a difficult period of financial turmoil. By 1971, Chevrolet was one of the most successful businesses in the entire automotive industry.

In 1972, DeLorean became the vice president of car and truck production for the entire GM line. It seemed certain that he'd become the company's next president, which caused significant strife amongst GM's other executives. On April 2, 1973, less than a year after his promotion to vice president, DeLorean resigned, stating he wanted to focus on business "in the social arena," which he was unable to do in GM's stifling corporate culture. It has also been suggested that DeLorean was being targeted for termination to prevent his further rise in rank at General Motors.

After General Motors

DeLorean started the DeLorean Motor Company (DMC) in 1973. He immediately set to work on a two-seat sports car prototype that featured gull-wing doors and a stainless-steel body. As the design evolved, it became known as the DeLorean DMC12.

Production delays prevented the DeLorean automobile from reaching consumer markets until 1981. Even then, inexperienced workers, quality-control issues in his Northern Ireland manufacturing plant, a depressed automotive market, and lukewarm reviews from automotive critics around the globe all prevented the DMC12 from earning the sales numbers he needed to recoup the millions owed to his investors. The DeLorean Motor Company was suddenly in serious financial trouble.

In October 1982, DeLorean was indicted on charges of allegedly trafficking approximately $24 million worth of cocaine after entering into an illegal business transaction with FBI informant James Hoffman. DMC was $17 million in debt at the time of his arrest, which led many sceptics to speculate whether John DeLorean had been attempting to sell drugs to make his company solvent again. The case went to trial.

On August 16, 1984, DeLorean was found not guilty by a jury of his peers on the grounds of police entrapment. Unfortunately, the DeLorean Motor Company had already declared bankruptcy by the time his trial ended. Its collapse resulted in more than 40 civil suits being filed against DeLorean on charges of fraud and tax evasion. Although he was eventually acquitted of all charges, the financial toll of his legal representation forced DeLorean to file for personal bankruptcy in 1999.

Despite his once-lavish lifestyle, DeLorean spent his remaining years in a modest condominium in Morristown, New Jersey. He died of a stroke on March 19, 2005, at the age of 80 years old.

In 1974, John Z. DeLorean was awarded a distinguished service citation by the Automotive Hall of Fame. It read: "He is honored for his foresight in the future needs of the automotive industry in engineering and safety, serving for 23 years in top leadership for Packard, Chrysler, and General Motors."

Originally scheduled to be unveiled as part of GM's display at the 1965 New York International Auto Show, the X-15 was later pulled from the lineup of cars being presented. It has never been put on public display, and its present whereabouts are unknown. (Photo Courtesy GM Media)

wheels at all four corners (each with equally prominent fenders), a tapered tail section, and a roof assembly that was fully integrated into the body.

Shinoda's team was required to design the new Shark around an existing second-generation Sting Ray chassis. The team was also informed that the car would be one of Chevrolet's star attractions at the New York International Auto Show in April 1965, which left them with only a few short months to conceptualize the design and build a functional prototype.

The Mako Shark II incorporated elements from past concept vehicles, including the Corvair Monza GT and the Pontiac Banshee. Beyond drawing upon these obvious design references, the car quickly took on a life, and a look, of its own. Mitchell frequented the design studio during the early stages of the car's development, and each

Developed from Shinoda's sketches and tape drawings, this early, full-size shaping buck of the Mako Shark II allowed designers to evaluate and adjust the car's final proportions before fabricating the full-sized clay model. (Photo Courtesy GM Media)

The full-size clay model of the Shark II had the addition of side-mounted exhaust pipes. This image, taken by GM staff photographer Neil Madler, provides a great overview of automotive design process, beginning with full-size renderings of the car (seen along the back wall), followed by the construction of a shaping buck (to the left of the clay model). (Photo Courtesy GM Media)

The revised version of the Mako Shark II clay model was used to fabricate the actual concept car's body panels. Note the car's pointed, slightly upturned nose and its signature front and rear fender flares. These features, subtly refined, became key design elements of the third-generation Corvette. (Photo Courtesy GM Media)

The Mako Shark II featured a boat-tail roofline and a rear window concealed behind six electronically operated louvers that could be opened by the driver whenever he or she needed to see out the back of the car. (Photo Courtesy GM Media)

visit was better than the last. He became enthralled with the car he saw taking shape under Shinoda's leadership. Although nobody knew it then, the Mako Shark II would become one of Bill Mitchell's personal favorites as well as one of the most iconic-looking Corvettes of them all.

Shinoda's team rolled an early model of the new Corvette concept out into GM's viewing yard in March 1965. This first example was a nonfunctional styling mockup that had been created to verify fitment of body panels and gain final design approval from Bill Mitchell. Many of GM's early photographs of the Mako Shark II (including those found on the internet today) were of this styling mockup and not the actual concept car.

The car's front end included a pointed snout, a pair of oversized front grilles, and a pair of dramatically flared front fenders. Its long, sweeping hood featured a centrally placed "power dome" assembly that included badges that read "MARK IV 396." The upper end of the hood included a set of grille openings that allowed warm air to dissipate from the engine compartment. A pair of cast-aluminum exhaust pipes protruded from the front fenders. The pipes were painted black, except for a series of polished "fins" that ran along the length of each pipe.

The Mako Shark II had a V-shaped glass windshield. It tapered upward to the car's roof line and was framed by a pair of narrow A-pillars. The roofline cascaded toward the rear of the car in a sweeping arch before tapering back to a point atop the rear deck assembly. A set of six electronically controlled louvers were installed within the upper portion of the rear deck area. These could be opened and closed during vehicle operation via controls inside the cockpit. They provided the only rearward view, as the car was devoid of any mirrors.

Its flared rear fenders began as part of the driver and passenger door assemblies and extended back to the car's twin ducktails. The wheel openings were filled with 7.5-inch aluminum wheels wrapped in 8.8-inch Firestone rubber radials up front and even wider 10.3-inch radials in the rear. The wheel design was similar to the optional aluminum wheels from the second-generation Sting Ray.

Painted in a graduated dark blue to white color scheme like the first "Shark," the completed Mako Shark II mockup was nothing short of spectacular. GM employees went out of their way to stop and inspect the car at the design studio. When it was officially unveiled on April 3, 1965, during the International Auto Show in New York City, the Mako Shark II became Chevrolet's star attraction and one of the biggest draws of the show.

Completing the Mako Shark II

After spending a week on display in New York, the Mako Shark II returned to Michigan, where it was paired with a complete and fully operational chassis. The only exterior modification made to the car was the removal of the black paint from its exhaust system. Ironically, the completed Mako Shark II's side pipes were nonfunctional. During chassis development, the exhaust system was routed along the car's undercarriage to a pair of tailpipes mounted neatly beneath the car's rear fascia.

A dressed-up-in-chrome 427-ci Mark IV V-8 engine provided power to the Mako Shark II. This same engine was offered as an optional powerplant in the 1966 Corvette. (Photo Courtesy GM Media)

An early rendering of the Mako Shark II's interior by GM designer James E. "Jim" Barron features many design cues that eventually became part of the third-generation Corvette, including the vertically mounted radio. (Photo Courtesy GM Media)

The Shark II was fitted with a 427-ci Mark IV V-8 engine and four-wheel disc brakes. The engine included a single, 4-barrel carburetor with a special air cleaner that used a custom-designed, rear-facing inlet specifically built to fit within the hood bulge. A 3-speed Turbo Hydra-Matic transmission transferred power to the car's rear wheels.

Accessing the engine was accomplished by unlocking the car's entire front end (via a release lever mounted on the lower left corner of the instrument panel) and tilting the assembly up and forward. The massive clamshell hood included two circular openings for checking/filling engine oil (on the right) and engine coolant (on the left). The leading edge of the hood also included a pair of concealed headlight assemblies.

The interior of the Mako Shark was a showcase of technology unlike any Corvette that had come before it. It featured a digital speedometer and a fuel gauge (a precursor to the dashboard introduced on the 1984 Corvette). The center console included a digital clock, the trip and main odometers, the radio head (with three prominent thumbwheel controls), the ignition switch, and an array of toggle switches that controlled the car's exterior and interior lights, the rear-window louvers, the windshield washer/wiper assemblies, a switch that extended elongated rear bumpers designed to protect the bodywork/paint when the car was parked, and a special servo that could rotate the rear license plate out of view.

Although the overall shape of its cockpit followed Barron's original design, the Mako Shark II's dashboard and center console used cutting-edge technologies far more advanced than the analog gauges and manual shifter depicted in his original rendering. (Photo Courtesy GM Media)

Barron's rendering of the Mako Shark II's interior showed the car's seats and center console as a single, fixed assembly. Also depicted were the car's roof-mounted headrests. (Photo Courtesy GM Media)

By the time that Bill Mitchell began driving the Mako Shark II as one of his personal cars, it had already become a fan favorite around the globe. General Motors received countless requests to build a production Corvette based on this design, which led to the creation of the 1968 Corvette Stingray. (Photo Courtesy GM Media)

The retractable license plate feature had allegedly been installed for occasions when the Mako Shark II was on public display, although it has also been speculated that it was purposefully installed for those occasions when Bill Mitchell, a known drag racer, wanted to push the car's limits on the open road.

The interior was equipped with nonadjustable driver and passenger seats. Instead of moving the seats, the pedals (along with the headlight dimmer switch) could be raised or lowered to accommodate most drivers. Steering wheel position could also be adjusted, as could the driver and passenger headrests. The headrests were affixed to the B-pillars, and each contained a pair of tiny speakers that broadcasted music and news from the car's AM/FM Multiplex radio.

Small, recessed servo motors mounted to the B-pillar allowed the car's single-piece roof panel to swing upward whenever occupants entered or exited the vehicle. The roof was activated by pressing a button mounted near the window and lock controls on the driver and passenger doors.

The Mako Shark II concept received an overwhelming positive response from fans in America and Europe. After its October 1965 debut at the Paris Auto Show, Chevrolet was flooded with requests asking them to transform the Shark II into the next Corvette. Other automotive manufacturers were equally smitten with the car. Giovanni Agnelli, then president of Fiat, reached out to Bill Mitchell to express his interest in driving the Mako Shark II. Special arrangements were made, and Agnelli piloted the car around an airport in Turin.

It seemed that Duntov alone felt the Shark II would be a lousy successor to the second-generation Sting Ray. He detested the car's long-hood, short-deck appearance. He also felt that the car's exaggerated fenders limited the driver's sight lines. Duntov took his concerns to Chevrolet General Manager Pete Estes, arguing that while the design might be appealing to consumers at first, turning the Mako Shark II into a production model would likely finish the Corvette program.

Zora Arkus-Duntov (left) and Bill Mitchell seldom saw eye-to-eye on anything pertaining to the Corvette. Their contentious difference of opinion during development of the 1963 split-window Corvette resulted in Duntov being banned from the styling department for several years. (Photo Courtesy GM Media)

Unbeknownst to Duntov, Mitchell had already sold senior management on the benefits of building a production Corvette based around his Shark design. The car was a head turner. Even better, it used the same chassis as the second-generation Sting Ray model, which saved General Motors millions of dollars in development and retooling costs.

Mitchell called Duntov with a compromise. He agreed to lower the fender heights and adjust other aspects of the car based on Duntov's earlier critiques. This placated Duntov's distaste for the Mako Shark II and lessened his angst at GM's decision to build a production Corvette based on Shinoda's design.

The Mako Shark II returned to the United States in early 1966. It became one of Bill Mitchell's personal vehicles for the next two years. It also served as the official pace car for several major racing events. But by the time the third-generation Corvette arrived in 1968, the Mako Shark II's distinctive, dramatic appearance had diminished, at least in the eyes of Bill Mitchell. It was time for a change . . .

The 1968 AstroVette

The AstroVette was introduced by General Motors at the launch of the third-generation Corvette Stingray in 1968. It was developed by Bill Mitchell's design team to study and improve the aerodynamic properties of the third-generation Corvette. Simply put, Bill Mitchell wanted "to see how slippery the Corvette could be made."

Development of a new concept vehicle usually follows the ground-up approach of car design. As we've already seen, it is a creative process that can take months, or even years, to complete. Although the AstroVette was admittedly more of an engineering study than a genuine concept car, it began life as a blue 1968 Corvette convertible and was developed over a very short period.

Outwardly, most of the factory Corvette's body panels were reworked or replaced to create the AstroVette's longer, airfoil-shaped body. Almost everything else—from the engine and chassis to the car's cockpit—was carried over from the production model.

Every element of the AstroVette's exterior was created to reduce drag. An elongated nose replaced the factory assembly. It included a minimized, contoured grille opening that directed air into the radiator and beneath the car. The factory hood was reworked to match the minimalist contours of the new nose assembly. It was flat and devoid of any badging that might generate air resistance. An abbreviated roadster windshield with an aggressive rake angle replaced the factory assembly. It mated with two additional glass panels to create a contoured, transparent windscreen that deflected air up and over the cockpit.

The car's front fenders remained mostly unchanged, although the factory gills were eliminated. Instead, four "flaps" were scribed onto the surface of the fenders. While the scribed flaps were purely a cosmetic detail on the AstroVette, they marked the location where actual pressure-actuated flaps (intended to eliminate engine compartment air pressure from building) would have been installed. The doors also remained the same, although the exterior door handle pockets were filled in, creating a smooth, unbroken surface along the top of the fender beltline.

The majority of the AstroVette's most dramatic body enhancements were at the rear of the car. The car's designers transformed the existing B-pillar into an arching airfoil behind the cockpit. Contoured, hinged skirts filled most of the rear fender wheel openings. The factory rear fascia and bumper were replaced with an extended, tapered rear end that swept downward from the rear of the cockpit and upward from behind the rear wheel openings before mating along the car's character line.

Although the AstroVette began life as a 1968 Corvette convertible, few of the original body panels remained on the heavily modified car. However, the interior remained virtually unchanged–including its blue finish (which can be seen in this early image of the car)–until Bill Mitchell elected to have the interior re-dyed black. (Photo Courtesy GM Media)

Every element of the AstroVette (from the refined fender flares to the low-slung windshield) was deliberately engineered to eliminate drag. Engineers even removed the raised Corvette hood emblem and replaced it with a decal.

The back half of the AstroVette was elongated and tapered downward to eliminate the formation of turbulence behind the car. Also, while a "sugar scoop" roofline was added, this feature functioned as an airfoil to help prevent lift while the car was in motion.

The AstroVette was on display at a regional auto show prior to being put into long-term storage by General Motors. Over the course of its lifetime, the AstroVette was repainted several times in a variety of different colors. It has since been restored to its original Pearlescent White. (Photo Courtesy GM Media)

For all of the modifications to its outward appearance, the interior of the AstroVette remained virtually unchanged, save for the installation of a new steering wheel. (Photo Courtesy GM Media)

Several additional measures were added to the car to help reduce drag. The factory wheels were replaced with narrow rims and tall Firestone tires reminiscent of those used on cars from the 1930s. Aluminum wheel covers, like those used on cars attempting land speed records at the Bonneville salt flats, were also installed. The car's designers even added partial front and rear belly pan assemblies to improve airflow beneath the car.

Mitchell had the AstroVette finished in Pearlescent White paint and ordered the car's factory interior to be dyed black. Besides the modified interior color and the installation of a three-spoke racing-style steering wheel, the car's interior remained unchanged. The car also maintained its 427-ci 400-hp V-8 engine and Turbo Hydra-Matic transmission.

The car was poorly received when first introduced in 1968. Keeping with Corvette's nautical naming conventions, critics began sarcastically calling the car "Moby Dick," referencing the car's exaggerated length and bold, white exterior. Despite GM's early indications that the car was to be used to advance "another area of automotive design," the car quickly became a misguided novelty. It made appearances at regional car shows for much of 1968 and then disappeared into storage at General Motors for many years.

During its internment at General Motors, the AstroVette was repainted bright orange. While there is not much information supporting the reason for the color change, it's possible that General Motors used the car to evaluate an orange paint scheme prior to introducing the color on a production Corvette. Whatever the reason, the AstroVette was restored to its original Pearlescent White in 1992. Today, the car is on display at the National Corvette Museum in Bowling Green, Kentucky.

It is worth noting that two styling features introduced on the AstroVette were eventually incorporated into the production model. The 1973 Corvette received a less exaggerated version of the AstroVette's nose after the decision was made to get rid of its front chrome bumpers. A year later, the Corvette's rear chrome bumperettes were also eliminated and a new fascia was introduced that resembled a subdued version of the AstroVette's rear end.

The 1969 Manta Ray

The 1965 Mako Shark II was arguably one of the most influential concept Corvettes in the history of the brand. But by the time the third-generation Corvette Stingray arrived in 1968, the Shark had lost much of its public appeal. It simply looked too much like the production cars it had inspired a half-decade earlier.

Instead of retiring the car or sending it to the crusher, Bill Mitchell decided it was time to breathe new life into his most beloved Corvette. He sent the Mako Shark II back to the GM design studio with a list of styling changes, most of which involved modifications to the back half of the car.

One of the most dramatic changes was the replacement of the Shark II's ducktail with a longer, tapered rear end reminiscent of the one introduced on the 1968 AstroVette. The Shark's rear louvers were replaced with a narrow, vertical rear window placed just behind the vehicle's cockpit. This rear window was framed by a "sugar scoop" feature that cascaded along the back half of the car before coming to a point just above the bumper. The fuel filler cap was relocated and placed in the middle of this feature.

Widened rear fenders each housed a new, flip-up brake light assembly that actuated during panic braking or when signaling a turn. The actual brake lights were set into the rear decklid beneath pop-up lids. Each lid was affixed with a mirror on its undersides that reflected the brake lights when activated. The car also included the traditional four-taillight arrangement first introduced on the 1961 Corvette.

The other major change to the Shark II was the installation of an all-aluminum, 427-ci ZL1 engine. The 7.0-liter ZL1 was an L88 engine built with an aluminum

In 1969, the Mako Shark II was transformed into the Manta Ray. It received Chevrolet's new ZL1 V-8 engine, chrome side pipes, a reimagined front grille, and a new-and-elongated rear end. (Photo Courtesy GM Media)

A narrow glass panel framed in a sugar-scoop roofline replaced the Mako Shark II's louvered rear window. A less-dramatic version of this styling element served as the basis of the third-generation Corvette's rear-window structure. (Photo Courtesy GM Media)

One of the most dramatic design elements of the Manta Ray was its pop-up mirrored taillight assemblies. In addition to the traditional rear taillights in its lower rear fascia, the Ray's concealed compartments opened during braking and reflected a pair of illuminated brake lights. (Photo Courtesy GM Media)

The Manta Ray's interior remained largely unchanged from the Mako Shark II, although it did receive a new steering wheel and updated badging depicting the Manta Ray logo. It also received an assortment of updated toggle switches and gauges representative of the evolving automotive technologies of that era. (Photo Courtesy GM Media)

block. Originally produced for Can-Am racing, the engine produced a massive 524 hp and 550 ft-lbs of torque. The exhaust system was removed from beneath the car and was instead cleverly tucked in along the chromed rocker panels below each door. Each exterior pipe assembly included a finned muffler and a downturned exhaust pipe just ahead of the rear wheels.

The car was rebadged during the winter of 1969–1970 and given the name "Manta Ray" (once more paying tribute to Bill Mitchell's passion for the ocean). Unique emblems depicting an actual manta ray were developed and added to the car's front fenders and right rear bumper assembly. The classic Corvette crossed-flags emblem was added to the fuel filler cap. It was also repainted dark blue with pearl white accents along its lower edges.

From a pure show car standpoint, the 1969 Manta Ray represented the last in a long line of dream/concept cars that began with the 1953 EX-52/EX-122 Corvette. While we'll explore a variety of concept Corvettes that followed the Manta Ray, there've been few examples built since that served as "an exercise in pure automotive form (which) could be taken at its own pace, for its own sake."

Today, both the Mako Shark I and the Manta Ray are carefully preserved as part of the GM Heritage Center Collection.

The Mako Shark and the Manta Ray remain two of the most iconic Corvette concept vehicles in the history of the brand. While it is unfortunate that the Mako Shark II no longer exists in its original form, these iconic cars inspired the generation of Corvettes that followed. (Photo Courtesy GM Media)

Bill Mitchell's fascination with marine life gave rise to the creation of the Manta Ray badging. This iconic emblem was the direct predecessor to the "Stingray" badging installed on every seventh- and eighth-generation Corvette to date. (Photo Courtesy GM Media)

CHAPTER 5

EVOLUTION OF THE MID-ENGINE CORVETTE: PART 1 (1960–1970)

Zora was driven by more horsepower, more RPM, better handling, another speed record—that was his adrenaline. For him it was a matter of how to get this done . . . all of these unusual engine combinations evolved because Zora was driven by that. His heart and this interest were in the right places for the right reasons.

—Herb Fischel, former head of GM's Motorsports Technology Group

On the evening of July 18, 2019, Chevrolet introduced the eighth-generation Corvette Stingray via an in-person and global live stream event in Orange County, California. From the moment it was officially announced that General Motors was going to produce a mid-engine Corvette as the successor to the seventh-generation Stingray, there was a massive (and massively diverse) response from Corvette enthusiasts around the globe.

In one camp, there were those who believed that a mid-engine Corvette was the next step in the natural evolution of a car that had, for all intents and purposes, reached its maximum potential in its traditional front-engine, rear-wheel-drive configuration. On the other hand, there were just as many who felt that GM's decision to develop a mid-engine Corvette was breaking with more than 65 years of tradition and would bring about the swift demise to the brand entirely.

The Chevrolet Engineering Research Vehicle (CERV I) was designed and built at the Chevrolet Engineering Center in Warren, Michigan. It was developed by Zora Arkus-Duntov to study ride and handling behaviors of a mid-engine vehicle in more rigorous environments. (Photo Courtesy General Motors LLC)

While that debate may have quieted since the mid-engine Corvette became commercially available in 2020, there are still factions of Corvette enthusiasts who denounce the mid-engine Corvette for breaking with tradition. It may come as a surprise to some to learn it was Zora Arkus-Duntov who first proposed the idea of transforming the Corvette into a mid-engine sports car more than a half-century ago. And, like so many of the design elements that have been integrated into Corvettes over the decades, Duntov's thoughts about placing the engine in the rear of the car had very practical beginnings.

The 1960 Chevrolet Experimental Research Vehicle/Chevrolet Engineering Research Vehicle (CERV I)

In an interview in *Esquire* magazine in November 1961, Duntov said, "CERV I is designed without limits. It is very fast. It is very sensitive. It amplifies all disturbances of steering and driver control, and all problems of transmitting power to the road. It is an admirable tool. It tells us, for example, what to put in a Corvette, for the highest margin of safety for the driver."

Duntov's first notions about placing the Corvette's engine behind the driver materialized while racing the Corvette SS at Sebring in 1957. Heat coming off the SS's

The Chevrolet Engineering Research Vehicle (CERV I) was one of the most important concept vehicles ever built by General Motors. The mid-engine, open-wheel race car prototype was Zora Arkus-Duntov's personal engineering test mule for the development of new automotive technologies. Here, Duntov drives the CERV I around Riverside International Raceway in California before the start of the 1960 U.S. Grand Prix. (Photo Courtesy General Motors LLC)

The CERV I is shown under construction at Chevrolet Engineering in Warren, Michigan. (Photo Courtesy General Motors LLC)

engine had produced blistering temperatures inside the cockpit. After fielding similar complaints from his codrivers, Duntov decided then and there that he'd begin development of a mid-engine race car. Unfortunately, his plan had to wait until 1959, when Chevrolet started to back down on its strict adherence to the AMA's ban on racing.

Development of the Chevrolet Experimental Research Vehicle (CERV I) coincided with Chevrolet's introduction of its rear-engine Corvair. Duntov sold GM's brass on the idea of building the car by claiming it could be used to validate the soundness of any rear-engine platform, not just those specifically built for high-performance driving conditions.

The realty of the situation (of which General Motors was blissfully unaware) was that he planned to build the car with two objectives in mind. First and foremost, it would be able to navigate the challenging twists and turns of the International Hill Climb at the summit of Pikes Peak in Colorado. Second, optimistic that General Motors would eventually allow the CERV I to race at the Indianapolis Speedway, Duntov wanted to build a car that would conform to the design requirements of that event.

Engineering "The Hillclimber"

Duntov, along with engineers Harold Krieger and Walt Zetye, started work on the CERV I in 1959. Early efforts on "the Hillclimber" (as it was commonly referred to by GM styling before receiving the CERV I designation) centered around the development of a chassis with a 60-percent rearward weight bias and a low polar moment of inertia (the close distribution of mass around the center of gravity). Both were achieved by grouping the driver, the engine, and the fuel tanks near the center of the car.

The Hillclimber was originally powered by a specialized 283-ci Chevy V-8 engine specifically developed for it. The engine featured several aluminum components including the block, heads, the flywheel, water pump housing, clutch pressure plate, and starter motor body. The block uses a high-silicon alloy that enabled the

The CERV I has been fitted with a total of seven different engines over the course of its lifetime. Its original engine, a Chevrolet small-block V-8, is similar to the current 6.2L V-8 small-block engine that's installed in the eighth-generation mid-engine Corvette Stingray. (Photo Courtesy General Motors LLC)

The CERV I currently uses a 377-ci V-8 Grand Sport engine along with a revised Rochester fuel injection system and wider tires. In this configuration, the CERV I was able to achieve a top speed of more than 200 mph.

The CERV I was built for a single purpose: to develop a low weight, low center of mass race car with a mid-engine configuration. The "bare bones" cockpit offered the driver just enough space to strap in and pilot the CERV I. (Photo Courtesy General Motors LLC)

pistons to travel in their individual cylinder bores without separate liners. This manufacturing process was unheard of in cast-iron engine assemblies. In addition, casting the block out of aluminum instead of iron resulted in a weight reduction of 90 pounds!

Duntov also used magnesium for the clutch housing, the fuel injection manifold, and the manifold adapter plate. The rear-engine placement allowed Duntov to install a taller manifold with 16-inch ram pipes. The longer pipes improved the engine's mid-range torque, which was of vital importance for hill climbing. Air fed into the engine via a pair of scoops that were positioned just behind the driver's headrest. Individual 40-inch headers were mounted to the exhaust manifolds and routed toward the rear of the car. There, they mated with a single tubular collector above each of the rear axles.

Despite its unique modifications, the engine was largely the same as the stock 315-hp V-8 used in the 1960 Corvette. It featured the same Duntov cam and the same stock lifters, pistons, connecting rods, and crankshaft found in the other engine. However, unlike the Corvette, the CERV I's engine weighed just 350 pounds fully assembled, which was roughly 175 pounds less than its cast-iron counterpart. It also produced 353 brake hp at 6,200 rpm, which translated into just over 1 hp per pound as well as 1 hp per cubic inch of displacement!

Power from the engine was transferred to the rear wheels via a mostly stock 4-speed synchronized transmission. Given the space limitations of the rear engine and axle assemblies, the mostly stock transmission incorporated a special transaxle housing that placed the reverse gears (normally positioned toward the rear of the transmission assembly) within the transmission's main case.

Duntov integrated elements from his SS Corvette racer project into the CERV I design. It used the same 3.28:1 overall rear axle ratio and the same inboard-mounted rear brakes. An experimental mercury switch (originally designed for the Corvette SS) was installed to sense the amount of deceleration the car was experiencing during braking. This switch operated a solenoid valve that prevented the car's rear wheels from locking during extreme braking conditions.

Tony Lapine (left) began his career with General Motors in 1951. He served as the studio engineer for the 1963 Corvette Sting Ray, at which point he gained the attention (and respect) of Zora Arkus-Duntov. Duntov and Lapine worked together on several concept Corvettes, including both mid-engine CERV prototypes. (Photo Courtesy General Motors LLC)

The CERV I had specially designed aluminum brake drums with cast-iron liners installed at all four wheels. A braking ratio of 57 percent in the front and 43 percent in the rear was regulated by a single master cylinder with an internal dual-piston assembly, which enabled one set of brakes (front or rear) to continue functioning even if the other set failed during operation. This same type of dual-cylinder master cylinder is almost universally used on most of today's automobiles.

The car's brakes could be actuated by one of two pedals. The first was mounted conventionally next to the accelerator pedal and the second was mounted for left-foot braking, which was a requirement at venues such as the Indianapolis 500.

The front and rear suspension used on the CERV I was heavily influenced by/directly borrowed from earlier concept Corvettes. A complete front suspension assembly was adapted from the Corvette SS and integrated into the car. It used variable-rate springs and hard-mounted Delco shock absorbers with interchangeable internal components that could be swapped out to adapt the car to varying road conditions. An 11/16-inch stabilizer bar interconnected the front wheels.

Despite borrowing from components originally developed for the Q-Corvette, the CERV I's independent rear suspension required a bit more consideration by the engineering team. Vertical movement of the wheels was controlled by two lateral links: an upper link that doubled as a driveshaft and a lower, tubular link that provided stability to the axle. Variable rate coil springs integrated onto the rear shock tower assemblies were mounted diagonally at each rear wheel. A third link assembly between each wheel hub and the car's frame was incorporated to transmit driving and braking thrust. This configuration became the basis of design for the 1963 Corvette Sting Ray's independent rear suspension.

Designing a Body for the CERV I

Larry Shinoda and German designer Tony Lapine were tasked with designing the body of the CERV I. Their objective was to provide the driver with uninterrupted visibility by creating an open cockpit while enclosing the car's engine, transaxles, and cooling system within a streamlined fiberglass shell. Where the car's structural rigidity was dependent upon its chrome-molybdenum steel tube chassis underpinnings, the CERV I's fiberglass body needed to be both aerodynamic and lightweight.

The car's cylindrical-wedge-shaped body was hand constructed using just two layers of fiberglass, making it appreciably thinner than the standard Corvette body panels of that era. The body assembly, consisting of just three major sections, completely enclosed the car's chassis and weighed just 80 pounds. Its front end featured

In 2021, the CERV I was on display at the National Corvette Museum in Bowling Green, Kentucky. If you think the car looks different than it did when first constructed, you're right! Larry Shinoda performed a restyle of the car's body, removing air scoops and streamlining its overall appearance. (Photo Courtesy Kolecki Photography)

The mid-engine CERV I was introduced a full year before the first mid-engine Indy cars came on the scene. Here, Zora Arkus-Duntov pushes the car through a high embankment, demonstrating that the car is equally comfortable on a racetrack or a road course such as Pikes Peak. (Photo Courtesy General Motors LLC)

three separate air inlet ducts. The forward-most of these provided airflow into a front-mounted aluminum radiator. The other twin ducts, placed just ahead of the front axle assemblies, directed cooling air to the engine oil pan.

The fully assembled, single-seater CERV-I had a dry weight of 1,450 pounds and a wheelbase that measured 96 inches in length. The body was finished in white with metallic blue stripes that ran the length of the car and highlight the car's single roll bar, which had been installed just behind the driver's seat.

Putting the CERV I to the Test

Testing of the CERV I began in September 1960 on the challenging roads of Pikes Peak. Initial time and speed results provided to Duntov and his crew after each test run up the mountain were so disappointing that the team elected not to compete in the actual event. It wasn't until the team received their official results from Pikes Peak that they discovered the times provided to them during testing had been inaccurate.

To rebound from their struggles at Pikes Peak, Duntov had the CERV I transported to the Continental Divide Raceway in Castle Rock, Colorado, for road course testing. There, he partnered with the Firestone Tire company to test the car's acceleration and cornering capabilities with tires of various heights and thicknesses. Duntov wanted to determine which tire setups worked best for the CERV I when encountering various driving situations. The outcome of this testing was so beneficial to all involved that the CERV I became an integral part of future tire testing programs for both Firestone and (later) Goodyear Tires. The results of this experimentation aided in the development of the modern, wider race tires used in open wheel racing today.

The CERV I was brought back to Detroit and overhauled. From there, it was shipped to Riverside Raceway in California for two weeks of additional testing before being showcased at the U.S. Grand Prix on November 20, 1960. Press releases documenting the CERV I's participation in the Grand Prix altered the car's name to "Chevrolet Engineering Research Vehicle." This name was used to shield the appearance of a Chevrolet automobile at a sanctioned race event during a time when the company was still participating in the AMA racing ban.

Over the course of its working lifespan, the CERV I was equipped with seven separate engines of varying sizes and horsepower. However, its original engine—the Chevrolet small-block V-8 comprised of lightweight aluminum engine components—was a direct precursor to the contemporary 6.2L V-8 engine, which was developed for the 2020 Mid-Engine Corvette Stingray.

This modern image of the CERV I shows the car fitted with wider tires than those first used at Pikes Peak. The car became a test mule to determine which tire widths worked best for use in racing programs such as Formula 1 and Indy. (Photo Courtesy General Motors LLC)

Zora Arkus-Duntov emerges from the CERV I looking pleased with the car's performance after an aggressive test drive around the Riverside Raceway. (Photo Courtesy General Motors LLC)

Zora Arkus-Duntov poses with the CERV I as part of a GM photo shoot to promote the new experimental research car. The expression on Duntov's face makes it easy to imagine he was already envisioning a mid-engine Corvette platform as the next step in the evolution of the brand. (Photo Courtesy General Motors LLC)

The 1962 XP-777: Corvair Monza GT

The Corvair Monza GT was not specifically developed as a Corvette concept vehicle. However, Larry Shinoda's unique GT design directly influenced future iterations of the Corvette (including other rear- and mid-engine prototypes, each of which positively impacted the evolution of the 2020 Mid-Engine Corvette Stingray). It is for that reason the Monza GT is included here.

The XP-777 Corvair Monza GT was powered by a new 6-cylinder engine specifically developed for the Corvair platform. Its body and powertrain were mounted to a steel monocoque chassis developed by Jim Musser of Chevrolet's research and development department. (Photo Courtesy General Motors LLC)

Larry Shinoda and Tony Lapine work on a full-scale rendering of the Corvair Monza GT. Note the smaller renderings above these men. Images of this type were created during early styling sessions and later used for visual reference when developing the final design. (Photo Courtesy General Motors LLC)

Ed Cole presented the Chevy Corvair to the world in 1960. The popular production model featured a rear-mounted engine, four-wheel independent suspension, and a transaxle, the last of which had been developed as part of the abandoned Q-Chevrolet concept car lineup a few years earlier. Chevrolet sold more than 1,000,000 examples of the Corvair from 1960 to 1963, which proved the marketability of a rear-engine automobile.

This engineering buck of the Monza GT helped GM's engineering team determine final placement and fitment of the car's underpinnings, including its cockpit, engine, drivetrain, fuel cell, suspension, exhaust system, and so on. (Photo Courtesy General Motors LLC)

The success of Chevy's new compact car inspired Bill Mitchell to develop a new, more radical Corvair based around the same rear-engine design. He employed the talents of his strongest designers—Larry Shinoda and Tony Lapine—to develop a car that included sharp leading/trailing edges and surface breaks with long, smooth curves. Shinoda, who had previously partnered with Mitchell on the Mako Shark, began laying out a new design that drew inspiration from the earlier Corvette concept.

Larry Shinoda poses in the lot outside the GM design studios with the full-sized clay model mockup of his Corvair Monza GT body design. (Photo Courtesy General Motors LLC)

The Corvair Monza GT (and SS, which is not pictured) were direct predecessors of the Grand Sport II developed by Frank Winchell and Chevrolet's research and development department. Given the Corvair's successes during testing, Chevrolet wanted to experiment with building a lightweight mid-engine sports car equipped with a larger V-8 powerplant. (Photo Courtesy General Motors LLC)

Many of the styling elements first introduced by Shinoda in the Corvair Monza GT resurfaced on future concept vehicles. The Corvair's louvered rear window was replicated on the Mako Shark II a few years later. (Photo Courtesy General Motors LLC)

The Monza GT was a well-engineered car that pioneered many concepts that have since found their way into other production automobiles. Its chassis used a deep platform frame like those found in Porsche-built race cars from that era. It came equipped with four-wheel independent suspension comprised of unequal A-arms connected via front and rear torsion bars. It sat on lightweight Halibrand magnesium alloy wheels and included disc brakes at all four corners. Its wheelbase was just 92 inches (2,337 mm), a full 16 inches shorter than the production Corvair.

The car's interior featured adjustable gas and brake pedals along with an adjustable/detachable steering wheel. These items allowed the cockpit to be configured to the individual needs of each driver, even with seats that were fixed in place.

The body of the Monza GT was equally innovative for its time. It was comprised of three major assemblies. The first included the header and nose panels; the front fenders; a pair of long sill plates mounted between the front and rear wheel openings; and a static, contoured body panel where the front hood/bonnet would normally have been. Each of these components was mounted separately to the car's chassis.

The central section consisted of a large, single-piece clamshell assembly with a wraparound windshield. This section of the car pivoted forward along a concealed hinge point, allowing vehicle occupants access into and out of the car's cockpit without the need for separate doors.

The third assembly was also its largest. A second, single-piece clamshell included the car's rear fenders, rear side windows, engine cover, exhaust pipes (which mated to the engine exhaust manifold when the canopy was closed), rear bumper, and taillights. In place of a rear window, the car employed special louvers that could be adjusted via a level mounted on the center console. This assembly swung open toward the back of the car on a pivot hinge mounted across the rear-most section of the car's frame.

GM Vice President of Design Bill Mitchell poses with the finished Corvair Monza GT. Although the Corvair did not make it to production, the car served as an early inspiration for Mitchell's Mako Shark II. (Photo Courtesy General Motors LLC)

Despite its dramatic styling, the Monza GT's powerplant was unremarkable. Its original engine was a standard 145-ci Chevrolet Turbo-Air V-6 that produced a paltry 102 hp. It was fitted ahead of the rear axle assembly in a mid-engine layout and paired to a rear-mounted transaxle. The Monza GT was fitted with other engines of varying horsepower throughout its life, suggesting that it also served as a mid-engine test mule at various points in its past.

Despite the early successes of the production Corvair, its popularity started to wane dramatically in 1964 and 1965. The rapid decline in sales numbers was the most plausible reason the 1962 Corvair Monza GT never moved beyond the concept vehicle phase. Elements from the Monza GT were later incorporated into other concept vehicles, including the 1967 Astro I. It also served as Shinoda's inspiration for the Mako Shark II, which in turn inspired the look of the third-generation Corvette.

Although the XP-777 Corvair Monza GT (silver, foreground) is the example most often associated with the history of the Corvette, both the mid-engine coupe and the rear-engine Monza SS roadster introduced numerous styling elements that literally shaped the look of the Shark II and the third-generation Stingray. (Photo Courtesy General Motors LLC)

Today, the 1962 Corvair Monza GT can be found at the GM Heritage Center.

The 1964 CERV II

Competitive advantage, and not "experimental research" (as the name indicates), was the primary driving force behind the development of the CERV II concept car.

Despite the AMA's ban on racing, Zora Arkus-Duntov and Chevrolet General Manager Bunkie Knudsen recognized a growing urgency to develop a Chevrolet-branded vehicle that could compete against the GT-40 race car Ford was developing for Le Mans. Duntov had invested considerable time and resources into the canceled Grand Sport Corvette program. Despite having personal reservations about developing another purpose-built race car after being reprimanded by GM's brass for creating the Grand Sport without their consent, Duntov was encouraged by Knudsen's general passion for racing, his conviction to defeat the Ford Motor Company, and his belief that Chevrolet's participation in racing would sell more automobiles.

Duntov envisioned the CERV II as a full-bodied, four-wheel-drive prototype race car with a mid-engine configuration and an automatic transmission. He was convinced that the benefits of installing four-wheel drive in a race car outweighed (literally in this case) the added weight of the extra powertrain components.

The CERV II was equipped with an all-aluminum 377-ci V-8 engine like the one first developed by Duntov for the 1963 Grand Sport Corvette. It used a Hilborn constant-flow fuel injection system and gear-driven, single overhead cams that operated two valves per cylinder via conventional rocker arms. The robust 6.2-liter engine was rated at approximately 490 hp.

One Engine, Two Transmissions

One of Duntov's first design challenges was determining how to distribute torque between the front and rear wheels. He decided that the CERV II would use two separate transmissions and two Powerglide torque converters: a 10-inch driving the front axle and an 11-inch driving the rear. Each was paired to the front and rear of the engine, respectively. The torque converters were then calibrated so they would distribute more torque to the car's rear wheels during hard acceleration and more balanced torque between all four wheels once the car had reached its desired speed.

Power was transferred to the asphalt via a set of Kelsey-Hayes magnesium wheels wrapped in a matched set of advanced Firestone race tires. The wider, 9.5x15-inch low-profile tires were still under development by Firestone (for use at the 1964 Indianapolis 500) when Duntov

The cockpit of the CERV II was intentionally configured with right-hand drive to better accommodate the clockwise configuration of most road courses. It also creates a more favorable weight bias and allows for greater driver visibility as he or she is seated closer to the apex of most turns. (Photo Courtesy General Motors LLC)

Officially developed as a second "engineering research vehicle," the CERV II was really Duntov's attempt to build a Le Mans–style race car that could compete with (and potentially defeat) Ford's GT40. (Photo Courtesy General Motors LLC)

acquired them. He convinced the tire manufacturer to provide him with the set, arguing that Firestone would reap the benefit of seeing how they performed on the CERV II.

Duntov equipped both the front and rear axles with compact, 2-speed gearboxes that could be controlled via a lever in the car's cockpit. With the lever engaged, the gearbox could be switched from direct drive to a 1.5:1 gear reduction. With the lower gear ratio engaged, the CERV II could achieve a 0–60 time of just 2.8 seconds. With the higher ratio engaged, the 0–60 time suffered but the CERV II could exceed 200 mph! Duntov achieved a top speed of 214.01 mph in the CERV II during a testing session at the GM Proving Grounds in Milford, Michigan.

Shinoda and Lapine Design the CERV II

Larry Shinoda and Tony Lapine were once more chosen to design the car's body. To maintain a short wheelbase of just 90 inches, Duntov directed the pair to place the cockpit seating in an upright position. This went against the design standards of then-current Grand Prix racers, but Duntov reasoned that the CERV II would be at its best during hard acceleration and cornering, which required less of a "swept-back" stance than other high-speed race cars.

Lapine and Shinoda sculpted the first CERV II model out of clay. They developed the car's Stingray-esque body lines around an upward-ducted radiator; a built-in roll bar; its unique mid-engine, dual-transmission powertrain; and Duntov's shortened wheelbase. Duntov's approval of the mockup led to the fabrication of a fiberglass body that closely resembled the clay model.

The body was constructed of three separate sections. The first section included the front bumper, flared front fenders (like those on the Mako Shark), and the hood assembly. The second section housed the car's two-seat cockpit and was the only section of the car firmly affixed to the chassis. The third section served as the bonnet

Zora Arkus-Duntov developed a dual-transmission configuration for the CERV II with one transmission mounted to each end of the engines. He earned a patent for this unique drivetrain arrangement. (Photo Courtesy General Motors LLC)

A full-sized clay model of the CERV II was developed under the direction of Tony Lapine and Larry Shinoda in the GM design studio. Many of the reference drawings posted behind it contain styling cues that eventually found their way into Winchell's Grand Sport II and Mitchell's X-15 concept vehicle. (Photo Courtesy General Motors LLC)

Members of GM's engineering department and design studio stand proudly together with the newly completed CERV II at the GM Technical Center in Warren, Michigan. (Photo Courtesy General Motors LLC)

to the car's rear-mounted engine. It included large side scoops in each quarter panel and a pair of rectangular openings behind the driver and passenger seats from which the car's inverted header pipes projected like porcupine quills.

CERV II versus Grand Sport II

The CERV II made its inaugural test run in March 1964 at the Rattlesnake Raceway in Midland, Texas. Despite some early challenges with the as-yet incomplete 2-speed gearbox, the car was successfully driven by Grand Prix racers Roger Penske and Jim Hall. Both men were impressed with the car's handling, and Penske marveled at how well the two separate drivetrains worked with one another. While the car still presented some engineering challenges, including a tendency to spin out uncontrollably when letting off the throttle at high speeds, the CERV II proved to be a viable race car.

To help improve the car's higher-speed instability, Duntov cut an additional opening into the rearmost body panel and installed a retractable spoiler of his own design. Dubbed the "cow tongue" spoiler when first introduced (based on how it emerged from the car when engaged), it created the necessary additional downforce to stabilize the car at speeds more than 150 mph.

Unfortunately for Duntov's new race car, the CERV II was not the only GM vehicle being tested at the Midland Texas raceway that March. Frank Winchell, one of Duntov's professional rivals within General Motors, developed his own mid-engine racer: the Grand Sport II. The GS II had succeeded to run wide open throughout its test session without exhibiting any issues like those suffered by the CERV II.

The edict came down from Bunkie Knudsen in the fall of 1964 that the CERV II would not be used to compete against Ford at Le Mans. Instead, Chaparral would represent Chevrolet at the 24-hour event in 1966 and 1967. Knudsen's decision to distance himself from the CERV II program was a painful blow to Duntov both professionally and personally. Knudsen had privately endorsed and encouraged Duntov's efforts to build the CERV II only to later abandon him and the fledgling race program in one fell swoop.

The CERV II was never afforded the opportunity to compete in a sanctioned race event. However, many of the technologies introduced on Duntov's compact, mid-engine racer were eventually repurposed during his final decade with Chevrolet. Although his quest to build a corporately sponsored race car may have been at an end, his determination to build a commercially viable mid-engine Corvette was just beginning.

Today, the CERV II resides at the GM Heritage Center. It is celebrated as one of the early pioneering milestones in the development of the 2020 mid-engine Corvette.

The CERV II is driven by legend Roger Penske during its inaugural test run at Rattlesnake Raceway in Midland, Texas. The CERV II was also test piloted by Grand Prix driver Jim Hall. (Photo Courtesy General Motors LLC)

Duntov inspects the engine and powertrain of the CERV II (with its body removed) at the Rattlesnake Raceway. Behind him is Frank Winchell's Grand Sport II. (Photo Courtesy General Motors LLC)

In an attempt to improve downforce on the rear of the car when operating at high speed, Duntov installed a "cow tongue" spoiler (shown in its extended position here). (Photo Courtesy General Motors LLC)

The 1964 XP-819: The "Ugly Duckling" Rear-Engine Concept

The creation of the XP-819 "Ugly Duckling" began as a design exercise to conceptualize a rear-engine sports car based on a short list of engineering specifications created by Zora Arkus-Duntov. With the number of available foreign automobiles (many of them sports cars) on the rise across the United States, Duntov wanted to determine whether a rear-engine Corvette would be a viable option to help differentiate the brand from its international competitors.

The objective: develop a production car that utilized a rear-mounted (located behind the rear axle) engine, sat on a 90-inch wheelbase (the same wheelbase as the CERV I and II), featured body lines to make its Corvette lineage apparent, and set the driver low in the car, allowing for a reduction in the car's overall height. Two design teams, each working independently, were tasked with developing their own variant of a rear-engine Corvette concept vehicle.

Shinoda Delivers an "Ugly Duckling"

The first team was made up of Frank Winchell and his Research and Development department. While Duntov planned on championing the effort himself, he became professionally entangled in several other projects. The second team was comprised of members from GM's design team. Henry Haga appointed Larry Shinoda as the project lead. Haga had seen Shinoda's earlier work on the Corvair Monza GT and SS concepts and knew his talents were exactly what this project needed.

The teams were given just a few short weeks to produce line drawings of their designs. These drawings were used to determine whether General Motors would build an actual prototype of the car. As the designs neared completion, Duntov and Haga scheduled a meeting and asked participants from each team to present their work.

Winchell's team presented first. Their design depicted a car with a high nose, a 1963 Corvette front windshield, and a cockpit more akin to a race car than anything being sold commercially. The car's mechanical systems, including the radiator, fan shroud, and condenser, were hung

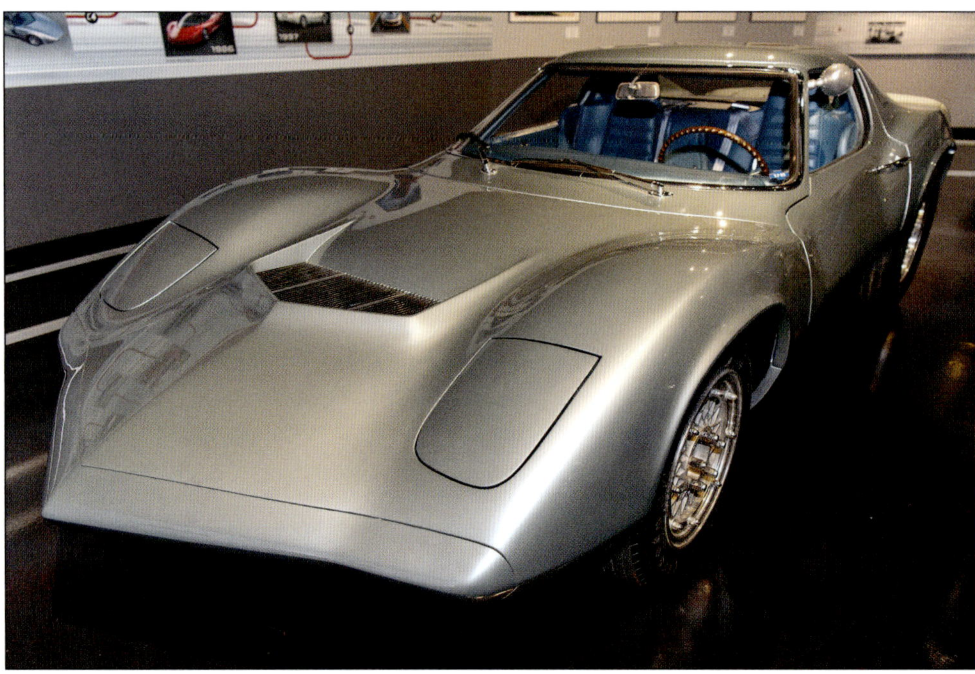

The XP-819 "Ugly Duckling" was designed by Larry Shinoda and John Schinella and was the first Corvette concept to feature a rear-mounted engine. Although it never made it past the concept phase, the Ugly Duckling is responsible for several technologies still used on current Corvettes. (Photo Courtesy Kolecki Photography)

Upon approval of Shinoda's design, the styling department wasted no time constructing a full-size clay mockup of the XP-819. (Photo Courtesy General Motors LLC)

Development of the full-size clay models provided several advantages to the design team. It allowed them to work out final placement of chassis and mechanical components. It also allowed for quick fabrication of the car's three major body assemblies out of fiberglass. (Photo Courtesy General Motors LLC)

Although the XP-819 represented one of GM's first efforts at a rear-engine production car, many of the Ugly Duckling's design elements evolved from Shinoda's work on the CERV II, the Grand Sport II, and the Mako Shark II, all of which can be spotted in the images on the wall behind the clay model. (Photo Courtesy General Motors LLC)

This GM press photo of the XP-819 clearly depicts the design similarities between the rear-engine concept car and the third-generation production Corvette, including its signature sugar scoop rear window and its round taillights. (Photo Courtesy General Motors LLC)

off the back of the car. The rest of the car looked a lot like the 1963 Corvette.

At this point in the presentation, the XP-819 landed its famous name. When Duntov saw the initial design proposal, he laughed and said, "Ha, it would be [a] very ugly duckling."

Most others present in that meeting agreed. However, Shinoda remained silent until he was approached by Irv Rybicki, director of design (below Bill Mitchell). When asked, Shinoda commented, "I think we could make it into a very beautiful car. When do you want to see it?"

Rybicki said he wanted to see it after lunch.

Although not yet complete, Shinoda committed to presenting his team's design as requested. When the group broke for lunch, Shinoda and his team rushed back to their studio and worked feverishly to finalize their drawings. Shortly thereafter, Duntov, Rybicki, Winchell, and his team arrived at the studio to see Shinoda's rear-engine design.

All were astonished by what they saw. Shinoda's design was rendered at a full 1:1 scale. Duntov immediately began taking measurements from the drawings, convinced that Shinoda's design had broken with the original engineering specifications. He even asked Shinoda, "Where did you cheat?"

It was decided right then and there that the XP-819 "Ugly Duckling" should be built.

Building the XP-819

Shinoda's design and the prototype that followed incorporated much of the same "Coke bottle" styling that had been previously introduced on his Corvair Monza GT concept. Winchell, who had recognized the XP-819 as an opportunity to influence the future look of the Corvette, had encouraged Shinoda to repurpose design elements from the earlier concept car. Shinoda and designer John Schinella had done just that.

The result was a car that was once more comprised of three major body assemblies like the Monza GT before it.

The forward-most section included a urethane front bumper, a pair of flared fenders with pop-up (concealed) headlights, and a static panel where the hood/engine bonnet normally resided. A large air duct was sculpted into this panel that allowed warm air to exit the radiator, which Shinoda had placed in the front of the car. The entire front assembly opened forward along a hinge point near the front of the chassis. This "clam shell" bonnet allowed for easy access when servicing the car's cooling, fast-ratio rack-and-pinion steering, and front suspension systems.

The car's windshield, removable roof, doors, and cockpit made up the central section of the car. Finished in blue vinyl, the interior was a dramatic departure from any Corvette that had preceded it. It featured fixed driver and passenger seats with a cascading center panel that doubled as the interior seat bolsters. The exterior bolsters were affixed to the driver and passenger doors, allowing vehicle occupants easier access when entering or exiting the car.

The accelerator and brake pedals were adjustable to accommodate drivers of varying heights. The same

The XP-819's front panel assembly includes an outlet duct for venting air up and away from the radiator. This feature reappeared 50 years later on the production model C7 Corvette Stingray. (Photo Courtesy Kolecki Photography)

The rear section of the XP-819 includes the sugar scoop assembly that became popular on the early C3 production car. However, the rear section of the car was hinged to open rearward, allowing access to the car's rear-mounted engine. It also included a unique snorkel feature to feed air into the engine. (Photo Courtesy Kolecki Photography)

Unfortunately, the XP-819 struggled with a significant front-to-rear weight bias disparity that caused the car to spin out of control during high-speed testing. This GM press photo was taken before that fateful day at the GM Milford Proving Grounds. (Photo Courtesy General Motors LLC)

was true for the steering wheel, which was affixed to a seven-position tilt-telescoping steering column. An exterior rearview mirror was mounted high on the driver-side A-pillar, which allowed for increased visibility behind the car.

The rearmost assembly covered the XP-819's powertrain. While nondescript compared to the other sections, the rear assembly included a raised airbox and a urethane ducktail spoiler/bustle wrapped around its trailing edge. Below the spoiler, a pair of taillights and a large screen mesh framed a centrally located license plate mounting panel.

The XP-819 originally featured a rear-facing 287-ci V-8 marine engine. Made of special alloys to reduce weight, it was mounted to and suspended from a modified Pontiac Tempest automatic transaxle specially designed to support the weight of the rear-engine powerplant. Power was transferred through the transaxle to the car's rear wheels.

Two-piece alloy wheels were installed at all four corners of the car. While the diameter of the front and rear wheels was the same, the width of the rear wheels was notably wider (10 inches in the rear versus just 6 inches up front). All four wheels were wrapped in specially ordered Firestone tires.

It took just two months to transform Shinoda's drawing into a fully realized fiberglass prototype. The finished car sat on a 90-inch wheelbase and weighed approximately 2,700 pounds. Even prior to testing, it was acknowledged that the Ugly Duckling had a rear weight bias that might be detrimental to the car's performance. Shinoda acknowledged the weight bias disparity but maintained that the varying front-to-rear tire widths had been specifically chosen to account for it.

The XP-819 had another strike against it. By 1965, the rear-engine Chevy Corvair had come under attack for being "unsafe." While many of the claims against it later proved to be false, they still put the production car's sales numbers into an unrecoverable tailspin. It left many Chevy executives questioning the wisdom of a rear-engine Corvette.

Despite these concerns, Winchell's research and development team presented the completed XP-819 to GM management in 1966 as an official proposal for a future Corvette. Stylistically, the Ugly Duckling was stunning. The executives loved what they saw but continued to admonish Winchell and Shinoda to proceed with caution, given the scrutiny that the Corvair had come under.

A Quick End to the Rear-Engine Corvette

Testing of the car was scheduled at GM's Milford Proving Grounds to alleviate these concerns. During its initial tests, the XP-819 performed solidly in steady-state cornering but struggled with transient handling maneuvers, such as high-speed lane changes. While performing high-speed maneuvers at the Proving Grounds, the car's driver lost control and smashed the XP-819 against a guardrail, causing considerable damage and ending any future discussion of the car being a viable option for the next Corvette.

Chevrolet General Manager Bunkie Knudsen sent the remains of the XP-819 to race car builder Smokey Yunick with the instruction that he could salvage whatever parts he wanted to use so long as he destroyed the rest of the car. Yunick dismantled the car as instructed and cut the chassis into several pieces. Fortunately, he had the foresight to hide the car's remnants at his shop in Daytona, Florida.

More than a decade later, Steve Tate, a Chevy dealer and Corvette collector from Missouri, purchased the remnants of the XP-819 from Yunick. The car was crudely reassembled by Tate (mostly guesswork) with the intent of showing the car at Bloomington Gold. Collector Ed McCabe acquired the car in 1990 and later lent it to the National Corvette Museum as a display piece. The car was purchased again in 2002, this time by Mike Yager of MidAmerica Motorworks fame. Yager contracted Kevin Mackay, owner of Corvette Repair Inc., to perform a frame-off restoration of the XP-819.

The fully (and properly) restored XP-819 was showcased at the 2020 Amelia Island Concours d'Elegance.

While Winchell's desire to see the XP-819 serve as the prototype for the next-generation Corvette was short-lived, there is no question that many of its design elements directly influenced Shinoda's styling choices for the 1965 Mako Shark II, which influenced the final look of the 1968 Corvette. More than that, design elements introduced on the XP-819 eventually found their way into other production Corvettes: the car's clamshell hood resurfaced on the fourth-generation Corvette, and its hood-mounted radiator duct was reintroduced with the 2014 Corvette Stingray.

Fortunately, the XP-819 survived the crusher and was instead dismantled by Smokey Yunick. The car changed hands several times before becoming the property of Mike Yager. Yager had the XP-819 reassembled, and it is now a frequent attraction at Corvette-related events (including the 2020–2021 Mid-Engine Corvette showcase at the National Corvette Museum).

The 1964 XP-817: Grand Sport II(b)

The Grand Sport II(b) was developed by Frank Winchell and Chevrolet's Research and Development Group at roughly the same time that Duntov and his engineering team were developing the CERV II. In both cases, the GS II and the CERV II were developed (unofficially) to compete against the Ford GT40 at Le Mans despite GM's ongoing involvement with the AMA racing ban. While the CERV II was presented to GM's top brass as a second "engineering research vehicle" (like the CERV I before it), the GS II was openly touted by Winchell as a "sports racer." Despite these facts, it was the GS II, and not the CERV II, that received the lion's share of funding from General Motors during its development.

There were two reasons for this. First, and probably most significant, Frank Winchell had fostered a strong (though clandestine) relationship with the Chaparral Racing team. The relationship afforded Chevrolet access to Chaparral's test tracks and facilities in Midland, Texas. It also allowed Chevrolet the opportunity to install its own hardware, including engines, transmissions, suspension, and other hardware, into the Chaparral race cars in the interest of "research and development."

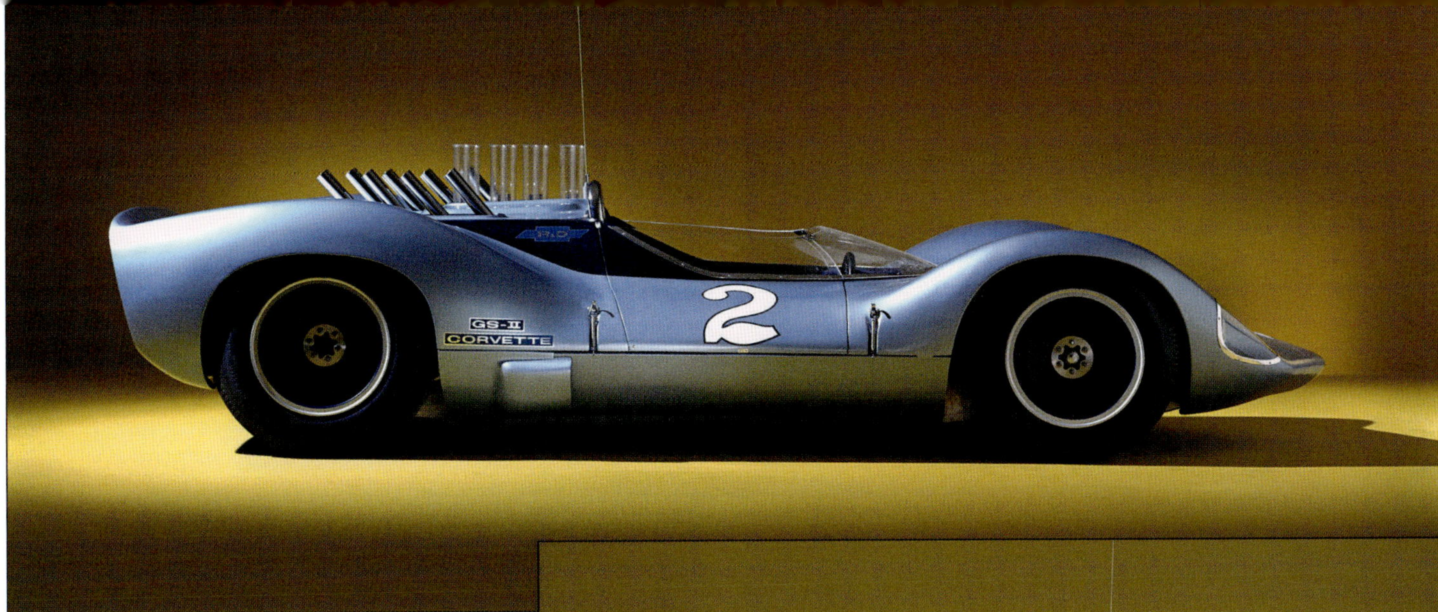

Larry Shinoda's design for the Grand Sport II was heavily influenced by the styling of Jim Hall's Chaparral II race car, although the Grand Sport II also featured signature Corvette design elements, including a high belt line and large, rounded front fenders. (Photo Courtesy General Motors LLC)

The Grand Sport II was powered by a custom-designed, all-aluminum, fuel-injected Mark IV V-8 engine and was built around an aluminum monocoque frame. Much of the GS II's frame design was repurposed by Chaparral in the development of their 2C racer. (Photo Courtesy General Motors LLC)

Frank Winchell's original take on the Grand Sport II closely resembled the CERV II, which caused most people at General Motors, including members of the design studio, to confuse the two cars. (Photo Courtesy General Motors LLC)

Second, Frank Winchell kept a low profile and worked better within GM's hierarchy than Zora Arkus-Duntov, who tended to be brash and constantly sought celebrity for his work on the Corvette. This dichotomy of personalities created an antagonistic relationship between the two men. Duntov's need to be in the limelight also created a rift with many members of GM's senior management, including Ed Cole.

Chapparal and Chevrolet

The evolution of the XP-817 started with a car being built by driver, engineer, and owner of the Chaparral race team Jim Hall. The car, the *Chaparral II* (sometimes referred to as the Grand Sport II[a]), was lent to Winchell and his research and development team so they could study the car in advance of starting work on their own. After an extensive evaluation, Winchell decided that General Motors could produce a similar car with an aluminum chassis and a fiberglass body.

Construction of the XP-817 was completed in Winchell's shop as a cooperation between Chevrolet and Chaparral. Frank Winchell selected Jim Musser, one of his chief engineers, to oversee the project and serve as a liaison between the two companies. It was during the construction of the car that the "Grand Sport II" name was chosen. In his book *Chevrolet = Racing?*, author Paul van Valkenburgh suggests that the name *Grand Sport* was selected by Winchell as a deliberate jab at Duntov's canceled Grand Sport race car project, while the "II" was added to "one-up" his rival.

Winchell placed an all-aluminum block 327-ci engine paired to a single-speed automatic transmission at the heart of the Grand Sport II racer. The car's chassis was simplistic in its design and weighed in at a mere 60 pounds. Although, based on a Chapparal chassis, it was appreciably less rigid. Between the chassis and the car's non-racing-compliant suspension, the GS II was eventually nicknamed "The Eyeball Jiggler."

Shinoda Refines Chapparal

Larry Shinoda was tasked with refining the body for the Grand Sport II. Jim Hall had already begun development of a racing body for the Chaparral II that featured an upturned nose and an inverted airfoil design. Despite his best efforts to counteract lift, Hall struggled to keep the car grounded at higher speeds. Shinoda and the research and development group refined Hall's initial design by installing a downturned nose. They also used spoilers and articulating wings (some of which had been developed by Hall) to keep the car glued to the road at high speeds and in tight corners.

The Grand Sport II body was a perfect fusion of Shinoda and Chaparral. Shinoda gave the car a flat, pointed snout and flared front fenders. Both resurfaced a year later on his Mako Shark II design. The quarter panels similarly flared up and around the rear wheels, framing the car's mid-engine exhaust ports and deck assembly. The rear of the car included an integrated, upturned ducktail spoiler. The rest of the car, including the single-passenger cockpit, sat low, long, and lean.

When the Grand Sport II was introduced in 1964, it was immediately compared to the CERV II (and vice

Chevy Engineer Jim Musser (left) attaches telemetry hardware to sensors in the Grand Sport II prior to putting the car through its paces at GM's Milford Proving Grounds. (Photo Courtesy General Motors LLC)

The Grand Sport II(b) featured highly stylized, ultra-thin GRP body panels that were bonded together with oven-cured 3M adhesive. The low and lean racer weighed in at just 1,450 pounds and reached a documented top speed of 198 mph during its testing sessions at the Milford Proving Grounds. (Photo Courtesy General Motors LLC)

versa). Many within General Motors had a hard time differentiating between the two cars. Duntov criticized Winchell's car for being too long and narrow. He was also frequently irritated when Winchell failed to acknowledge the engines that his team provided to the Research and Development Group. Winchell, on the other hand, criticized the CERV II's twin-transmission arrangement as being "too complicated."

Much of Duntov's frustration with Winchell really stemmed from his own envy of the budget that had been afforded to the development of the Grand Sport II. Ultimately, Duntov conceded that Winchell had developed a well-engineered car, although he never expected it to outperform his CERV II racer. But it did.

Driven by Jim Musser, the Grand Sport II achieved a top speed of 198 mph on its inaugural run. It performed consistently throughout its day-long testing at the Midland, Texas, raceway. Despite this, the Grand Sport II was not selected to compete at Le Mans the following year. That distinction was awarded to another of Jim Hall's Chaparral race cars.

There has been considerable speculation that GM funded Winchell's Grand Sport II as a means of tempering Duntov's strong-willed determination to build unsanctioned race cars (including the 1963 Grand Sport Corvette, which he'd developed without the consent or knowledge of GM's top brass). However accurate or inaccurate this claim may be, the GS II remained an experimental vehicle for the remainder of its functional days with General Motors.

Today, a restored version of the Grand Sport II can be seen in the Chaparral Gallery at the Permian Basin Petroleum Museum in Midland, Texas.

The 1966 Mid-Engine Styling Proposal

By 1965, both Duntov and Mitchell had begun championing the development of a third-generation Corvette. While Mitchell was developing cars inspired by his exploits on the ocean, Duntov redoubled his efforts to advance the development of a mid-engine Corvette. If nothing else, Shinoda's Ugly Duckling and Winchell's Grand Sport II proved that GM's top brass was still receptive to the idea, despite the recent downturn in sales of the Chevy Corvair.

Another of Shinoda's concepts, the Corvair Monza GT, provided a viable and much-needed chassis from which to hang additional mid-engine Corvette body concepts. GM's styling staff worked in conjunction with Duntov's engineering team to flesh out several design studies, many of which drew inspiration from elements introduced on the Monza GT and SS bodies.

One of the most dramatic mid-engine styling proposals was introduced in 1966. It had the familiar Coke-bottle front-end styling combined with a fighter jet–inspired rear section complete with large air intakes behind the doors and full fender skirts that concealed all but the bottom-most section of the car's rear wheels.

The car's cockpit included a 180-degree windshield with small side lights behind virtually non-existent B-pillars. It also featured a pair of gull-wing doors that

The Mid-Engine Styling Proposal was fabricated in GM's design studios. The completed clay model was presented in March 1966. Given the continued commercial success of the current Corvette combined with the high cost of re-tooling that would be required to build this one, the proposal was ultimately rejected. (Photo Courtesy General Motors LLC)

Bill Mitchell's styling department developed the Mid-Engine Styling Proposal concept during the winter of 1965–1966. The car featured several aircraft-inspired styling components, including a pair of large air scoops at the leading edge of the rear nacelles and a two-piece, wraparound windshield canopy. (Photo Courtesy General Motors LLC)

The Mid-Engine Styling Proposal lacked a rear window. Instead, the car was meant to use an integrated periscope mounted in the coupe's tapered roofline. This periscope provided the driver with the only means of viewing what was happening behind the vehicle. (Photo Courtesy General Motors LLC)

Although it is not catalogued as a genuine Corvette concept, the Astro I was a pivotal first link in the evolution of the mid-engine Corvette platform. It incorporated many of the latest design cues of its time and presented the world with its first taste of GM's mid-engine offerings. (Photo Courtesy General Motors LLC)

opened along a centrally mounted hinge point built into the car's roof. A carefully concealed periscope replaced the car's nonexistent rear window.

GM's styling department built a full-size clay model of the 1966 Mid-Engine Corvette with the intent of seeking design approval from management. Despite his support of their efforts, Duntov felt the design was too extreme to be a viable option for the next-generation Corvette. The executives at General Motors agreed and rejected the 1966 Mid-Engine Styling Proposal.

The 1967 XP-842 Astro I Experimental

According to Chevrolet's Astro I advertising literature, circa 1967, "Chevrolet's Astro I 'design study' car, a pure research vehicle, represents an advanced approached to the ultimate passenger car."

Like the XP-819 before it, the Astro I is often regarded as one of the earliest, fully engineered, mid-engine Corvette styling studies in the history of the brand. Ironically, the car shares a closer lineage to its predecessors

This is an early sketch/styling study of an "Advanced Corvette." This sketch (and others like it) provided the basis of design for the Astro I experimental vehicle. (Photo Courtesy General Motors LLC)

of the Corvair Monza GT and SS concept vehicles. Even so, its two-seat cockpit and exterior design were representative of the styling cues being considered for the next-generation Corvette.

Though technically designed under the direction of Bill Mitchell, Roy Lonberger and Larry Shinoda were the individuals most responsible for the development of the Astro I in January 1966. Developed from a sketch created by Lonberger, their objectives were to design a car with a very low drag coefficient and to investigate the visual potential of automobile aerodynamic characteristics. In a very real way, the Astro I was one of the earliest cars to adopt the mantra "form follows function," which has since become a cornerstone of Corvette design.

As can be observed through the images mounted above the clay model, the development of the Astro I's body lines was the synthesis of several vehicles, including the Corvair Monza GT and the Grand Sport II, which preceded it. (Photo Courtesy General Motors LLC)

A Shinoda Design Based on a Shinoda Design

Drawing inspiration from the Monza GT concept and the Mako Shark II, Shinoda gave his new concept car a long, low front end with a downturned nose to counteract lift. The frontal area was framed by two convex fender flares that helped direct air back and over the car's laid-back windshield and roofline. The roofline extended back along a contour that was previously introduced on the second-generation Corvette Sting Ray but without a rear window. A three-element periscope was used in its place.

The rear of the car sat higher (relatively speaking) and included more prominent fender flares with integrated side skirts designed to reduce drag at the rear wheels. An almost vertical rear fender/fascia assembly was also used to eliminate back-end buffeting during operation at high speeds or in windy conditions.

Under its massive canopy and rear bonnet assembly, the Astro I was equipped with a modified version of the production Corvair's horizontally opposed 6-cylinder engine. The smaller engine was chosen in lieu of a more powerful V-8 because of the car's low profile. Chevrolet engineers expanded the engine's bore from 3.43 to 3.56 inches, which increased the engine's overall displacement to 176 ci. New cylinder heads, a belt-driven SOHC valvetrain, inclined valves, and hemispherical combustion chambers were also incorporated into the engine, all of which improved the car's output and rev potential. When completed, the Astro I's 2.9-liter flat-six engine was rated at 240 hp at 7,200 rpm.

When introduced at the New York Auto Show in 1967, the Astro I was an instant hit with everyone in attendance. It forced General Motors to begin looking more closely at a potential mid-engine Corvette program, and it helped give rise to the creation of the Astro II platform the following year. (Photo Courtesy General Motors LLC)

Unveiling the Astro I

The Astro I made its public debut at the 1967 New York Auto Show. Spectators were enthralled with the low and long, futuristic-looking sports car. Featuring an all-fiberglass body finished in a bright red with black accents, the Astro I sat just 35.5 inches high (with the canopy closed) on a wheelbase of 88 inches with an overall length of 176.75 inches. The car also had a wide stance with track widths of 54.68 inches up front, 55.9 inches in the rear, and an overall width of 72.24 inches at its widest point.

Many of the auto show attendees questioned how vehicle occupants could enter or exit such a mis-proportioned automobile; that is, until the car's clamshell entry system was introduced. When activated, the rear half of the car's body opened automatically, raising up along a hydraulic lift assembly concealed beneath the back of the car.

As the clamshell opened backward, the driver and passenger seats rotated up and forward to a near vertical position. Once the vehicle occupants had entered the vehicle and fastened themselves to the seats, the entire process reversed itself, lowering the seats (and their occu-

Because of its extremely low profile, entry into and out of the Astro II required the car to bring the seat to its occupants! As seen here, the rear of the car opened like a clamshell, enabling the driver and passenger seats to rise upward and outward for easier access. (Photo Courtesy General Motors LLC)

The interior styling of the Astro I was almost as radical as its exceedingly low-profile exterior. Its cockpit included a twin-grip aircraft-style steering control, which added significantly to the car's futuristic styling. (Photo Courtesy General Motors LLC)

Although this has never been confirmed, Chevy designer Roy Lonberger attests that the Astro I was originally designed as a potential racer for use at the 24 Hours of Le Mans. When the AMA ban went into effect, only then did General Motors repurpose the design as a mid-engine concept vehicle. (Photo Courtesy General Motors LLC)

pants) back into a sitting position. Now seated inside the car, the driver was presented with a twin-handgrip control in lieu of a conventional steering wheel. Both the handgrip control and the vehicle pedals could be adjusted to accommodate drivers of varying heights.

Although General Motors never intended to produce the Astro I, its contributions to the development of future mid-engine platforms (including the Astro II and III) are immeasurable. It is still considered one of the most innovative concept cars in the history of General Motors. The Astro I now resides at the GM Heritage Center and makes occasional appearances at various Chevrolet-sanctioned events.

The 1968 XP-880 Mid-Engine Astro II

The Astro II was the second in a series of experimental mid-engine sports cars developed by Chevrolet in the late 1960s. It was developed under the direction of Frank Winchell as a potential competitor to the production version of Ford's Le Mans–winning GT40. Winchell also saw the XP-880 as an opportunity to develop a potential mid-engine Corvette production prototype as a joint venture between his own Research and Development team and Bill Mitchell's styling department.

This early, full-size rendering shows the Astro II concept. Frank Winchell directed Larry Nies and Larry Shinoda to design a car that was similarly proportioned to Ford's Mach 2 concept. Interestingly, Shinoda incorporated many similar design elements into the 1970 Mach 2C after he left General Motors to join Ford that same year. (Photo Courtesy General Motors LLC)

The evolution of the Astro II concept began after the Ford Motor Company introduced its mid-engine Mustang Mach 2 in 1967 and announced its intentions to build a limited series of Mark III GT40 sports-racing cars. Frank Winchell wanted to make certain the Corvette was properly postured to compete with either car were they ever manufactured by Ford. (Photo Courtesy General Motors LLC)

Although nearly a half decade separates the creation of these two cars, there is no denying the similarities between the Astro II (foreground) and the XP-819 Ugly Duckling (in the background). Larry Shinoda's fascination with the Coke-bottle styling carried over into many of his designs, including the third-generation Corvette. (Photo Courtesy Kolecki Photography)

Unlike its less-conventional predecessor, the Astro II was designed for easy accessibility. Conventional driver and passenger doors with built-in side bolsters ensured drivers could easily enter/exit the car. The larger rear clamshell assembly also allowed for easy access to the car's engine, transmission, and rear suspension. (Photo Courtesy General Motors LLC)

Because of his work on the rear-engine XP-819 Ugly Duckling, Larry Shinoda was specifically requested by Winchell to design the XP-880. Winchell also appointed Chevrolet Engineer Larry Nies from research and development to work with Shinoda on the design and to lay out the mechanics of the car's mid-engine platform.

Work on the XP-880 commenced in May 1967. Nies led the research and development team in constructing a viable chassis. One of the first issues he had to resolve was how to mount the engine. It had already been decided that the Astro II would feature a 427-ci big-block V-8, but all the engine accessories (alternator, water pump, smog pump, drive pulleys, etc.) initially forced Nies to place the engine over the rear axle to ensure adequate space between it and the rear wall of the cockpit. Instead, Nies decided to rotate the engine 180 degrees and mount it backward in the car. This enabled the engine to sit farther forward in its compartment since it now required less than 3 inches of clearance from the rear cockpit wall.

Nies's team also developed a welded steel backbone frame for the Astro II. The frame accommodated the large V-8 engine, a radiator mounted in the rear of the car, and a 2-speed automatic transaxle. While the front of the chassis received mostly off-the-shelf parts, including wishbone suspension and disc brakes, the rear suspension and braking components had to be specially developed for the car.

A Shinoda Design Based on a Shinoda Design: Part 2

Larry Shinoda designed the Astro II's body from information provided to him by Nies and the research and development team. Shinoda's renderings depicted a car that was a cross between the Monza GT and a far-less radical version of the Astro I. Unlike its predecessor, the Astro I included a front storage compartment, side doors, and a smaller rear bonnet that could be opened to allow access to the car's engine. It also incorporated several of the signature styling cues that Shinoda had previously introduced on the XP-819 and the Mako Shark II.

The Astro II included many conventional styling cues found on Corvettes of that era, including their trademark flared front fenders. With an overall height of just 43.7 inches and an overall width of 79 inches (compared to the 1967 Sting Ray's 49.8 inches and 74 inches, respectively), the Astro II was a good deal shorter and wider than its production counterpart. (Photo Courtesy Kolecki Photography)

The rear end of the Astro II continued to use styling motifs, such as the sugar-scoop rear window and rounded taillights, first introduced on the Ugly Duckling and later on the production 1967 Sting Ray. Aside from its extended rear end, its most notable difference was the assortment of vents/grilles added to the rear decklid and facia assemblies. (Photo Courtesy Kolecki Photography)

The experimental Astro II was spruced up by Bill Mitchell's styling department and finished with a Firefrost Blue paint job prior to being presented as Chevrolet's latest concept car at the New York International Auto Show in April 1968. (Photo Courtesy General Motors LLC)

The car's exterior featured the now-familiar Coke-bottle styling, but with less radical fender flares than those found on earlier concept models. Notably absent from the car's front end was any type of grille or air intake. A pair of running lights mounted low in the front fascia and the gap around the front storage bonnet were the only features that broke-up the car's otherwise smooth-surfaced front end. The Astro II shared the same rear window and sugar-scoop features as the production Corvette, although its rear section was appreciably longer to account for the mid-mounted engine and transmission assemblies. It also included a series of inlet and outlet grilles to allow the engine compartment to breathe.

The interior of the Astro II was similar to those installed in the third-generation Corvette. It was equipped with the same, three-spoke, woodgrain steering wheel. It also used many of the same analog gauges, including its speedometer and tachometer, although many of the secondary gauges were placed in different groupings. Even the seats and interior upholstery were reminiscent of production cars from that era, save for two notable differences. First, the seat side bolsters were large cushions mounted to the driver and passenger door panels. Second, a massive center console divided the driver and passenger areas.

The completed Astro II's body was constructed out of fiberglass and was painted Le Mans blue with a black interior. It sat on a wheelbase of 100 inches and had an overall length of 181 inches. Despite being several inches taller than its predecessor, the low-slung car still had an overall height of just 43.7 inches, which was more than 5 inches shorter than a 1968 Corvette coupe.

Could This Be the Next Corvette?

The XP-880 Astro II made its public debut in April 1968 at the New York Auto Show. When the car was unveiled for the first time, it included Corvette badging on its nose and rear decklid assembly. The presence of the crossed-flags emblems left many spectators wondering whether the Astro II concept was, in fact, a prototype of the next-generation Corvette.

The answer might have been "yes" had it not been for the runaway success of the third-generation Corvette. Chevrolet was selling every Corvette they produced. GM executives argued that they couldn't justify incurring the substantial additional costs to retool their production efforts to build a mid-engine platform when the current Corvette continued to sell so well.

While the Astro II never moved past the concept phase, it will forever have the distinction of being the first, true mid-engine Corvette prototype. Today, the Astro II resides at the GM Heritage Center.

The XP-880 was test driven extensively to determine its viability on the road. All reports indicated that the Astro II handled extremely well and offered decent power/acceleration despite having an outdated automatic transaxle. It is still considered one of the best mid-engine concepts to date. (Photo Courtesy General Motors LLC)

CHAPTER 6

EVOLUTION OF THE MID-ENGINE CORVETTE: PART 2 (1970–1975)

A large part of a sports car appeal is its resemblance to a race car. . . . Corvette lost it when the front-engined racers became antiquated.
—Zora Arkus-Duntov (excerpt from a memo to Alex Mair, Chevrolet Chief Engineer, March 21, 1967)

The arrival of the 1968 Corvette was delayed a full year (it was originally slated for 1967) due to a variety of lingering quality control issues. Many of these issues, from body squeaks and rattles to drivetrain-related problems to challenges with the vacuum-actuated windshield wiper doors, were directly attributed to Zora Arkus-Duntov's removal from the Corvette program a year earlier.

Zora Arkus-Duntov served as Corvette's first-ever chief engineer from 1967 until his retirement from General Motors in 1975. He used his position to advance the mid-engine Corvette toward becoming a viable production vehicle. His efforts paved the way for the creation of the eighth-generation Corvette Stingray. (Photo Courtesy General Motors LLC)

Despite being nearly 50 years old, the 1973 Four-Rotor Aerovette remains one of the most poignant, beautiful, and contemporary-looking Corvette concepts of all time. From its gull-wing doors to its swept-back appearance, the Aerovette has inspired many of GM's top designers and engineers, including Dave McLellan, Ed Welburn, and John DeLorean. (Photo Courtesy General Motors LLC)

Corvette's Chief Engineer

In March 1967, Duntov drafted a memo to Chevrolet Chief Engineer Alex Mair challenging his decision to produce the third-generation Corvette. Duntov believed the new Corvette lacked the innovation needed to maintain its relevancy. He argued that Ford had the vision to partner with former racer and car builder Alejandro DeTomaso to develop and market the mid-engine Pantera sports car. If the Corvette was to remain competitive in the marketplace, he believed it also needed to transition to a mid-engine platform immediately. He concluded that he, along with his engineering group, should replace Mitchell's design studio as the Corvette's future innovators.

What to Do with Zora Arkus-Duntov?

The memo ruffled more than a few feathers within GM's hierarchy. Duntov had openly challenged the decisions of many key personnel responsible for the success of the Corvette program. It wasn't long before Chevrolet General Manager Pete Estes was directed by Mair to reassign Duntov to another division within General Motors.

Duntov was initially offered an opportunity to transfer to the German-based Opel division in early 1967. Despite being a potentially lucrative move for him, Duntov declined the position, stating that he did not want to leave the Corvette program. Estes responded by first disbanding Duntov's Corvette engineering group and then reorganizing the entire engineering department.

Because of Duntov's massive public appeal, Estes created a special public relations position for him beginning April 1, 1967. While the role enabled Duntov the opportunity to work both as a press spokesperson and an engineering consultant, it also severed most of his direct ties to the Corvette program. Duntov accepted the role begrudgingly and began a three-month press junket across Europe to discuss the imminent arrival of the 1968 Chevy Corvette.

Back in the United States, Duntov's sudden absence impaired the continued development of the third-generation Corvette. Many of the mechanical and design issues that Duntov normally resolved on his own now festered without his involvement. Although it had not been recognized by either Estes or Mair before his reassignment, Duntov's management of the Corvette program had been one of the cornerstones of its success. In a very real way, Duntov had served as the Corvette's chief engineer for years, even if he'd never formally held that title.

Fearful of the bad press that Chevrolet would receive if the new Corvette failed in Duntov's absence, Estes rescinded his earlier decision and instead elected to formally promote Duntov to Corvette chief engineer on December 1, 1967. It marked the first time in Chevrolet's history that a chief engineer had been tasked with managing an individual brand. Duntov now had authority over all major aspects of the Corvette.

Duntov and DeLorean

Forty-four-year-old John Z. DeLorean replaced Pete Estes as Chevrolet general manager on February 1, 1969. From the start, Duntov saw DeLorean as a fellow visionary who took a nonconformist approach to product development when it suited his purpose. He hoped that DeLorean might finally be the ally he needed to propel the mid-engine Corvette program forward.

Before DeLorean entertained any notions of a future Corvette program, he first needed to rein in the issues surrounding production of the current third-generation model. Despite his promotion to Corvette chief engineer three months earlier, Duntov had done little to improve the quality issues that plagued the current production model Corvettes. DeLorean recognized that while Duntov

Forty-year-old John DeLorean was promoted to general manager of the Pontiac Motor Division on June 24, 1965, making him the youngest man to hold that title in any of GM's corporate divisions. He was named general manager of Chevrolet in 1969. (Photo Courtesy General Motors LLC)

John DeLorean (left) and Zora Arkus-Duntov inspect the newly assembled XP-882 Corvette concept outside the design center at GM's Technical Center in Warren, Michigan. (Photo Courtesy General Motors LLC)

was a brilliant engineer, he lacked the know-how to manage the production quality of the cars being built at the St. Louis manufacturing plant.

He tasked Duntov with correcting any design or engineering issues that plagued the third-generation Corvette. At the same time, DeLorean systematically addressed issues within plant operations and made sizable investments into the quality control infrastructure of the plant itself. Within a year, the St. Louis plant was transformed from one of the worst plants owned by General Motors into one of its finest.

While he and DeLorean each worked to improve the quality of the Corvette program, Duntov began to experience issues with his health. In June 1969, while attending the wedding of Bunkie Knudsen's daughter in Bloomfield Hills, Michigan, Duntov suffered a stroke that left him without the ability to speak for several weeks and required him to undergo months of therapy. He spent the remainder of the year regaining his ability to speak fluently. While he resumed his engineering responsibilities at General Motors a little at a time, his efforts to advance the mid-engine Corvette program were delayed once more.

It wasn't until October 1969 that Duntov was fully re-engaged in the Corvette chief engineer role. Now he had just five years left before his mandatory retirement from General Motors at age 65. Duntov needed to act quickly and decisively if he was ever going to transform his vision of a mid-engine Corvette into reality.

The 1970 XP-882 Corvette Concept

Duntov's relentless determination was the sole driving force behind the continued development of the mid-engine Corvette. GM's leadership had rejected every rear- and mid-engine Corvette concept car to date,

The XP-882's unique drivetrain arrangement earned Zora Arkus-Duntov a patent, which was granted to him in May 1971. Although it is commonplace today, the XP-882 featured one of the first transversely mounted powertrains in automotive history. (Photo Courtesy General Motors LLC)

and there was no indication they'd approve a similarly designed car in the foreseeable future.

Despite these truths, Duntov never lost hope. Shortly after his promotion to Corvette chief engineer, he and his engineering division began work on an experimental prototype that eventually became Chevrolet's answer to Ford's mid-engine Pantera platform. He knew that this car, officially designated the XP-882, would likely be his personal "swan song," and he was determined to see it through, regardless of the forces working against him.

Engineering a Mid-Engine Powertrain

There was one major obstacle working against Duntov: General Motors had yet to develop an actual mid-engine powertrain he could use. Further, the research and development and tooling costs (to say nothing of the time) to develop the necessary automatic and manual transaxles would be prohibitively expensive. If Duntov hoped to produce a commercially viable mid-engine Corvette, he'd have to design a powertrain using existing GM hardware.

Duntov started with a 454-ci V-8 engine and a Turbo 400 front-wheel-drive transmission originally developed for the Oldsmobile Toronado. While the Chevy powerplant produced the desired horsepower, Duntov claimed that the conventional placement of the engine caused

The clay model of the XP-882 sits in the courtyard outside of GM's design studios. John DeLorean initially canceled the XP-882 project in August 1969 in favor of making Corvettes more profitable by building them on the new, less-expensive Camaro chassis. (Photo Courtesy General Motors LLC)

Although many of the styling elements introduced on Zora Arkus-Duntov's original XP-882 clay model were a complete departure from the generations of Corvettes that preceded it, Duntov's mid-engine concept car motif still captured the spirit of its forebearers. (Photo Courtesy General Motors LLC)

The completed XP-882 Mid-Engine Corvette concept carried forward much of Zora Arkus-Duntov's original design. It also incorporated more traditional Corvette styling elements, including its signature round rear taillights, the Corvette crossed flags, and "Stingray" badging. (Photo Courtesy General Motors LLC)

it to sit higher than the car's profile allowed. Additionally, the Toronado's transmission was only available as an automatic.

Solving the engine placement issue proved to be relatively simple. Duntov turned the engine sideways and mounted it transversely. He located the car's transmission behind the passenger compartment while the car's differential was mounted behind the driver-side rear axle. To connect the two, Duntov ran the axle shafts through the center of the engine's oil pan. Final-drive gears were then centrally placed in an aluminum housing between the car's rear wheels.

With the mechanics of the car mostly sorted out, Duntov turned to GM's design team to stylize the car's body around his specifications. The XP-882 was to have a wheelbase of just 95.5 inches. This dimension was critical, as earlier mid-engine prototypes had been accused of being "too long." Duntov achieved the shorter wheelbase by fully using the lateral space around the engine, even providing enough additional real estate to allow for a trunk compartment to be placed at the back of the car.

The styling group developed a look for the XP-882 that was sleek and low-slung. While it drew inspiration from many of the concepts that came before it, the new car was more refined and looked more chiseled, more futuristic, more production-ready, than any of them. Most important of all, it still looked like a Corvette. Upon Duntov's fervent approval of their design, two prototype cars were approved for construction, and work commenced on each in the spring of 1969.

And then, just a few months later, development of the XP-882 prototypes came to a grinding halt.

DeLorean Pulls the Plug

As Duntov underwent a long and slow recovery from his stroke, there were production challenges at the St. Louis manufacturing plant. So, DeLorean interceded and temporarily canceled the XP-882 project in August 1969.

He argued that moving to a mid-engine platform would be a costly undertaking. He elected instead to begin looking for ways to reduce the Corvette's production costs, going so far as to suggest developing a next-generation Corvette that utilized the new-and-inexpensive Camaro chassis.

Fortunately for Duntov, Ford announced its plans to begin selling the DeTomaso Pantera through the Lincoln-Mercury dealerships across North America. With the assistance of both Mitchell and Mair, Duntov convinced DeLorean that his mid-engine Corvette could outperform the Pantera.

As 1969 drew to a close, DeLorean agreed to reinstate the XP-882 program. He gave Duntov the order to have one of the XP-882 prototypes finished in time for the 1970 New York Auto Show.

Work resumed on the XP-882 in earnest. The completed coupe-only concept car was 8 inches shorter, 5.8 inches wider, and nearly 700 pounds lighter than the 1970 Corvette. It featured a gas tank mounted between the front wheels with a filler cap in the center of the front decklid. It also came equipped with a new, louvered, fastback roofline. Finished in silver and riding on a set of aluminum wheels with vent slots like those introduced on the 1976 Corvette, the XP-882 looked capable of out-performing anything that Ford (or anyone else) could throw at it.

Could This Finally Be It?

The XP-882 made its public debut to a surprised audience on April 2, 1970, at the New York International Auto Show. Because of GM's last-minute decision to showcase the car, the car wasn't even given a proper name. Instead, it was unveiled simply as the "Corvette Prototype."

The Corvette Prototype was an instant crowd favorite. It completely upstaged the Pantera (along with every other car on display). Given the overwhelming public reception it received, DeLorean initially approved the development of a 4-speed manual gearbox for the car. Plans were created to market the XP-882 with a 400-ci version of the small-block V-8 engine.

But then reality once more asserted itself. There were many at Chevrolet who argued that the cost of building the car far exceeded any performance gains the car could offer, especially equipped with an automatic transmission. They also countered that the DeTomaso/Ford Pantera posed no real threat to the existing Corvette program.

It seemed that the XP-882—and the future development of a mid-engine Corvette—was finished.

The 1972 XP-895 "Reynolds Aluminum Concept"

After the XP-882 project was abandoned, Duntov was directed to relinquish the chassis of both prototypes for use on other projects. The first was slated to be modified for the installation of a four-rotor engine platform (see "The Four-Rotor Concept/Aerovette" later in this chapter). The second chassis was earmarked for a collaborative project between General Motors and the Reynolds Metals Company.

John DeLorean wanted to explore the advantages of constructing Corvette bodies out of alternate materials. He authorized Bill Mitchell to create a new body based on the earlier XP-882 design that was more dramatic than its predecessor. The new car (designated the XP-895) featured more prominent fender flares, incorporated a rear roof/window sugar scoop treatment, included a pair of NACA-style air inlets in the hood (for improved cooling), and had a teardrop contour from front to back. Additionally, he wanted the first XP-895's body to be built out of steel.

The finished car weighed nearly 3,500 pounds, which was approximately 100 pounds heavier than a production-model Corvette. It needed to be lighter. Enter Reynolds Aluminum. Reynolds already had a longstanding agreement with General Motors to supply the automotive manufacturer with aluminum alloy for engine fabrication. This included specialized aluminum alloys used in the creation of ZL1 engine blocks and L88 heads.

Tragically, both examples of the original XP-882 Corvette concept were repurposed for other projects. The first was assigned to Bill Mitchell, and its chassis became the foundation for the Four-Rotor concept. The second was transformed into the Reynolds Aluminum Corvette. (Photo Courtesy General Motors LLC)

The XP-895 Reynolds Aluminum Corvette was the second in a series of mid-engine concepts built by General Motors in the early 1970s. It was developed as a joint venture between Reynolds and General Motors to demonstrate the weight-saving benefits of an all-aluminum body. (Photo Courtesy General Motors LLC)

A full-size clay model of the XP-895 Corvette was assembled in the heart of Bill Mitchell's design studio. While this new car shared many of the same styling cues as the XP-882, a new sugar scoop rear window assembly and functional National Advisory Committee of Aeronautics (NACA) scoops were introduced on this iteration of the car. (Photo Courtesy General Motors LLC)

The first XP-895 Corvette's body was constructed almost entirely out of steel. When the steel Corvette proved to be too heavy, each of the car's body panels were removed, reverse engineered, and then replicated in Reynolds aluminum. (Photo Courtesy General Motors LLC)

A Corvette "Wrapped" in Reynolds

Early in 1972, DeLorean contracted the Reynolds Metals Company to fabricate a duplicate XP-895 body out of a special aluminum alloy designed to be spot weldable. DeLorean wanted to determine how much weight could be saved by building a car out of aluminum. Reynolds was happy to oblige. The company wanted to showcase the potential of building automobile bodies out of aluminum and saw the XP-895 project as the perfect opportunity.

Duntov was skeptical as to whether the Reynolds body would provide the same structural integrity as the steel body. Further, he was reluctant to see the Corvette move away from using fiberglass body panels. However, DeLorean's interest in the feasibility study showed real promise that a mid-engine Corvette was in the works.

The front end of the XP-895 included NACA ducts cut into the hood that fed air into the radiator. It also had new tuckaway headlights with pockets that were now long and narrow versus the short and wide version introduced on the XP-882. (Photo Courtesy Kolecki Photography)

The XP-895 featured softer, more rounded surfaces than its predecessor. While there's no denying the lineage between these two cars, the XP-895 lacked some of the aggressive styling introduced by Zora Arkus-Duntov and his engineering group on the original XP-882. (Photo Courtesy General Motors LLC)

While it undoubtedly looked futuristic when first introduced, the interior of the XP-895 featured several styling concepts that eventually found their way into other GM products. A version of the car's steering wheel was used in the fourth-generation Corvette from 1984 to 1989, and its center console was reintroduced in the third-generation Camaro. (Photo Courtesy Kolecki Photography)

After sitting in storage for nearly a half decade, Corvette Chief Engineer Dave McLellan discovered the XP-895 hidden away. He had it restored to driving condition. Despite being outdated by 1979, the car allowed McLellan to study and better understand the aluminum construction process that had been used by General Motors and Reynolds. (Photo Courtesy Kolecki Photography)

Reynolds Metals assured Duntov that it would produce a body that would be as strong as its steel counterpart. To achieve this, all the panels needed to maintain a minimum thickness of 0.125 inch. For the next several weeks, the Reynolds team worked out of a small Detroit-based prototype shop called Creative Engineering to recreate each of the XP-895's body panels out of the company's unique 2036-T4 aluminum alloy.

The completed aluminum body panels were returned to General Motors in June 1972 for final assembly. Because the aluminum components were exact replicas of the steel panels, everything fit together flawlessly. The fully assembled Reynolds Aluminum Corvette looked beautiful in its silver paint. More importantly, the aluminum body was approximately 38.9 percent (approximately 450 pounds) lighter than its steel counterpart!

While the prospect of building a mid-engine Corvette out of aluminum alloy was satisfactory to Duntov, the XP-895 project was mothballed as soon as the study was completed. While aluminum provided definite weight savings, it proved to be prohibitively expensive to mass-produce. The conventional manufacturing standard of a steel chassis and fiberglass body was still the most economically viable option for Corvette. The XP-895 was put into storage at the end of 1972 and would not resurface for many years.

Several years after Duntov's retirement from General Motors in 1975, Corvette's new chief engineer, Dave McLellan, discovered the Reynolds Aluminum XP-895 in storage. When he learned it was still drivable, he had it rebuilt.

The Reynolds Aluminum Corvette Concept is now part of the GM Heritage Center collection.

Initially conceived by General Motors as the Chevrolet GT, the XP-987 GT was developed to showcase the Wankel rotary engine at the 1973 Frankfurt Auto Show. The car was rebadged with Corvette "two rotor" nameplate decals (instead of chrome badges) just days before the Frankfurt Auto Show opened to the public. (Photo Courtesy Kolecki Photography)

The XP-987 GT Two-Rotor Corvette

They say timing is everything. On November 10, 1970, Ed Cole purchased the patent rights to develop the Wankel rotary engine as a potential future GM offering.

This is an early rendering of the Wankel GT by GM Designer John Wasenko. While there is no question that Wasenko used elements of the Manta Ray and XP-882 concepts to create this design, his Wankel GT design also included new elements that were incorporated into both the Two-Rotor and Four-Rotor concepts, which demonstrates how automobile design evolves from one model to the next. (Photo Courtesy General Motors LLC)

Although there has been a lot of conjecture over the years claiming the XP-987 GT was developed as a less-expensive companion car to the Corvette, John Wasenko's drawing clearly depicts the Corvette logo, both on the car's front plate and along its front fender. (Photo Courtesy General Motors LLC)

Originally conceived by German engineer Felix Wankel in the mid-1950s, the small and powerful rotary engine had fewer moving parts than a traditional piston engine.

"Fewer parts" meant "less expensive to produce," which suited Cole just fine. He envisioned the rebranded powerplant, the General Motors Rotary Combustion Engine (GMRCE), becoming GM's sole future engine offering. However, the current iteration of the Wankel engine needed development. It was both inefficient and suffered from poor fuel economy.

Cole tasked Duntov with developing improved high-performance versions of the GMRCE engine in one-, two-, three-, and four-rotor configurations. Despite his initial frustration with the assignment, Duntov quickly recognized that a mid-engine Corvette might be the perfect platform to showcase the Wankel powerplant. He presented his idea to Cole. Cole agreed with Duntov's idea and instructed Mitchell's design department to begin developing a pair of rotary-powered Corvette concept cars.

The Two-Rotor Chevrolet GT?

Work on the first of the mid-engine car designs began in February 1971. Its development was executed as a collaboration between GM's design and engineering departments. John "Kip" Wasenko, of GM styling, was tasked with designing the first of the Wankel-powered cars, a smaller, mid-engine coupe officially designated the XP-987 GT but more commonly referred to as the "Chevrolet GT."

Wasenko developed the Two-Rotor Corvette's profile and body design around the dimensions of a modified Porsche 914 chassis. The reason was simple: Porsche had been building mid-engine sports cars for decades. General Motors had not. Using an existing Porsche chassis enabled Wasenko to expedite his design, which was critically important to Ed Cole. Cole intended to use the two-rotor Corvette to gain public acceptance of the Wankel rotary engine, which he envisioned as the primary powerplant for all future GM automobiles.

The Porsche 914's wheelbase was shorted from 96 inches to 90 inches and its floorplan was shorted to match. The chassis was then fitted with McPherson strut front suspension, rack-and-pinion steering, and trailing arm independent rear suspension. Special 7x15-inch rims were developed for the car by American Racing.

GM's design staff completed a full-size fiberglass mockup of the Chevrolet GT in June 1971. They also developed a highly realistic-looking, full-size model of

This early, full-size mockup of the XP-987 GT depicted a car with very pointed front and rear ends and an almost nonexistent beltline around the sides of the car. This study, more so than the concept car that followed it, captured the essence of the earlier XP-882 and XP-895 concepts in its overall design. (Photo Courtesy General Motors LLC)

A second full-sized clay model of the XP-987 GT was completed in June 1971. This model accurately depicted the final look of the soon-to-be concept car. The proportions of both clay models were developed around the modified chassis of a Porsche 914. (Photo Courtesy General Motors LLC)

Most of the clay model's front-end styling carried forward onto the final XP-987 GT concept car. The car's front fenders, windshield, doors, and rear-quarter assemblies were reworked and/or replaced with hardware that was more sensible than that showcased in the original design. (Photo Courtesy General Motors LLC)

Using the clay model and a highly detailed "space buck" (not pictured) for reference, GM's design studio constructed a full-sized fiberglass mockup of the Two-Rotor Corvette around its completed chassis. (Photo Courtesy General Motors LLC)

The fiberglass mockup of the XP-987 GT, more commonly called the Chevrolet GT at this point in its development, was on display at GM's design studio in June 1971. Both the fiberglass model and the space buck (not pictured) allowed detailed engineering and design changes to be made to the body design prior to fabrication by Pininfarina in January 1972. (Photo Courtesy General Motors LLC)

the car they called a "first-class space buck." This model included a detailed breakdown of where each of the car's components would be located. Both the fiberglass model and the space buck were shown to GM's top executives and directors later that same month. It was decided at this meeting that the XP-987 should be transformed into a complete, running car.

The Pininfarina Corvette Concept

Bill Mitchell was intrigued by the idea of developing a new sports car, especially one that could be built overseas and marketed globally. He contracted Italian design firm Pininfarina to build the XP-987 GT's steel body. Known for developing many of Ferrari's body designs, the respected Italian coachbuilder had the resources to

The completed XP-987 GT hatchback coupe was stunning in its red paint and gold-colored trim. Many of GM's designers thought the car, with its short wheelbase and low stance, looked more like a Ferrari 246 Dino than a Chevrolet Corvette. (Photo Courtesy Kolecki Photography)

The plaster-bodied Two-Rotor Corvette was fabricated in GM's design studio in December 1971. It was shipped, along with the car's chassis and a mockup of the Wankel rotary engine, to Pininfarina in Turin, Italy. Each of the plaster panels were replicated in steel, carefully fitted together, and reassembled to create the finished body of the XP-987 GT concept. (Photo Courtesy General Motors LLC)

Despite being smaller in height and shorter in length than the third-generation Corvette, the XP-987 GT offered its occupants more shoulder and legroom, as well as better ergonomics for the driver. (Photo Courtesy Jonny Bens)

One of the biggest benefits of the Wankel rotary engine was its compact size. Despite being 6 inches shorter than a Porsche 914, the Two-Rotor Corvette was easily able to accommodate a mid-mounted engine while leaving enough rear storage space for luggage and/or golf clubs. The engine depicted here is a Mazda 13B rotary engine. (Photo Courtesy Jonny Bens)

complete the job far more quickly than GM's own design department, and at a fraction of the cost.

The chassis of the XP-987 GT, equipped with a mockup of the Wankel rotary engine (the actual engine was still under development) was flown to Turin, Italy, in January 1972. It was accompanied by a supervisory team from the styling department and a full-sized plaster model of the car. Using the plaster model and Wasenko's drawings for reference, Pininfarina constructed the car's body out of steel (while its hood, doors, and hatchback were made of aluminum), in just 12 weeks.

The completed hatchback coupe was breathtaking to behold. Shorter in length (166 inches), width (65.6 inches), and height (43.3 inches) than the current third-generation Corvette, the well-proportioned XP-987 GT looked more like a Ferrari than anything being produced in Detroit. It featured recessed-but-exposed quad headlights, a first for a US-based "production" automobile. It also came equipped with concealed windshield wipers, specially designed doors that wrapped around its A-pillars, a longer hatchback that gave spectators a view of the engine through its rear glass, subtly positioned air intakes in the rear quarter panels that fed air into the engine compartment, and outlet ducts above the rear fascia that allowed that same air to escape.

The completed car was flown back to Detroit in October 1972, where it was introduced to GM executives. It was decided that its public unveiling would wait until the Frankfurt Auto Show the following year. This decision was likely made because of the Temporary Importation Bond that was placed on the car. Because so much of the car was built in Italy, the XP987GT was imported into the United States under a temporary bond that excused General Motors from paying duty for the work performed by Pininfarina. The bond allowed General Motors to keep the car in the United States for a period not to exceed 365 days.

While in Detroit, the car was fitted with a transversely mounted Wankel two-rotor engine mated to a 3-speed Hydra-matic transmission. The engine, a GMRCE-type RC2-266, which translated into 266 ci of displacement, had six 1,090-cc combustion chambers. It was equipped with a single Rochester Quadrajet carburetor, side inlet ports, and a twin ignition setup. The engine was rated at an estimated 180 hp at 6,100 rpm.

The Two-Rotor Premieres in Europe

The XP-987 GT was officially introduced at the Frankfurt Auto Show in September 1973. Less than a week before its premier, GM's top brass decided the car should be renamed the "Corvette Two-Rotor." Nameplates were quickly rendered using decals instead of traditional badging. Now finished in metallic red with a fawn-colored leather interior and gold-colored wheels, the car was an instant crowd favorite. Like the Corvette Concept before it, the Corvette Two-Rotor left many auto show

A pair of air intakes were cut into the door and quarter panel assemblies to feed air into the rotary engine. This feature was added after General Motors fabricated the full-size fiberglass mockup of the car during the summer of 1971. (Photo Courtesy Kolecki Photography)

The Two-Rotor concept, seen here on display in the Claremont Corvette showroom at Snodland in Kent, England, was one of the first Corvettes to include a rear hatchback decklid assembly. While a hatchback wouldn't be offered on a production Corvette until 1982, there is little doubt that the idea originated with the XP-987 GT. (Photo Courtesy Jonny Bens)

Exterior badging on the XP-987 GT was limited to the "two rotor" decals on its front and rear fascia and on its quarter panels. Despite being marketed as a Corvette, the absence of Corvette badging only adds to the speculation that the Two-Rotor was originally going to be branded as the Chevrolet GT. (Photo Courtesy Kolecki Photography)

attendees wondering if Chevrolet would produce their newest mid-engine sports car concept.

According to Ludvigsen's book *Corvette: America's Star-Spangled Sports Car*, Duntov ridiculed the Corvette Two-Rotor as being underpowered and complained that the car had a "lack of space, both in the luggage compartment and in the car itself: in case of rain you are forced to disrobe outside of the car and shove the raincoat in the trunk—there is no space to store the coat."

Despite Duntov's criticisms, General Motors seriously considered building a production version of the Corvette Two-Rotor as a 1975 model-year production car. Unfortunately, Arab members of the Organization of Petroleum Exporting Countries (OPEC) imposed an embargo against the United States in retaliation for the US decision to support the Israeli military during the 1973 Arab-Israeli war. The 1973 embargo caused US fuel prices to skyrocket.

While the Wankel rotary engine proved to be a viable powerplant in the lightweight Corvette Two-Rotor, it required a lot more fuel to run than a standard internal combustion engine. It also failed to meet the EPA's increasingly stringent federal emissions standards. Given these challenges, the Corvette Two-Rotor program was canceled. Cole eventually abandoned the Wankel rotary engine program in its entirety.

Tom Falconer Saves the XP-987 GT

Given the cost of the taxes and tariffs required to allow the Corvette Two-Rotor back into the United States, General Motors elected instead to remove the car's rotary engine and transmission and put the car into storage at the Vauxhall design center in England. There the car remained, largely forgotten, for the next 10 years. When the car was eventually rediscovered in the early 1980s, General Motors planned on sending the XP-987 GT to the crusher.

Instead, the Corvette Two-Rotor was purchased by UK Corvette collector Tom Falconer. Falconer equipped the engineless sports car with a Mazda 13B rotary engine coupled to a Cadillac front-wheel-drive automatic transmission. It spent years touring car shows in Europe and the United States, eventually making an appearance at the 2019 Amelia Island Concours d'Elegance. In 2020, the XP987 GT was acquired by the National Corvette

Today, the XP-987 GT Two-Rotor Corvette is part of the National Corvette Museum's private collection, along with its original Wankel rotary engine, which is displayed next to the car. There are plans to restore the Wankel engine and eventually reinstall it in the Two-Rotor Corvette. (Photo Courtesy Kolecki Photography)

Museum thanks to the fundraising efforts of the Lone Star Corvette Club and the Texas Corvette Association.

The Four-Rotor Concept/Aerovette

Duntov's mandatory retirement from General Motors at age 65 was foremost on his mind when he scheduled an appointment with Ed Cole in December 1971 to discuss resurrecting the canceled XP-882. He knew the Concept Corvette was his last, best chance to build a production-model mid-engine Corvette. He also knew that convincing Ed Cole to go along with his plans would be paramount if he ever hoped to make it happen. Surprisingly, Ed Cole agreed with Duntov's pleas but with one stipulation: the XP-882 would be fitted with a Wankel rotary engine.

Duntov's engine group had already invested a fair amount of time working to improve the Wankel two-rotor engine's output and efficiency. Thanks largely to their advances, it was slated to become the primary powerplant of the Chevy Vega. Duntov argued that the Corvette should not share the same engine as the Vega. Cole countered back that Duntov should develop a larger four-rotor version of the Wankel engine to satiate the Corvette's power requirements.

Recognizing that he'd reached a stalemate with Cole, Duntov accepted the terms of their arrangement and set about developing a four-rotor engine to power his XP-882 concept car. He tasked his lead chassis engineer Gibson "Gib" Hufstader with the task of preparing the retired show car's chassis for fitment of two two-rotor GM Wankel engines with the car's unique Toronado-based Turbo Hydra-matic transaxle assembly. Work on the Wankel-powered XP-882 began in March 1972.

Four Rotors Equal More Power

Gib assembled a single four-rotor Wankel engine from a pair of two-rotor units. The newly minted engine was transversely mounted across the engine bay of the XP-882. Gib connected the two engines via a custom-built chassis made of plate steel. The "steel box" chassis housed the output shafts of both engines and mated them to an internally splined steel driveshaft. A cog on the central driveshaft drove a splined rubber belt, which in turn operated the engine's Delco-Remy distributor, alternator (mounted at the top of the engine assembly), and single-pressure oil pump (mounted at its bottom). Two V-belts mounted on the right side or "front" engine drove everything else, including the A/C compressor, the power-steering pump, and the dual-outlet water pump (specially designed to cool both engines).

The 1973 Aerovette directly influenced the look of both the fourth-generation Corvette and the DMC-12 DeLorean, which was manufactured by John DeLorean after he resigned from General Motors. (Photo Courtesy General Motors LLC)

The completed engine had a displacement of 9.5 liters (roughly 585 ci) and produced an estimated 360–370 hp at 7,000 rpm. It bore the distinction of being the largest Wankel engine ever mounted in an automobile up to that point in time.

Hufstader's custom-built four-rotor engine assembly was successfully paired with the XP-882's original Turbo Hydra-matic 425 transmission. Power was transferred to the transmission via a torque converter mated to the left engine. The torque converter was specifically developed by Hufstader to handle the increased stall speeds of the higher-revving rotary engine. The transmission's output shaft then ran back through a separate opening in the engine's steel box chassis to a differential mounted at the rear of that same assembly. Its final-drive gear ratio was 3.55:1.

Ed Cole and Zora Arkus-Duntov test drove the resurrected XP-882 Four-Rotor in July 1972. The car accelerated smoothly to a peak speed of 148 mph at GM's Milford Proving Grounds. According to both Duntov and Cole, the car was accelerating quickly when Cole lifted his foot from the accelerator pedal. The rotary engine's performance was doubly impressive given that Gib Hufstader had assembled the custom powerplant in just three months. He received a patent for his uniquely devised powerplant on December 10, 1974.

Immediately following the test drive, Cole approached Bill Mitchell and insisted his design team freshen the look of the aged XP-882. Mitchell permitted several of his stylists to drive the car that summer as a means of inspiring them before they began work on the design. As expected, his staff was enthralled by the experience.

The XP-882 Becomes the Aerovette

Mitchell had previously assigned designers Jerry Palmer and Henry Haga the task of streamlining and updating the aged XP-882's body (with instructions to put the engine out front) for consideration as a possible next-generation Corvette. Haga's studio was already well underway with their new design when Duntov approached them about maintaining the Concept Corvette's original mid-engine placement for use with the four-rotor test mule.

When designing the back end of the Aerovette, Mitchell drew inspiration from race cars like the Porsche 907L, which had an airfoil profile and an extremely long tail. This styling motif found its way into several of Mitchell's designs, including the 1968 AstroVette and the 1969 Manta Ray. (Photo Courtesy General Motors LLC)

"In February of 1973," said Duntov in *Corvette: America's Star-Spangled Sports Car*, "I said, 'let's inject some more life in this job. I have the four-rotor Corvette. Let's put a body on it.' And subsequently no work was done. In mid-July, I cornered Bill (Mitchell): 'Let's put a deadline: Paris Show.'"

Mitchell agreed with Duntov's idea of using the XP-882 as a platform to showcase the four-rotor powerplant. However, Mitchell wanted to incorporate several of his own ideas into the design, many of which were inspired by the European race cars he was passionate about in his youth.

The new XP-882 was to have a swept-back, airfoil-shaped design with a long nose and a tapered rear end. Early renderings of the new concept depicted a car with an immensely long tail, not unlike the Porsche 907L race car from the late 1960s. While the "stretched airfoil" design provided a streamlined racing profile for the track, its aesthetic was impractical in a production vehicle. Palmer and Haga shortened the car's exaggerated rear end with each new iteration while attempting to maintain Mitchell's preferred aesthetic. They also had to balance Mitchell's desires with the federally mandated bumper standards required for any production vehicle.

Palmer and Haga presented Mitchell with the design that evolved into the Four-Rotor Corvette in April 1973. The car's profile included the

Designers Henry Haga (seated) and Charles Jordan inspect the Four-Rotor Aerovette concept in the backlot of the design studios at GM's Technical Center in Warren, Michigan. (Photo Courtesy General Motors LLC)

The Aerovette's doors were a bifolding gull-wing design and included a lower door sill, all of which made it easier for occupants to enter or exit the vehicle. The largest drawback to the bifold design was that the door windows could not be raised or lowered due to the absence of a window pocket inside the two-piece door. (Photo Courtesy General Motors LLC)

When it was publicly introduced at the 1973 Paris Auto Show, the Four-Rotor concept was a showstopper. It left many hopeful attendees wondering if they'd glimpsed the next-generation Corvette. Unfortunately, ongoing challenges with the Wankel rotary engine combined with the Organization of Petroleum Exporting Countries (OPEC) energy crisis of 1973 brought the Aerovette program to a quick and final end. (Photo Courtesy General Motors LLC)

desired tapered front and rear ends and a swept-back windshield set at a dramatic 72-degree slope. In addition to being aesthetically stunning, the car was extremely aerodynamic with a drag coefficient of just 0.325, which was a remarkable achievement for that time.

Production of the Four-Rotor concept began in earnest immediately following Mitchell's approval of the design. GM designer Charles M. "Chuck" Jordan was responsible for designing the car's unique bifold gull-wing doors. A concealed slot in the door skin allowed occupants to unlatch each door. They then swung out-and-up like a traditional gull wing, except that the lower part of the door swung inward on a hinge located just beneath the side windows.

The interior of the car featured suede and leather seats that could be adjusted automatically via a single toggle to the needs of the driver. Moving the toggle up or down adjusted the seat position around a front-mounted pivot. Moving the toggle forward or back adjusted the pedals to accommodate drivers of varying heights. Similarly, the car featured a tilting/telescoping steering wheel. The dashboard featured a series of digital displays, including the speedometer in the main display, a selectable oil pressure/fuel level display to its left, a coolant temperature/

battery voltage meter to its right.

The GM design staff fabrication shop built the car's body panels out of fiberglass (GRP) and mounted them on a framework of steel and aluminum tubing. They assembled the complex body and interior in less time (roughly four days sooner) than it took Pininfarina to assemble the Two-Rotor's body. This distinction was both a point of pride for the fabrication team and a mandatory schedule requirement as Bill Mitchell planned to publicly introduce the Four-Rotor Corvette concept at the Paris Auto Show in October 1973.

In 1976, one year before his mandatory retirement from General Motors, Bill Mitchell decided to resurrect the XP-895 concept. He replaced its four-rotor engine with a 400-ci (6.6L) V-8 engine and had the rest of the car inspected before returning it to the auto show circuit. Its sudden appearance left enthusiasts and critics alike wondering if a mid-engine Corvette was finally on its way. (Photo Courtesy General Motors LLC)

The Wankel Engine Abandoned

The Four-Rotor Corvette looked stunning in its metallic silver paint. It sat on 10-port aluminum wheels that were a design carryover from Duntov's original XP-882, albeit with a deeper stance on the new car. Parked next to the XP-987 GT, the cars attracted the largest crowds at that year's Paris Auto Show. The pair became Chevrolet's centerpiece at car shows across Europe for the remainder of the year.

Like the XP-897 GT, the Four-Rotor Corvette was adversely and irrevocably impacted

The Aerovette was greenlit (at least briefly) to begin production in 1980 as the fourth-generation Corvette. Corvette Chief Engineer David McLellan rejected the idea, arguing that the car would be too costly to manufacture and that it arrived on the coattails of the Middle East energy crisis. (Photo Courtesy General Motors LLC)

by the OPEC energy crisis of 1973. The four-rotor engine, like its two-rotor counterpart, suffered from massive efficiency issues (Duntov claimed fuel consumption averaged 6 mpg). It also deteriorated rapidly during testing, leaving many to question its long-term durability as a viable option for the car. The rotary engine program continued into 1974, but it became clear that it would never meet increasingly stringent federal emissions standards.

Ed Cole, who had been the single largest driving force behind GM's use of the Wankel engine, retired on September 29, 1974. Not long after his retirement, Chevrolet's involvement in the rotary engine program was abandoned.

For Duntov, the collapse of the rotary engine program meant the end of his Four-Rotor prototype. This came as a harsh personal blow to Duntov. He had spent his final years with Chevrolet developing the Wankel-powered mid-engine Corvette under the belief that Ed Cole would eventually approve the car as a production vehicle. Once more, his dream was snuffed out by a situation well beyond his control.

In late 1975, Bill Mitchell resurrected the Four-Rotor project after he'd spotted the car sitting abandoned in the design center garage. Recognizing the work that had been put into its development and recalling the fact that structurally the Four-Rotor was little more than a reworking of the earlier XP-882, he elected to have the car refitted with a 400-ci small-block V-8 engine. During this reworking on the car's powertrain, Chuck Jordan rechristened it the "Aerovette."

By the mid-1970s, the third-generation front-engine Corvette proved to be a commercial success with steady year-over-year sales number growth. Because of this and the massive cost of retooling the Corvette production line to build a mid-engine car, the Aerovette was relinquished once more to become a "turntable" queen at car shows across the United States.

Zora Arkus-Duntov retired from General Motors on December 24, 1974. During his retirement dinner the following January, he was presented with a beautifully recreated scale model of the Aerovette assembled by GM's design studio. Despite his disappointment in not seeing the car become a reality, Duntov considered the 1973 Aerovette one of the greatest concept Corvettes, along with the 1957 Corvette SS race car, ever produced.

The Aerovette directly influenced many of GM's future engineers and designers, including Corvette Chief Engineer Dave McLellan and GM Vice President of Design Ed Welburn, both of whom were still relatively new to General Motors when the Aerovette was introduced. It also served as Jerry Palmer's inspiration when designing the fourth-generation Corvette.

The Aerovette is now part of the GM Heritage Center Collection.

For those fortunate enough to visit GM's Heritage Center in Sterling Heights, Michigan, the 1973 Aerovette remains one of the highlights of its entire collection. The car also makes infrequent appearances at various Corvette events across the United States throughout the spring and summer months. (Photo Courtesy General Motors LLC)

CHAPTER 7

THE CHANGING OF THE GUARD

There is no more important relationship in the concept phase of a new car program than the one between styling and engineering. Either department can cause a project to fail, but it takes both, working together, to make it succeed.
—Dave McLellan (excerpt from Corvette from the Inside*)*

Duntov's retirement from General Motors on December 24, 1974, marked a major turning point in the evolution of the Corvette. GM's leadership knew the role of Corvette's chief engineer needed to be filled by someone who could continue to advance Duntov's vision while simultaneously propelling the Corvette program forward in entirely new directions. Although filling such an iconic position might have proved to be a daunting challenge, senior management had already picked a young engineer named Dave McLellan to succeed Duntov in the role.

Dave McLellan: Corvette's Next Chief Engineer

A native of Munising, Michigan, McLellan attended Wayne State University in Detroit, where he earned his Bachelor of Science in Mechanical Engineering. Upon graduating, he joined the GM Corporation's Milford Proving Grounds Noise and Vibration Laboratory on July 1, 1959.

During the early years of his career, McLellan worked on improving the dynamics of both production and military vehicles. In time, he was promoted to manager of

David R. McLellan joined General Motors in 1959 and became Corvette's second chief of engineering in 1975. During his time as chief engineer, he oversaw the creation and evolution of the fourth-generation Corvette and the launch of the Corvette Assembly Plant in Bowling Green, Kentucky. (Photo Courtesy General Motors LLC)

the newly completed Black Lake Vehicle Dynamics Test Area.

His continued successes at General Motors over the next decade afforded him the opportunity to join the Chevrolet Engineering Center. In this new role, McLellan developed the chassis for the Camaro Z28 and led the team that finished the 1970½ Camaro. His achievements with the Camaro caught the attention of John DeLorean. McLellan was reassigned to the GM Technical Center, where he was tasked with managing a project promoted by DeLorean that explored building a shared chassis for both the Camaro and Corvette.

McLellan was promoted to assistant staff engineer of Chevrolet Passenger Cars in April 1972. In 1973, he took a leave of absence after being extended an opportunity by General Motors to attend the Massachusetts Institute of Technology (MIT) as an Alfred P. Sloan Fellow. He graduated a year later with a Master of Science in Management. Equipped with his new degree, McLellan was promoted to staff engineer. At this point in his career, he was assigned to work with Zora Arkus-Duntov.

Six months later, Dave McLellan was officially appointed to the position of Corvette chief engineer.

Bill Mitchell's Retirement and the New Vice President of Styling

After Duntov's departure from General Motors, there weren't many left within the corporation who felt convicted to continue building Corvettes with the massive high-horsepower V-8 engines that

Upon his retirement from General Motors in July 1977, Bill Mitchell (pictured here with his Sting Ray racer), made this proclamation: "It's the kids I care about. They know what the Corvette is all about. Corvette owners see the car as a vehicle of personal expression, an extension of themselves, a car that is individually their own." (Photo Courtesy General Motors LLC)

Corvette Chief Engineers David Hill (far left), Zora Arkus-Duntov (left), and Dave McLellan pose with the highly stylized 1986 Corvette Indy concept on the Long Wharf in Boston, Massachusetts. This Corvette concept, more than any other in this book, remains one of the best examples of pure automotive design without limits. (Photo Courtesy General Motors LLC)

Jerry Palmer served as chief designer of the Chevrolet Studio No. 3 after receiving the promotion from Bill Mitchell in 1974. In this role, he worked directly with Dave McLellan to define the shape and to sort out the aerodynamics of the fourth-generation Corvette. (Photo Courtesy General Motors LLC)

had made them popular to begin with. Instead, GM management was looking for ways to make the Corvette more economical and fuel efficient. Bill Mitchell and Dave McLellan openly disagreed with this change of direction, but both faced significant pressures from management to operate within the increasingly stringent governance concerning fuel economy and emissions regulations. To make matters worse, Bill Mitchell was facing his mandatory retirement from General Motors.

By 1977, Mitchell had lost much of his personal conviction about the seemingly inevitable downsizing of the Corvette powerplant. He even started defending the decision, arguing that Ferrari and Mercedes-Benz continued to achieve great success after introducing smaller engines in their cars. However, after driving a mid-engine V-6 powered test mule, he spent the remainder of his days at General Motors defending the continuance of the V-8 powerplant as the only viable option for the Corvette.

Prior to his retirement, Mitchell promoted Henry Haga to head the Opel studio in Europe and handpicked Jerry Palmer to lead the Chevrolet Studio No. 3 as its chief designer. Palmer had trained under Haga and had been heavily involved in the development of the Four-Rotor Corvette. Mitchell knew that Palmer would continue the high standard of styling and design that made the Corvette great. He also believed that Palmer would forge a similar partnership with Dave McLellan to the one he'd developed with Zora Arkus-Duntov decades earlier, thereby ensuring the continued success of the brand.

Bill Mitchell retired from General Motors in July 1977.

Rybicki Replaces Mitchell

On August 1, 1977, Mitchell was succeeded by Irv Rybicki, a conservative designer who had never worked on the Corvette and knew virtually nothing about it. It has been claimed that Rybicki was given the vice president of GM styling position because of his known reputation for being a "team player." GM's executive leadership wanted greater control over the styling of the company's new cars, including the Corvette. Mitchell had been loud, flamboyant, and had often proceeded without the consent of upper management. Rybicki was his opposite. From management's perspective, Rybicki was the perfect man for the job.

Fortunately for the Corvette program, Rybicki's lack of enthusiasm was buffeted by strong engineering and design leadership from Dave McLellan and Jerry Palmer. Even so, the road ahead was uncertain and would present both men with a variety of new and unique challenges.

Irv Rybicki replaced Bill Mitchell in 1978 as GM's vice president of styling. Prior to his promotion, he worked as a designer on GM's larger car lines. Rybicki suffered from debilitating back problems, which led to his general disinterest in the Corvette. The fourth-generation Corvette was developed during his time in the vice president of styling role. (Photo Courtesy General Motors LLC)

Designing for a New Generation

Development of the fourth-generation Corvette began in 1979 under the leadership of Dave McLellan. Despite having personal reservations about the continued development of a mid-engine Corvette, McLellan took stock of the considerable research and development that had been performed by his predecessors and decided he would let public opinion dictate the future of the brand. After polling an assortment of Corvette owners and enthusiasts, he quickly discovered that consumer opinion was divided. Some supported a mid-engine platform, but a great deal more argued that the Corvette was, and always should be, a front-engine, rear-wheel-drive sports car.

McLellan helped usher in a new era of Corvette performance by forging a relationship with Reeves Callaway in the mid-1980s and through his work on the fourth-generation Corvette ZR1. He retired from General Motors on August 31, 1992, and was inducted into the National Corvette Museum's Hall of Fame on September 1, 1999. (Photo Courtesy General Motors LLC)

Ultimately, McLellan's research (along with strong personal preference) dictated that the next-generation Corvette should continue to follow in the traditional format of its predecessors.

Chevrolet's research and development team was tasked with improving the third-generation Corvette's chassis design. Meanwhile, McLellan began acquiring other sports cars, including a Porsche 928, a Ferrari 330 GT, a Maserati Ghibli, and a Lamborghini Muira. These cars were evaluated by the research and development team to identify which design characteristics worked well and which should be avoided while developing the new Corvette. He also had the research and development team resurrect the XP-895 Reynolds Aluminum concept. They drove it extensively at the Milford Proving Grounds and gleaned a great deal of information about its performance and handling characteristics under various conditions.

Form Follows Function

Increased emissions standards and fuel economy requirements became a significant part of the fourth-generation Corvette's development. As the EPA placed additional restrictions on all automobile manufacturers, McLellan and his team scrambled to identify engine, transmission, and exhaust arrangements that would satisfy emissions requirements without completely debilitating performance. For this reason, the Doug Nash 4+3 manual transmission was introduced on the fourth-generation Corvette.

Even with McLellan in Corvette's top seat, GM styling continued working on Duntov's mid-engine Corvette. The team introduced this design in 1978 as a potential 1984 model. Although McLellan steered the Corvette away from the mid-engine platform, this design was reimagined by Pontiac engineers as the Fiero. (Photo Courtesy General Motors LLC)

Brian Decker, a member of Chevrolet's research and development department, was tasked with chassis development. One of the major challenges facing Decker was the need to improve the car's structural stiffness while also meeting crash/safety requirements, reducing mass, and improving the car's interior roominess. Decker developed a new program that became known as the GM Research Laboratories. GMR applied analytical optimization techniques to the development of the Corvette chassis. It marked one of the first times that computer modeling was used in the Corvette's development.

In the fall of 1979, McLellan partnered with Jerry Palmer to develop the shape of the new Corvette's body. Palmer started by creating a series

One of Jerry Palmer's early color renderings shows the fourth-generation Corvette. This drawing was one of probably hundreds of concept renderings created during the early development of the C4. (Photo Courtesy General Motors LLC)

of sketches that depicted a swept-back profile based on Decker's chassis. By the following spring, GM's top brass wanted to inspect the progress being made on the car. A drivable chassis, McLellan's sketches, and Decker's computer models were presented to Howard Kehler, group vice president of engineering, styling, and research. Kehler's only question was "Can you fit a 4-cylinder engine?"

Palmer's design work moved forward in earnest, and it wasn't long before he began transforming his sketches into clay models. He moved the Aerovette into his studio for reference and reused many facets of his previous design on the new Corvette. Unlike the Aerovette, which had a back end that was nearly as long as its front, this new car received a blunt "Kamm" tail.

Developed in a Wind Tunnel

A series of quarter-scale models were constructed for wind-tunnel testing. These models were used to determine the best aerodynamic profile for the car. Several examples, each varying in form from the others, were tested until a model with an optimal drag coefficient of 0.365 was identified. A full-size clay car was then sculpted by Palmer and his design team. It was also subjected to extensive wind-tunnel testing (over 100 tests in all) that resulted in a design profile with a drag coefficient of 0.330 and an appreciable reduction in vehicle lift.

Through the combined efforts of McLellan's engineering group and Palmer's design staff, a pre-prototype version of the fourth-generation Corvette began to take shape. The decision was made to build six test mules (though budget constraints limited production to three). Each incorporated Palmer's then-current styling cues, which included a T-bar roof assembly, a forward-raked B-pillar, and a series of very defined (sharp) edges throughout.

The assembly of the pre-prototype Corvettes took place in McLellan's Engineering center. Each part was designed in detail, mocked up out of cardboard and/or wood, and then replicated in the actual materials used to build each car. As each of the cars took shape, the question that loomed on everyone's mind was whether they'd meet the approval of Chevrolet's new Product Policy Group (PPG).

The PPG was made up of GM's top officers. They decided whether this latest Corvette would become a production vehicle or disappear into obscurity. The PPG effectively (or ineffectively, depending on who you ask) replaced the decision-defining feedback that General Motors once received from Motorama spectators, racing enthusiasts, and the like.

Palmer's drawings of the 1983 Corvette were transformed into a full-size clay model inside Chevy Studio No. 3. This model was presented to GM's corporate management on April 22, 1980, and it was approved for production that same day. (Photo Courtesy General Motors LLC)

1973 Chevrolet XP-898

Despite looking like an early iteration of the fourth-generation Corvette, the XP-898 was a two-seat sports coupe developed by Chevrolet Chief Engineer Ed Mertz and Project Engineer Brook Lindbert. Its creation was part of a feasibility study to explore alternative methods for building fiberglass-bodied automobiles.

The basic outward structure of the XP-898 consisted of four lightweight fiberglass body panels (a floor pan, a firewall, an upper front section, and an upper rear section) bonded together by urethane and a foam substructure. Prior to assembly, each of the four panels were mounted onto a specially shaped foam mold. Liquid urethane was then injected between the foam mold and the fiberglass panels, bonding them together into a single, rigid structure.

Once the urethane cured (which took approximately 15 minutes), the body assembly was removed from the mold and fitted with a complete powertrain, suspension, doors, and a hood. Each of these components was bolted to metal attachment plates bonded to the inside of the fiberglass body. Many of the mechanical components installed in the XP-898, including its 4-cylinder engine, came from a Chevy Vega.

Although the early notchback styling of the car was pretty basic, the Chevy Studio Three developed the XP-898's stylized coupe body from some of the previously assembled prototypes. They added dramatic elements to the car's front and rear ends, including a stylized cowl on the hood and a fastback assembly with removable hardtop. The finished car had a 90-inch wheelbase and an overall length of 166 inches.

The XP 898 was virtually devoid of squeaks, rattles, and vibrations during operation. Better still, its foam/fiberglass construction prevented the car from sustaining catastrophic damage at speeds up to 50 mph. This dramatically improved crashworthiness caused some GM engineers to consider recommending the car for production. Unfortunately, the XP-898's production process was far too time consuming to be a viable solution for General Motors.

The chassis of the XP-898 is exceptionally rigid, without the creaks and groans commonly heard when driving a car made from multiple body panels. Moreover, the inner and outer shells of the body were filled with foam, which reduced outside noise and improved energy absorption in the event of a crash. (Photo Courtesy General Motors LLC)

The XP-898 concept was a two-seat, targa-top coupe built by General Motors that used an experimental assembly process wherein body panels were bonded together via polyurethane to create a single-piece outer shell. (Photo Courtesy General Motors LLC)

From Pre-Prototype to Pilot Car

On the morning of April 22, 1980, the PPG met in Jerry Palmer's Chevrolet Studio Three to evaluate the new Corvette. The car was immediately approved as presented.

Further development toward a final production-model prototype continued for the next two years. Unlike earlier iterations of the Corvette, which had largely evolved from the specific vision of either an individual or a small

This is a side-by-side comparison of the 1983 Corvette concept (right) and a 1979 third-generation Corvette outside the Design Dome at General Motor's Technical Center in Warren, Michigan. (Photo Courtesy General Motors LLC)

The 1983 Corvette concept's (left) overall length and height were shorter by 9 inches and 2 inches, respectively, as compared to the then-current third-generation model. GM Vice President of Design Irv Rybicki insisted that the new Corvette was to be smaller than its predecessor. While this initially presented some challenges to McLellan's engineering group, the product they delivered was very well received. (Photo Courtesy General Motors LLC)

The similarities between the 1983 Corvette concept and the third-generation model are essentially limited to the two pairs of round taillights. Everything else, including the straightedge styling, the integrated exhaust ports, even the "turbo-corvette" badging, were new additions to the fourth-generation prototype. (Photo Courtesy General Motors LLC)

The pre-prototype 1983 Corvette concept included a forward-raked B-pillar, a centrally located air inlet framed by integrated cornering/turn signals in the front fascia, and sharper body lines than the production model. Side fender louvers were notably absent from this early design. (Photo Courtesy General Motors LLC)

group of designers/engineers, the fourth-generation Corvette evolved through a more robust "prototype program." This afforded the project team with additional engineering resources to solve mechanical, structural, and performance problems throughout preproduction. During this period of development, Corvette's Z51 suspension option was born.

The fourth-generation Corvette's press reveal was scheduled for fall 1982 at the Riverside International Raceway. As the date neared, there were still many unknowns about the car, including when production of the new Corvette would begin, what it would cost, and how it would be marketed—as a 1983 model or possibly as a 1984 Corvette. The answer to the model year question was determined, not surprisingly, by federal emissions regulation standards.

The next iteration of the 1983 concept included many of the styling cues that ended up on the final design. Still absent from the front fascia was the integrated front license plate assembly and recessed running/turn signal lights. Additionally, the front fender flares and hood cowls lacked the definition of the production model. (Photo Courtesy General Motors LLC)

Each year, the federal government establishes new emissions certification rules that all manufacturers must adhere to. Because a variety of testing, including exhaust and emissions refinements, was still being completed as 1982 ebbed into 1983, it was decided that the engineering team should be given extra time to make the new Corvette the absolute best car it could be. This meant Corvette would skip a year of commercial production. It also meant that Chevrolet could build the new Corvette to meet 1984 federal emissions certification standards so long as they started production on/after January 1, 1983, and they could do so without the added (and sizable) cost of having the car recertified in 1984.

Even with the decision to delay production for a year, Chevrolet produced 14 test mules and 43 pilot line cars with 1983 vehicle identification numbers. These cars were driven extensively to determine many of the fourth-generation Corvette's performance and handling limits. They were also used at press events and to evaluate consumer opinion of the new Corvette.

The 1983 Corvette: The "One and Only"

Forty-three 1983 Corvettes were built at the Bowling Green Corvette Assembly Plant as part of a pilot program to streamline production of the fourth-generation model. As each car rolled off the line, it was assigned a unique vehicle identification number (VIN) and prepped for transportation. In the case of the "one and only," it was dispatched to GM's Milford Proving Grounds for additional shakedown/testing by the Corvette engineering and design teams. The car was then scheduled to be returned to Bowling Green and summarily destroyed.

The earlier forward-swept B-pillar design had been reversed on this prototype version to enhance the car's swept-back aesthetic. Farther back, the car's rear fascia still featured a protruding rear bumper with a low-positioned license plate housing molded into its center. (Photo Courtesy General Motors LLC)

There has been considerable debate among Corvette enthusiasts as to what happened next. What follows are a couple of the more popular stories surrounding the survival of the "one and only" 1983 Corvette.

As development of the fourth-generation Corvette neared completion, former GM President Lloyd Reuss demanded that the car have a targa top instead of T-tops. To make this possible, the car's frame rails had to be increased in size, which is the reason C4 Corvettes (including the "one and only" 1983 Corvette seen here) have small doors and massive door sills. (Photo Courtesy Kolecki Photography)

A New Pair of Boots

General Motors reportedly rented a mobile crusher and had it delivered to the Bowling Green Assembly Plant with the express purpose of destroying the 1983 test mules and pilot cars upon their return. Work commenced, and the 1983 Corvettes were systematically destroyed one after the next. As the day progressed, the weather turned steadily worse until a torrential downpour began to soak much of southern Kentucky.

The facilities engineer overseeing the destruction of the 1983 Corvettes shut down the day's operations as pooling water began to soak his brand-new pair of expensive cowboy boots. Allegedly, all but one of the cars had already been crushed, but he decided the remaining car could wait until the following morning when work could resume under fairer weather conditions. Upon returning to the plant the next day, he discovered that the mobile crusher had been removed from the facilities (as the scheduled destruction of the 43 Pilot Corvettes had been assumed complete).

Sometimes referred to as RBV098, the sole surviving 1983 Corvette was number 4 of the 43 pilot cars manufactured by General Motors. This car was shipped to GM's Automotive Proving Grounds, where it underwent extensive testing in August and September 1982.

Fearful of any implications he might face should the oversight be discovered, the engineer decided to inform his supervisors of the mishap. The car was relocated to the manufacturing plant's back lot and abandoned, only to be discovered a year later by the plant's new GM Paul Schnoes.

Upon discovering the 1983 Corvette, Schnoes had the car moved from the back lot to safer keeping inside the plant. There it remained until the opening of the National Corvette Museum in 1994.

The Covert Rescue Mission

Another variation on this story depicts a more intentional act of rescue by members of the Bowling Green Assembly Plant staff. As before, the cars were returned to the plant and scheduled to be destroyed via a mobile crusher. Prior to their destruction, members of the plant staff agreed to relocate one of the 1983 Corvettes to a non-trafficked area of the back lot and cover it with a tarp.

The reasoning behind their decision? The 1983 Corvette represented Corvette's 30th anniversary and many of the plant workers felt it a grievous injustice that Chevrolet had elected not to produce a Corvette to celebrate the milestone year. By keeping one of the 1983 Corvettes tucked away "out of sight, out of mind," they reasoned they would eventually negotiate a reprieve from its destruction with GM management once enough time had passed.

What Happened Next

However it happened, the "one and only" Corvette did survive the crusher and became a resident of the Bowling Green Assembly Plant for nearly a decade. It was given a "star-and-stripes" paint job and received a set of

The "one and only" 1983 Corvette is on display in the National Corvette Museum's rotunda. Since being donated by General Motors in 1994, the 1983 Corvette has remained a key attraction for many of the museum's visitors.

The 1986 Corvette Indy is a concept car in its purist form. Designed without regard of federal safety and/or crash regulations, Tom Peters's wildly inventive "Indy" concept was a showcase of GM's latest technologies and the epitome of 1980s-era styling. (Photo Courtesy General Motors LLC)

directional 16-inch wheels from the 1984 model year. It was put on display inside the plant from 1984 to 1994 and became a celebrated piece of the plant's history among its employees.

The "one and only" was donated to the National Corvette Museum to celebrate its grand opening on September 2, 1994. The car's exterior was returned to its original white paint color and its original 15-inch wheels were reinstalled. The car continues to be a highlight of the museum's collection.

The 1983 Corvette (and its production counterparts a year later) marked the first time in the brand's history when virtually every aspect of the car followed the mantra "form follows function." The car had a drag coefficient of just 0.341, the lowest coefficient in the history of the brand. It had the most acute windshield rake (64.7 degrees) of any production vehicle from that era. It was the first Corvette to introduce a removable one-piece roof and one of the first Corvettes to introduce a frameless rear glass window that doubled as a hatch. It had a curb weight (with a full tank of gas) of 3,192 pounds, which was a marked improvement over the outgoing 1982 model at a weight of 3,342 pounds.

Most importantly, the 1983 Corvette represented GM's willingness to focus on "getting it right over simply getting it done."

The 1986 Corvette Indy

The Corvette Indy was the creation of GM Designer Tom Peters and Vice President of Design Charles M. "Chuck" Jordan. It made its public debut at the 1986 Detroit Auto Show and marked two unique milestones: it was the first genuine concept Corvette since the 1974 Aerovette and, like many of the earlier concepts that preceded it, the Corvette Indy was a mid-engine car.

Pure Design Meets Cutting-Edge Technology

When Peters started designing the Corvette Indy in late 1985, he saw it as an opportunity to design a completely unique and decidedly unconventional sports car that didn't require consideration of driver ergonomics, providing adequate interior space, or even allowing for cockpit accessibility. From the beginning, Peters's renderings depicted a car that showcased futuristic design motifs and exotic, supercar-style proportioning.

GM management saw the Corvette Indy as a platform to outwardly showcase GM's participation in several key technology development programs. The largest of these was Lotus's "Active Suspension" platform, a technology that Lotus developed to enhance the handling of its Formula 1 race cars. General Motors acquired the technology when it purchased Group Lotus (Lotus Cars Inc.) in 1986. It was also the ideal platform to highlight Chevrolet's upcoming 2.65-liter Indy V-8 engine, which had been under development by Ilmor Engineering when the new Corvette concept project was first announced.

An early, full-scale rendering of the Corvette Indy concept was created by Tom Peters. Although much of this design was revised over the course of the car's development, this drawing shows Peters's intention to place the engine behind the driver and to include a sloping, wedge-style nose, as well as military aircraft-inspired side air scoops as a dominant feature of the design. (Photo Courtesy General Motors LLC)

This second rendering of the Corvette Indy concept by Tom Peters provided the basis of design from which the rest of the car would evolve. Incidentally, the wheels showcased on this drawing were designed by Peters in 1984 as a stand-alone component. They were introduced on the 1988 Corvette and represent this first part manufactured by General Motors based on one of his designs. (Photo Courtesy General Motors LLC)

A full-size clay model of the Corvette Indy began to take shape under the watchful eye of Jack Schwarz and Chevrolet's special vehicles studio. (Photo Courtesy General Motors LLC)

The look of the Indy concept takes shape. Jack Schwarz and Chevrolet's special vehicles studio constructed a fully rendered, full-size clay model of the Corvette Indy concept in just six weeks. (Photo Courtesy General Motors LLC)

A silver "skin" is applied to the Corvette Indy clay model, allowing Tom Peters and his design team to visualize more fully what the actual car would look like once assembled. (Photo Courtesy General Motors LLC)

A detailed, composite body of the Corvette Indy concept is fabricated from clay and fiberglass in preparation for the 1986 Detroit Auto Show. The show car presented in Detroit was a non-running mockup, although it featured the same engine and technologies that would be installed in the running versions of the car. (Photo Courtesy General Motors LLC)

Tom Peters inspects the Corvette Indy concept car ahead of its public unveiling at the Detroit Auto Show. The show car included a mocked-up (non-running) version of the 2.6L, DOHC V-8 Ilmor-Chevrolet Indy racing engine. (Photo Courtesy General Motors LLC)

With its incredibly low profile, its massive air intakes, its open-air cockpit packed full of technology, and its bright silver exterior, the 1986 Corvette Indy concept became an immediate fan favorite from the moment it was introduced in Detroit. (Photo Courtesy General Motors LLC)

The overwhelming success of the Corvette Indy concept in Detroit motivated GM's management to order two running examples of the car. Although both of these later examples maintained the overall appearance of the original prototype, neither was as dramatic in form as the 1986 show car. (Photo Courtesy General Motors LLC)

The fiberglass-bodied and fully operational Corvette Indy concept was powered by a Lotus-sourced 32-valve DOHC 5.7-liter V-8 engine. This car has a documented top speed of 210 mph (per General Motors) and a 0–60 time of 4.6 seconds. Despite these impressive numbers, this car was primarily used as a show piece at public events. (Photo Courtesy Kolecki Photography)

In addition to its Lotus V-8 engine, the Corvette Indy concept was fitted with a 3-speed automatic transmission, which many would-be consumers had considered an unusual choice for such a high-performance machine. Had the car moved past the concept stage and into production, it is reasonable to assume a manual gearbox would also have been offered. (Photo Courtesy Kolecki Photography)

Tom Peters's radical concept car was given the name "Corvette Indy" because it was meant to showcase the Ilmor-Chevrolet Indy engine. Its primary purpose was to power the race cars at the Indianapolis 500. (Photo Courtesy Kolecki Photography)

As Tom Peters's renderings of the Corvette Indy concept neared completion, Chuck Jordon tasked Jack Schwartz of Chevrolet's special vehicles studio to create a clay model of the car's exterior. Schwartz embraced the challenge and led the efforts to fabricate a full-scale model based on Peters's highly stylized, swooping design in just six weeks.

Peters and Schwartz also oversaw development of the car's two-passenger interior, which contained a driver's seat surrounded by a CRT-based instrument display. The dashboard included a military-grade,

The Corvette Indy's cockpit used several CRT displays, including one that served as a rearview mirror by displaying video footage from a rear-facing camera on the back of the car. Additional screens provided vehicle operating information (speed, fuel economy, etc.) and GPS navigation. (Photo Courtesy General Motors LLC)

Each of the two Corvette Indy prototypes were fitted with a Lotus-sourced 32-valve DOHC 5.7L V-8 engine as well as Lotus's active suspension system, which used hydraulic dampers (instead of shocks and springs) to regulate ride control.

Like many of the high-end exotics of the 1980s, the Corvette Indy had scissor-style doors that opened vertically, allowing easier access into/out of the car's cockpit. Each door included half of the Corvette Indy's fixed, bubble-shaped canopy, which lowered into place with the door along a centrally mounted T-bar. (Photo Courtesy General Motors LLC)

Tom Peters

Tom Peters was GM's head of exterior design for performance cars. During his 35-plus-year career as an automotive designer for General Motors, Peters contributed to many of the company's most exciting brands, including the Chevy Camaro and Silverado, the Cadillac XLR, and of course, the Corvette. (Photo Courtesy General Motors LLC)

While attending the ArtCenter College of Design, Tom Peters was awarded an internship at GM design studio. Chuck Jordan (not pictured) was so impressed with Peters's work during his internship that he offered him a permanent position with General Motors upon his graduation in 1980. (Photo Courtesy General Motors LLC)

Like many of the Corvette designers before him, Tom Peters developed a passion for drawing when he was a young child. He filled sketchbooks with anything that caught his attention, but his favorite subjects to draw were aircraft and automobiles. He was intrigued by how these vehicles could be designed to be works of art while simultaneously providing a reliable means of transportation.

Peters had his first encounter with a Corvette when he was still in grade school. It was an experience that defined his career.

"I remember getting off the bus with my friends and seeing what looked like a silver flying saucer-spaceship coming in for a landing," Peters said. "It was a 1963 Sting Ray Corvette. The door opened, and it was the local rich kid. We just stopped in our tracks and stared at this amazing car as his dad drove off. Often, we waited outside for the chance to see it again."

Peters spent his first two years in college as an advertising/illustration major. He continued to draw cars and began to work on them as well, mostly to gain a greater understanding of how the mechanical underpinnings of an automobile complimented its outward aesthetic. Midway through his college career, he happened upon a catalog for the ArtCenter College of Design in Pasadena, California, a school that specialized in developing artists and designers. He created a portfolio of his work and submitted it to them along with his application for enrollment. They accepted him right away.

While the ArtCenter provided Peters with the education for which he'd been searching, it also proved to be an expensive endeavor. He soon discovered that he lacked the funds needed to complete his education. Eager to keep going, Peters discovered a paid internship at General Motors for juniors and seniors. Despite only being a sophomore, he submitted his portfolio and was awarded the position at General Motors.

Working as an intern at the design studio was a dream come true. It enabled Peters to work with actual automotive designers and to gain real-world experience that helped him advance his skills beyond anything he might have learned in school. His own work at General Motors resulted in a design portfolio that earned him a scholarship that paid for the rest of his education.

Peters's work at the design studio also caught the attention of Chuck Jordan, GM's vice president of design. After graduation, Jordan presented Peters with a permanent position at General Motors. Elated, Peters started work at the Advance Design studios in 1980.

While he loved his work at the ArtCenter, he loved his wife more. When she failed to find employment at General Motors, the couple moved to Lubbock, Texas, after she received a job offer from Texas Instruments. The couple

Tom Peters works on the exterior of the sixth-generation Corvette. While Corvette Chief Engineer David Hill was responsible for the car's underpinnings, it was Peters who gave the car its aggressive outward appearance and reintroduced exposed headlights as a design element on the sixth-generation model. (Photo Courtesy General Motors LLC)

worked at Texas Instruments for two years. A letter arrived in the mail from Chuck Jordan offering Tom and his wife a job at General Motors. Delighted by the offer, the couple packed their bags and headed to Detroit.

"I could feel the electricity in a studio led by Jerry Palmer," Peters said. "One of the first assignments he gave me was to work on a Corvette mid-engine concept using the Lotus Indy engine. When we were done, I looked at it and remembered the 1963 Sting Ray spaceship I saw as a kid way back when, and here I am in this exclusive, hallowed area working on this vehicle."

Peters's continued successes at General Motors, his teamwork-based attitude, and his genuine passion for design led to his eventual appointment as chief of design for the sixth-generation Corvette and the seventh-generation Stingray. He also served as the director of design for the eighth-generation, mid-engine Corvette.

In addition to his work on the Corvette program, Peters designed many of GM's other product offerings during his 30-year career, including the Chevy Camaro, Chevy Silverado, the Pontiac Aztek, and the Cadillac XLR. Additionally, his portfolio included several incredible concepts, including the 1986 Corvette Indy show car, the 1988 Pontiac Banshee, the Cadillac Sixteen, and the Buick Velite.

In 2013, Peters was awarded a lifetime achievement award for his work at General Motors from the ArtCenter College of Design. He was inducted into the National Corvette Museum Hall of Fame in September 2019. After retiring from General Motors in 2020, Peters accepted a position as a Consulting Curator of Exhibits at the National Corvette Museum.

Like Harley Earl before him, Tom Peters was inspired by the lines/shapes of contemporary military aircraft, especially the YF-22 Raptor. His vehicle designs (which include the sixth- and seventh-generation Corvette and the fifth-generation Camaro) incorporate many of those fighter-jet styling cues into their exterior and interior aesthetics. (Photo Courtesy General Motors LLC)

ETAK-satellite navigation system (remember this was years before GPS was approved for civilian use), a rearview television monitor, door-mounted displays for climate and audio controls, and selectable all-wheel steering.

The car presented at the Detroit Auto Show was a nonfunctional prototype, complete with a mocked-up version of the 600-hp twin-turbo 2.6-liter DOHC V-8 Ilmor-Chevrolet Indy racing engine mounted transversely behind the cockpit and fully visible through the car's wraparound rear glass window. The car's high-tech cockpit was similarly visible thanks to the raked-back windshield and the massive glass panels that made up the top half of the driver and passenger doors. The rest of the car, from its curvaceous front fascia to its long, low, and wide rear end, was outwardly finished in a brilliant silver and a light grey with black accents interior.

One Concept Car Begets Two More

The public's reaction to the Corvette Indy was so overwhelmingly positive that it inspired the creation of two additional cars. The first was a fiberglass-bodied example used primarily for publicity purposes. This car was finished in bright red with black accents and a black interior. It is on extended loan from General Motors to the National Corvette Museum, where it remains on permanent display. The second car was created as an engineering test mule for cutting-edge automotive and computer technologies still under development by General Motors.

Instead of using the 2.6-liter Indy race engine, the prototypes were instead powered by a Lotus-sourced 32-valve DOHC 5.7-liter V-8 that produced 380 hp and 370 ft-lbs of torque (a variation of this same engine eventually made its way into the fourth-generation ZR1 Corvette). Both cars were also equipped with Lotus's active suspension system, which used microprocessor-controlled hydraulics to adjust ride stiffness and wheel position based on acceleration values and road conditions.

Although neither of the prototype powerplants could produce the alleged 600 hp of the original Ilmor 2.6-liter, the cars were still incredibly fast with an estimated top speed exceeding 180 mph and sub-5-second 0–60 times. Unfortunately, the car's low, 43-inch height and its long, wide stance made it far more practical for use on a racetrack than the open road.

Still, many styling elements of the 1986 Corvette Indy Concept found their way into other GM production vehicles. The car inspired the front-end styling of the fourth-generation Camaro, and several of its design elements appeared on the fifth-generation Corvette. The Chevrolet-Ilmor Indy V-8 engine became a dominant force in CART racing and won multiple championships. Additionally, the Corvette Indy Concept/Prototypes were a precursor to Chevrolet's next engineering research vehicle: the 1990 CERV III.

The 1990 CERV III

When it was introduced in 1986, the Corvette Indy concept gave consumers their first tantalizing glimpse at some of the advanced computer-powered technologies

Just as the Corvette Indy was a product of one man's unbridled imagination, the 1990 CERV III was the metamorphosis of that fantastic vision into a vehicle that could exist and operate in the real world. (Photo Courtesy General Motors LLC)

under development by General Motors. Four years later, the 1990 Corporate Experimental Research Vehicle III (CERV III) provided consumers with a fully realized vision of where those automotive technologies were headed.

The CERV III made its public debut at the Detroit International Auto Show in 1990 and was touted as a "fully operational research vehicle utilizing state-of-the-art technology to explore the outer reaches of automotive performance." The car showcased the advances that Chevrolet had made in engine performance and vehicle handling, its acquisition of Lotus, and its own advances in computer-controlled technologies.

Many of the styling elements found on the CERV III, from its dramatic air scoops to its elongated rear end, were repurposed from the Corvette Indy's design. Other areas, including its shortened front end, more traditional doors with operable side windows, and fixed roof assembly were introduced to meet federal safety requirements. (Photo Courtesy General Motors LLC)

The teams at Lotus and GM Advanced Solutions started having discussions about building the CERV III in 1985. They recognized that Tom Peters's Corvette Indy concept provided a worthwhile foundation for the new car. The clay model (pictured here) was constructed during the Corvette Indy concept program. Note the similarities in its profile compared to the CERV III. (Photo Courtesy General Motors LLC)

Changes to the CERV III's front end included a shortened, less dramatic front bumper/fascia assembly for improved ground clearance, recessed/flip-up headlights relocated farther up the front fenders, a separate front access panel, and a pair of side-mounted rearview mirrors at each of the doors. (Photo Courtesy General Motors LLC)

It also presented attendees with a look at the latest automotive styling concepts from GM's design studio. Despite its ultra-futuristic aesthetic, many wondered if the CERV III was actually a "sneak peak" at the next-generation Corvette.

A "More Practical" Corvette Indy

Development of the CERV III began in 1985 when GM's Advanced Engineering Vice President Don Runkle and Lotus's Tony Rudd (both of whom had been involved with the Corvette Indy program) began considering how they might use the earlier concept car as a platform to showcase new technologies each of their respective teams had been busy developing. Runkle believed that automobiles equipped with computer-assisted powertrains, braking systems, and the like would soon provide consumers with a superior and safer driving experience.

Jerry Palmer was tasked with reworking Tom Peters's original Indy design while GM engineer (and liaison to Lotus) Richard L. "Dick" Balsley was tasked with engineering and managing the project. Runkle challenged Balsley to use "extreme technologies" that would, in Balsley's own words, "(provide) top performance in a car that was predictable and able to forgive driver error."

Most of the CERV III's major styling changes were made out of necessity. The Corvette Indy's nose was shortened and raised to meet federal bumper standards. Its exposed front headlights were relocated atop the fenders and transformed into concealed, pop-up assemblies. The front fender openings were enlarged to allow sufficient wheel clearance during suspension travel and while turning the front wheels lock-to-lock. The fixed, curving, side windows that made up the top half of the Corvette Indy's doors were replaced by flattened windows that could be fully raised and lowered. The rocker panels were reshaped to allow easier access to the interior and to accommodate the dry-sump oil system and the side-mounted 23.3-gallon (combined) fuel cells.

Dimensionally, the CERV III remained faithful to the Corvette Indy in all areas except overall height and length. Where the Corvette Indy sat squat at 42.9 inches, the CERV III's height was increased to 45.15 inches to better accommodate vehicle occupants. Also, as the CERV III required a proper rear bumper, its overall length

The CERV III repurposed the scissor doors concept found on the 1986 Corvette Indy. The car's side windows were flattened out, and window pockets were installed inside the doors, which allowed vehicle occupants to raise and lower the windows at will. (Photo Courtesy General Motors LLC)

The CERV III was engineered with front and rear bumpers that met federal crash regulations. Most of the car's underbody was constructed of carbon fiber and Kevlar, both of which added to the car's structural rigidity. A thin layer of fiberglass was applied to the outer exterior to give the car a smooth finish. (Photo Courtesy General Motors LLC)

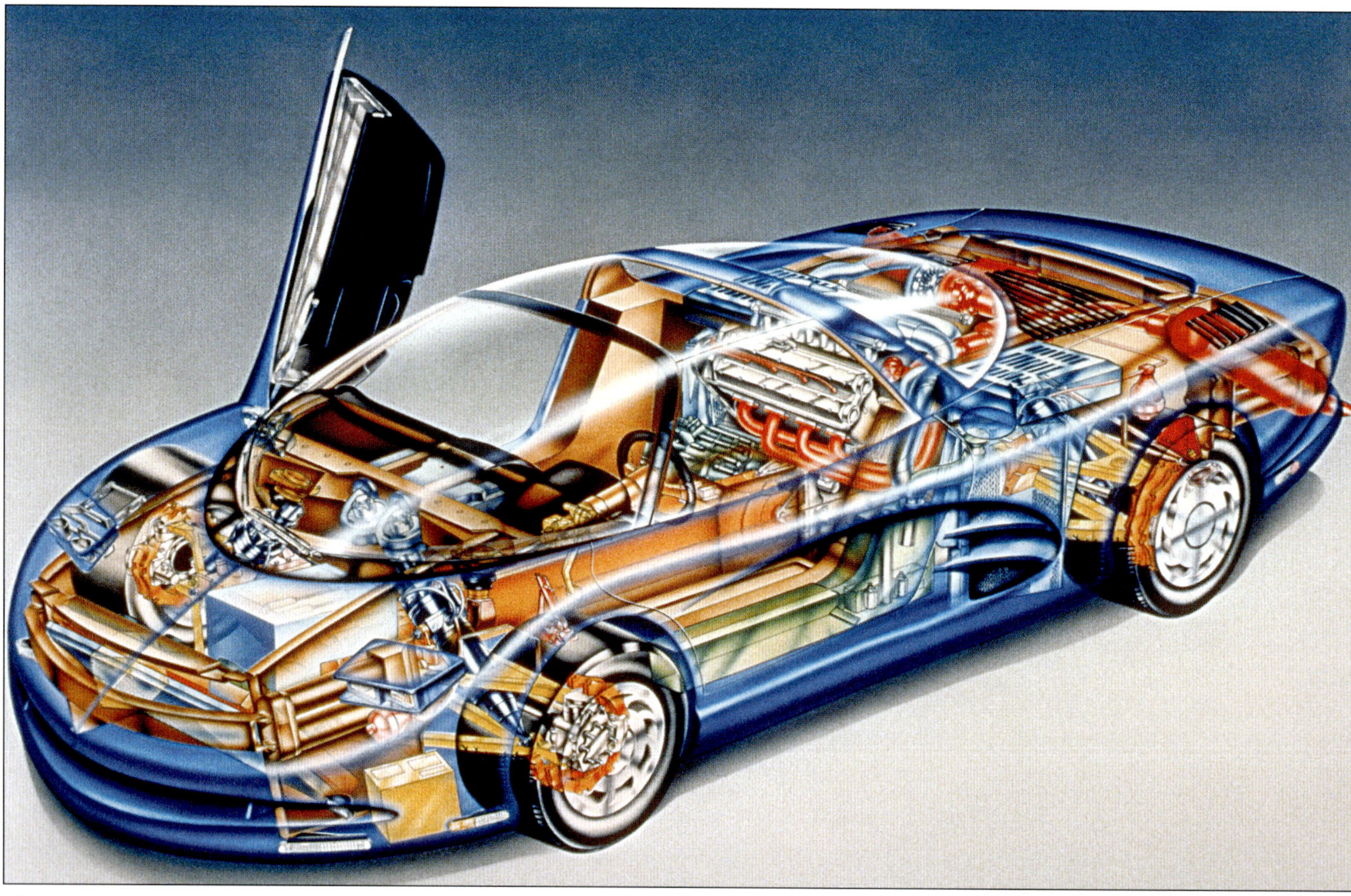

This see-through view of the CERV III provides an outstanding overview of the complex engineering involved in the assembly of this car. Of special interest is the placement of the engine directly behind the cockpit and the 23.3-gallon fuel cell near the front of the car, the latter of which required the rocker panels to be reshaped to accommodate its placement there. (Photo Courtesy General Motors LLC)

increased to 193.5 inches (to the Corvette Indy's 189 inches).

Inspired by Lotus

Production of the CERV III was heavily influenced by Lotus manufacturing standards. It featured a backbone chassis constructed of carbon fiber wrapped in fiberglass that weighed just 37 pounds. Honeycomb aluminum was also used to add structural rigidity. The car was equipped with double wishbone suspension at all four corners along with adaptable hydraulic dampers and titanium springs, the latter of which was only installed to maintain ride height when the car was stationary.

The car's body was also constructed of carbon fiber, Kevlar, and Nomex. It was fabricated as an entirely separate assembly from the rest

The CERV III received a modified version of the Lotus-derived LT5 DOHC V-8 engine. Equipped with a pair of Garrett T3 turbochargers that produced 12.0 psi of boost each, the car produced a documented 650 hp and 655 ft-lbs of torque on the dyno. (Photo Courtesy General Motors LLC)

Corvette Chief Engineer Dave McLellan (C3 and C4), Chevrolet General Manager Jim Perkins, Corvette Chief Engineer Dave Hill (C4, C5, and C6), and Corvette Chief Engineer Zora Arkus-Duntov (C1, C2, C3) pose with the CERV III. (Photo Courtesy General Motors LLC)

Like the Corvette Indy before it, the CERV III's engine was placed behind the driver in a transverse orientation near the middle of the car. Lotus provided a fortified and turbocharged version of its 5.7-liter 32-valve DOHC LT5 V-8 engine as the car's powerplant (a naturally aspirated version of this engine would be used in the fourth-generation Corvette ZR1 from 1990 to 1995). Two Garrett T3 turbochargers increased the CERV III's engine output to 650 hp and 655 ft-lbs of torque!

Engine power was transferred to all-four wheels through a crankshaft-mounted torque converter to the car's transverse 6-speed automatic transmission. The transmission was a compound system comprised of a 3-speed Turbo Hydra-matic mated to a 2-speed automatic gearbox that worked in sync with one another. A carbon fiber prop shaft ran the center section of the backbone chassis to provide power to the front wheels. The entire operation was managed via an onboard computer mounted in the car's front end.

A pair of scissor-style doors provided easy access to the CERV III's cockpit. Once inside, vehicle occupants were treated to a vast array of the latest technologies being offered by General Motors in 1990. The car came equipped with full climate control and entertainment systems, a sophisticated navigation system, and a message center designed to provide the driver with a broad assortment of information including engine diagnostics, active suspension parameters, torque split, individual wheel-steer angles, and a variety of performance measurements.

The interior of the CERV III lacked the dramatic styling of its exterior. Instead, Chevy engineers repurposed elements of the fourth-generation production model Corvette's interior, including its steering wheel and stereo head unit. Despite being packaged with a significant amount of technology, the interior of the CERV III was far less dramatic than its Corvette Indy predecessor. (Photo Courtesy General Motors LLC)

of the car. Once complete, the body was placed upon four hydraulic struts affixed to the chassis. All electric wiring and fluid hoses were configured with quick-disconnect hardware. Whenever the CERV III required service, the entire body could be lifted off the chassis, allowing for easy access to the car's underpinnings, including its engine and transmission.

The "One-Million-Dollar Corvette"

Prior to its unveiling at the Detroit Auto Show, the completed CERV III was driven more than 2,000 miles by several members of GM's design studio and research and development department. It was determined that the 3,400-pound CERV III had a 0.277 coefficient of drag, a 1.1-g skid pad, and could go from 0–60 mph in just 3.9 seconds and reach a calculated top speed of 225 mph! This level of performance wouldn't be seen in a production Corvette until the introduction of the sixth-generation ZR1 in 2009!

Sadly, General Motors had no intention of manufacturing the CERV III as a production Corvette. Although it was designed to be a more sensible version of the wholly impractical Corvette Indy, its performance capabilities and onboard technologies vastly exceeded anything

Like the CERV I and II before it, the CERV III helped advance Chevrolet's mid-engine powertrain technologies. Although it was another 30 years before General Motors commercially produced and marketed the 2020 mid-engine Stingray, each of these amazing "engineering research vehicles" played a pivotal role in making the newest Corvette a reality. (Photo Courtesy General Motors LLC)

being commercially produced at that time. But what really killed any consideration of moving the car beyond its concept phase was cost. A production version of the CERV III would have sold for between $300,000 and $400,000 each, putting it out of reach for most Corvette owners.

Today, the "One-Million-Dollar Corvette" (as it is often referred) is carefully preserved and maintained as part of GM's Heritage Center Collection.

The Stingray III concept, also known as the "California Corvette," was developed at the direction of Chuck Jordan, Chevrolet's vice president of design. He staged a competition among three of his studios to design a car with classic Corvette styling that was more economical than the poorly performing fourth-generation model. (Photo Courtesy General Motors LLC)

The 1992 Stingray III (California Stingray)

As difficult as it is to imagine today, there was a period during the late 1980s in which General Motors considered canceling the Corvette program as part of a larger corporate restructure aimed at improving the company's market share after a decade of significantly declining sales.

At GM's 1989 executive conference in Traverse City, Michigan, it was decided by GM's new president Jim Stemple that development of a fifth-generation Corvette should be indefinitely postponed. Serious consideration was given to rebranding, or even canceling, the fourth-generation Corvette platform due to poor sales numbers. Fortunately, Chevrolet General Manager Jim Perkins reasoned that the public still viewed the Chevrolet Corvette as the division's flagship brand. His compelling argument convinced most in attendance that canceling the fourth-generation program would only further damage the company's already-volatile public image.

While Perkins fought for the continuation of the Corvette program, GM's vice president of design Chuck Jordan had begun exploring alternative styling viewpoints for a fifth-generation model. In October 1989, Jordan staged a contest to see which of GM's design studios could create a new proposal that best contemporized the Corvette's styling for a new generation of consumers.

A Downsized Corvette Concept

John Schinella, director of Chevrolet's Advanced Concept Center in Los Angeles, California, decided its design proposal should depict a car that was smaller

Despite being a departure from the (then) current model Corvette, the Stingray III concept nonetheless included enough styling elements to commemorate its Corvette heritage. Its oval taillights likely inspired the taillights that were installed on the fifth-generation Corvette beginning in 1997. (Photo Courtesy General Motors LLC)

The Stingray III is packed full of high-tech features, including a high-performance hybrid drive, interactive touch controls to manage the power and efficiency of the car, a rearview camera with night vision enhancement, an in-car camera system, and advanced telematics. (Photo Courtesy General Motors LLC)

than the current fourth-generation model. After making some general decisions about chassis and drivetrain configuration, he began defining the look of the California Corvette (a nickname given to the project after Schinella posed the question "what would a California Corvette look like?") in a series of quickly rendered sketches. These sketches were presented to his team at the Advanced Concept Center, where they were reviewed, critiqued, and returned to Schinella with advised improvements. It was during this process that the new car, officially known as the Stingray III, started to take shape.

The completed design included styling elements that paid homage to cars that came before it, including Bill Mitchell's Manta Ray concept. Schinella understood the importance of incorporating classic Corvette elements into his design while simultaneously creating a new aesthetic that used contemporary design standards and could be built using modern construction materials.

A prototype was assembled from Schinella's design drawings. The Stingray III concept included a stretched wheelbase with wider proportions, a bobbed tail, and a steeply raked windshield. Its entire front end was comprised of fluid, sweeping curves that swept up and over its front axles. A clamshell hood and scissor-style doors afforded easy access to the engine and cockpit areas. Behind the cockpit, a rounded decklid concealed a separate trunk area. Four elliptical taillights and a stylized rear bumper made up the rear of the car. It sat on cast-aluminum wheels wrapped in 285/35ZR-18 tires.

The Stingray III concept lacked the massive side frame rails of the fourth-generation Corvette. Instead, low side sills allowed for improved interior accessibility. Likewise, the left side of the dashboard articulated upward when the driver's door was opened, providing the car's pilot with improved knee clearance when entering or exiting the vehicle.

The car's instrument panel contained a mixture of analog and digital gauges. Black, kidney-shaped pods were mounted on either side of the speedometer/tachometer display. Each contained a dense collection of dials, illuminated buttons, and toggle switches to operate the car's many onboard technologies, including an in-car camera system with built-in telemetric storage. Both the instrument cluster and the adjoining pods were positioned directly within the driver's field of view thanks to the near-recumbent positioning of the car's fixed, ergonomic seats. Like earlier Corvette concepts, the steering wheel and pedals of the Stingray III were adjustable to meet the needs of virtually anyone wishing to drive it.

A variety of advanced technologies were also incorporated into the Stingray III's chassis/underpinnings, including all-wheel-drive steering and a newly developed active suspension system. The latter used four optical sensors mounted to the car's undercarriage to continuously sample road/driving conditions. The collected data was then relayed to the computer-controlled coilover suspension system that adjusted the amount of shock damping required for optimal performance.

The 1992 Stingray III was originally designed to accommodate a high-output V-6 engine. Although the

With a body built almost entirely of carbon fiber, the Stingray III's exterior was both rigid and strong. The car featured a clamshell hood, scissor-style doors, ergonomic seats, and four-wheel steering with active suspension. (Photo Courtesy General Motors LLC)

V-6 was admittedly smaller than the Corvette's traditional V-8 engines, it would have provided plenty of power in Schinella's proportionately smaller concept car. However, when others within General Motors argued that a V-6-powered Corvette was a "step backward," the Stingray III was instead fitted with the next-generation LT1 engine, a 5.7-liter V-8 that produced 300 hp (this same engine went on to power the 1992 and later fourth-generation Corvette).

Well Received but Overpriced

Chevrolet introduced the Stingray III Concept at the 1992 North American International Auto Show in Detroit as a potential design for the next-generation Corvette. The car was well received by the public and got favorable reviews from much of the automotive press. Unfortunately, there were many within General Motors (and most especially within Chevy III's team of designers) who strongly disliked the car. They argued that the Stingray III, in addition to being developed solely as a roadster, lacked the styling elements that tied it to the second- and third-generation Stingray coupes that had defined the brand in the first place.

The Stingray III never moved past the concept/prototype phase. Despite being a crowd favorite, General Motors estimated that the car would cost nearly $300,000 per unit, putting it out of reach for most consumers, including current Corvette owners.

Even so, the concept car wasn't completely forgotten. Its body lines and basic profile provided the basis of design for the 1995 Chevy Cavalier coupe and convertible. As for influences on future Corvettes, its functional rear trunk first appeared on the 1998 Corvette convertible and again on the 1999 Fixed Roof Coupe (FRC) models. Its elliptical taillights found their way onto the fifth-generation Corvette. In 2005, a version of the Stingray III's exposed headlights was introduced on the sixth-generation Corvette.

Today, the Stingray III resides at the GM Heritage Center.

Although development of the "California Corvette" never moved beyond the concept phase, its creation directly influenced the look/design of other cars built by Chevrolet, including the third-generation Cavalier and the fourth-generation Camaro. (Photo Courtesy General Motors LLC)

CHAPTER 8

NEW CENTURY, NEW CONCEPTS

There is a certain magic about Corvette. It's more than a product. When you design cars like this, you're creating an individual with personality. When cars are done right, people relate to them on an emotional level.
—Tom Peters, Director of Design for the GM Performance Car Studio

By the dawn of the 21st century, the practice of building concept cars to gauge public interest in a potential design or technology offering was on the decline. Given the advances in computer-aided drafting software to expedite the automobile design process, along with the constant need to mitigate cost wherever possible, fewer and fewer automobile manufacturers saw the decades-old medium as being practical or profitable.

That's not to say that the notion of the concept car, which played such a major role in automotive design for more than a half-century, was completely dead. While the idea of building one-of-a-kind, over-the-top automobiles like the Biscayne, Manta Ray, or even the Corvette Indy may have largely fallen out of favor, General Motors continued to introduce concept vehicles that previewed technologies and/or styling elements that were about to be introduced on a next-generation model or as part of a

Tom Peters is arguably one of the most influential designers of the modern-era Corvette. Although many of his designs, including this styling study from the late 1990s, never evolved past the clay modeling stage, his direct influence over the look of the sixth-, seventh-, and eighth-generation Corvettes cannot be overstated. This model's body side coves, large air intakes, and wedge-shape profile are all signature elements found on a Tom Peters Corvette. (Photo Courtesy General Motors LLC)

The 2009 Corvette Stingray concept looks like something straight out of a science-fiction movie, and it should! Designed by Tom Peters, this beautiful concept was "born" to star as the Autobot Sideswipe in Michael Bay's blockbuster Transformers II: Revenge of the Fallen. *It was not, as many speculated, an early design concept for the seventh-generation Corvette. (Photo Courtesy General Motors LLC)*

mid-generation refresh. As history has proven at least a handful of times during the last 20-plus years, you can't keep a good design (or designer) down.

The 2008 Corvette Z06 E85 Concept

The Z06 E85 concept was one of three Corvettes selected as the official pace cars of the 2008 Indianapolis 500. It was specially engineered to run on E85, a domestically produced alternative fuel similar to the E100 fuel used in all the IndyCar Series race cars. It made its public debut alongside its counterparts, a black Corvette coupe and convertible, on May 25, 2008, during the race's opening pace laps. The E85 concept was piloted by two-time Indianapolis 500 champion Emerson Fittipaldi.

"Although not a production FlexFuel vehicle, the Corvette Z06 E85 concept pace car is a high-performance example of Chevrolet's gas-friendly to gas-free initiative, demonstrating viable fuel solutions," said Chevrolet General Manager Ed Peper. "As an ethanol refiner in his native Brazil, Emerson Fittipaldi is the fitting Chevrolet champion to help support GM's efforts with E85 and celebrate 30 years of the Corvette pacing the Indianapolis 500."

The Corvette Z06 E85 concept pace car was based on a production 2008 Z06 coupe. It was mechanically stock save for a specialized fuel system and powertrain controller that enabled it to operate on high-level ethanol gasoline. Outwardly, the pace car featured a unique Gold Rush Green color-shifting paint scheme that appeared to change colors when exposed to different types of light. It featured special "E85 ETHANOL" badging across its front fascia and along the top of the left and right fenders. Following the tradition of the pace cars that came before it, the E85 concept also included official "Indianapolis 500 Pace Car" badging, along with a checkered flag graphic down its sides.

The Z06 E85 was considered a concept by General Motors because it represented the first "production" Corvette to run on an alternative fuel source (besides traditional, high-octane race fuel). E85 is a blended fuel comprised of 85 percent ethanol and 15 percent gasoline. It provides several benefits, including the reduced

On May 25, 2008, two-time World Champion and two-time Indy 500 Champion Emerson Fittipaldi piloted the E85 Corvette concept before the start of the 92nd Indianapolis 500. (Photo Courtesy Vette Vues *Magazine)*

The 2008 Corvette Z06 E85 concept pace car was the tenth Corvette to lead the field at the Indianapolis 500. The E85 Concept was joined by two specially designed black-and-silver Z06 Corvettes that commemorated Corvette's 30th anniversary as the official pace car of this historic race. (Photo Courtesy Vette Vues *Magazine)*

The only significant difference between a stock Z06 and the E85 concept is the latter car's ability to burn ethanol fuel as its primary source of energy. (Photo Courtesy Vette Vues *Magazine)*

emission of greenhouse gases when burned, a decreased dependence on petroleum, and a renewable energy source produced from corn crops.

Although it was never intended to evolve past the concept car phase, the 2008 Corvette Z06 E85 pace car reiterated Chevrolet's ongoing commitment to manufacture vehicles that could operate on alternative fuel sources. At the time of this publication, Chevrolet has several vehicles in their portfolio that are engineered to operate on E85 fuel.

The 2009 Corvette Stingray Concept and Corvette Centennial Concept

The latter half of the first decade of the 21st century was one of the darkest periods in the history of General Motors. By late 2006, automobile sales had reached an all-time low due to record-high gas prices, poor product offerings, and a worldwide credit crunch that threatened the global economy. Thanks to fixed cost contracts with the United Auto Works Union, aging company pensions, and legacy healthcare costs, the century-old corporation was unable to adapt to the rapidly declining market. It suffered massive financial losses throughout 2007 and 2008 equaling more than $30 billion. By the end of 2008, General Motors was forced to file bankruptcy and seek federal assistance.

The U.S. Treasury Department and President George W. Bush's (and later President Obama's) automotive task force performed a meticulous audit of GM finances. Throughout the process, they eliminated entire divisions of the corporation (including Pontiac, Hummer, Saab, and Saturn) after deeming them unprofitable. Nothing was off the table, including the Corvette, and it was understood that the auditors had the final say in the decision-making process.

Although development of a new Corvette was indefinitely halted even before General Motors filed bankruptcy, Ed Welburn, GM's global vice president of design, recognized the importance of continuing work on a next-generation concept, even if it meant working "off the radar" for the time being. And so it was, under orders of absolute secrecy, that Welburn invited designers from every GM design studio around the globe to create and submit their own design sketches depicting the look of the next-generation Corvette.

GM exterior designer Kirk Bennion was tasked with collecting the sketches and beginning a formal review

The 2009 Corvette Stingray concept was developed by General Motors at the request of Michael Bay. Despite facing unprecedented financial hardships, Ed Welburn, GM's global vice president of design, saw this as an outstanding opportunity to showcase a new Corvette in Bay's second Transformers *movie and reach a global audience of prospective GM customers in the process. (Photo Courtesy General Motors LLC)*

Kirk Bennion (pictured) is the exterior design manager for the seventh- and eighth-generation Corvette Stingray. Bennion led the exterior design team on the 2020 mid-engine Corvette alongside Tom Peters and Tadge Juechter. He's worked at General Motors for 37 years and started with the Corvette program in the early 1990s. (Photo Courtesy General Motors LLC)

process of more than 300 individual submissions. Many of the renderings received depicted cars that were each radically new in form yet still unmistakably Corvette. Designers who'd never seen a Corvette in-person had captured the essence of GM's flagship sports car and breathed a new vitality into it.

Hollywood Superstar

The evolution of the 2009 Corvette Stingray concept really got underway when Hollywood director Michael Bay came knocking at GM's door. Bay had previously featured the 2007 Chevrolet Camaro concept as the character Bumblebee in his first *Transformers* movie. The massive box office success of his action-packed, cars-transform-into-robots film demanded a sequel. And this time, the script for *Transformers 2: Revenge of the Fallen* included a character named Sideswipe who could transform into a Corvette.

Even before he'd started filming the first *Transformers* movie, Michael Bay spotted a scale model of a reimagined, split-window Corvette while visiting the GM's design studios. The model was both contemporary and visceral, drawing on elements from the original Sting Ray while also presenting bold, futuristic styling cues that

One of the 2009 Corvette Stingray concept clay model styling bucks. While most of its exterior detail was complete, there were still a handful of design elements, including its sideview mirrors and headlight assemblies that still needed to be refined. (Photo Courtesy General Motors LLC)

The 2009 Corvette Stingray was only ever intended to be a stand-alone concept car. Despite sharing some similarities with the seventh-generation Stingray, the 2009 concept was developed purely as a "what if" design exercise. When director Michael Bay came calling, the concept got some added momentum behind it, as a running prototype was needed for use on screen. (Photo Courtesy General Motors LLC)

Tom Peters included the split rear window element as an homage to the 1963 Corvette coupe. The Stingray concept also incorporated elements from other past Corvettes, including the dramatic front and rear fender humps of the third-generation Stingray and the side vents/body side coves of the fifth- and sixth-generation models. (Photo Courtesy General Motors LLC)

The straightedge, sharp corner styling of the 2009 Stingray concept was representative of the body styling found on most production cars from that era. This Stingray styling buck was used to showcase alternate design elements being considered for the car, such as the two different taillight alcoves seen here. (Photo Courtesy General Motors LLC)

Bay felt were ideal for his *Transformers* film. He recounted the model when developing the script for the sequel, at which point he contacted General Motors.

Welburn, Bennion, and the GM design team were thrilled by Bay's request. They saw it as an opportunity to create a car that pushed the limits of design, much as the Corvette Indy had, while simultaneously updating decades-old styling cues to create a futuristic-looking Stingray that drew its inspiration from the 1963 split-window Corvette.

A Fusion of Old and New

Tom Peters, who now served as director of exterior design for GM performance cars, was tasked with creating a "modern interpretation of the 1963 Split-Window Sting Ray and the original 1959 Stingray Racer." He put his design team to work, challenging them to incorporate design elements from other past Corvettes as well. The completed design was presented to Welburn. He was so impressed with the car that he ordered a full-size clay model, and later a running prototype, be fabricated from the design team's drawings.

The 2009 Corvette Stingray concept car was assembled on the chassis of a production C6. The car used an assortment of existing hardware pulled from the Corvette parts bin as well as hand-fabricated parts developed specifically for it. Although the original designs called for the body to be fabricated from an assortment of composite materials, the finished concept car was constructed almost entirely of fiberglass.

The final look of the car's exterior was intended as an homage to many of the Corvettes that came before it. The front grille and fascia assembly was a modern reinterpretation of the 1959 Stingray Racer's front end. The front and rear fender humps were a fusion of the ones introduced on the Manta Ray and the second-generation Sting Ray. The roofline looked remarkably like the "double-hump" panel introduced on the fifth- and sixth-generation models. The body side coves and the car's hood bulge were an exaggeration of those used on the C6. And most notable of all was the reimagined rear split window, which drew its inspiration from one of the most iconic Corvettes ever: the 1963 Split-Window coupe.

The Stingray concept was 3.1 inches longer, 5 inches lower, and 6.6 inches wider than the production C6 Corvette. It sat on massive front and rear wheels: 20x9.5-inch wheels wrapped in 275/30R20 tires up front, and 21x13-inch wheels wrapped in 355/30R21 tires in the rear.

Like many of its earlier counterparts, the Stingray Concept used a reverse clamshell hood and scissor doors for greater ease of access to the car's engine and cockpit, respectively. Unlike the earlier cars, each of these assemblies could be opened and closed with the touch of a button.

A stock LS3 engine powered the Stingray Concept. Despite the "Hybrid Stingray" badging stamped into its fuel injection rail covers, the car was not a hybrid in any conventional sense of the word. Instead, the "hybrid" referenced the introduction of new technologies, including

Although many elements of the 2009 Corvette Stingray concept's bold body design never evolved beyond the concept car phase, there is no mistaking the styling similarities between this car, the 2010 Chevy Camaro, and the seventh-generation Corvette Stingray, all three of which were designed by Tom Peters. (Photo Courtesy General Motors LLC)

Tom Peters repurposed several design elements from the 2009 Stingray concept into the final design of the C7 Corvette Stingray, including its taillight assemblies, the shape of the door glass and B-pillars, the flared fender duct extensions as a feature of the doors, its squared-off rear end, and of course, the Stingray logos on the front fenders. (Photo Courtesy General Motors LLC)

The Stingray concept's doors and clamshell hood open and close automatically via motorized hinges mounted along the frame. Each assembly can be opened separately using either the car's key fob remote or via separate, internal switches inside the cockpit. (Photo Courtesy General Motors LLC)

cylinder deactivation and (possibly) electric/battery assist when being driven in stop-and-go traffic for improved fuel economy.

Although the technical specifications of the Stingray Concept's engine have never been published, it is assumed that the car's LS3 V-8 produced the same 430 hp and 424 ft-lbs of torque as its production counterpart. It was mated to a stock, 6-speed automatic transmission.

The interior of the Stingray Concept was stunning. It featured carbon fiber and chrome trim with integrated LED lighting and custom-designed seats with substantial side bolsters (likely developed in response to complaints General Motors received about the substandard seats installed in the sixth-generation Corvettes). The cockpit was appointed with technology offerings that included a massive infotainment system equipped with GPS and media interfaces and a customizable instrument cluster with advanced telemetrics and interactive touch controls.

Like so many of the Corvette concepts before it, the 2009 Stingray concept's interior was meant to be a technology showcase. In addition to its mixed analog/digital gauge cluster, the car features a massive media/infotainment center that included internet connectivity, navigation system, a personal digital assistant (PDA), ideal track line telematics, stereo controls, and more. (Photo Courtesy General Motors LLC)

Not the Next-Generation Stingray

The Corvette Stingray concept was introduced at the Chicago Auto Show on February 11, 2009. Ed Welburn introduced the car to the press as "a new automotive superstar: the Chevrolet Stingray concept." As its cover was pulled away, spectators were introduced to a beautifully proportioned car finished in silver

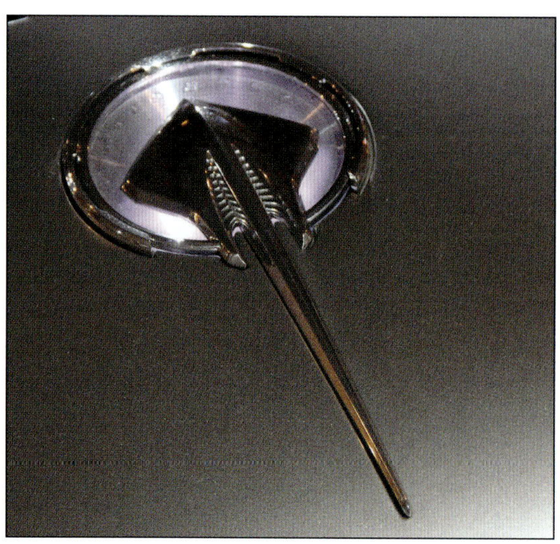

The Stingray emblems featured on the fenders and rear decklid of the 2009 Corvette Stingray concept were added as an homage to the original emblems installed on Bill Mitchell's 1969 Manta Ray. This emblem, virtually unaltered since its introduction in 2009, was included on the front fenders of the seventh-generation Stingray. (Photo Courtesy General Motors LLC)

and minimally badged with a newly imagined Stingray emblem.

Crowd reactions to the car were overwhelmingly positive, inspiring many to ask if they were looking at the next-generation Corvette. Welburn's response was simply, "No. It was a great styling concept with a role in (a) movie." As good as the Stingray concept's design was, Welburn believed that his styling team could still do better.

Michael Bay's *Transformers 2: Revenge of the Fallen* premiered on June 24, 2009, with the Stingray front and center in much of the action as the character Sideswipe. Despite the film being poorly received by fans and critics alike, one of the movie's highlights was the brilliant cast of GM vehicles, including the latest Corvette concept.

Many of the styling cues introduced on the 2009 Corvette Stingray Concept found new life in future GM offerings. The car heavily influenced the fifth-generation Chevy Camaro, as well as the seventh- and eighth-generation Corvette Stingrays. Today, the car is part of the GM Heritage Center collection, although it still makes frequent appearances at various Corvette-sanctioned events.

The 2009 Stingray Concept also represents the last of the true concept Corvettes produced by Chevrolet to date. Although there have been other "concepts" introduced since the Stingray's introduction, none of these cars advanced new design or technology initiatives. Instead, each was a unique customization to an existing model that introduced new styling or performance elements for a specific model year.

The 2011 Corvette Jake Edition Concept

From a design standpoint, the Corvette Jake Edition Concept wasn't a concept car at all. It was a stylized 2011 Corvette Grand Sport coupe finished in black paint and fitted with Competition Gray Z06 wheels, a matte "Jake" hood graphic from the GT1 commemorative model, and a variety of other unique accessories. It was introduced by General Motors to demonstrate how consumers might customize a Corvette to create their own Jake special editions by using parts available through GM's "Genuine Corvette Accessories."

"Jake" is the Corvette Racing team's unofficial mascot. Jake came into being in 2005 after its creator, Eddie Jabbour of Kick Design, scribbled the fifth-generation Corvette's crossed flags on a cocktail napkin and then drew the outline of a human skull around it, all while watching the team compete at Le Mans in 2004.

Jabbour believed the mascot captured the team's "Take No Prisoners" mentality. The team agreed and adopted the mascot immediately, adding the first Jake graphic to the cars for the 2005 running of the 24 Hours of Le Mans. Since that time, the mascot and the "take no prisoners" mantra have become integral parts of the Corvette Racing program.

In addition to paying tribute to Corvettes of the past, Tom Peters's 2009 Stingray concept was designed to commemorate GM's 100th anniversary. As such, the car is sometimes referred to as the "Corvette Centennial" concept. (Photo Courtesy General Motors LLC)

The 2011 Corvette Jake Edition concept was a production Grand Sport fitted with lots of available GM accessories designed to commemorate the Corvette Racing Team's championship during the 2009 American Le Mans Series season. (Photo Courtesy General Motors LLC)

One of the most dramatic aspects of the Jake Edition concept is the custom two-piece hood graphic, which featured Corvette Racing's "Jake" mascot in grey and black framed by a separate yellow border stripe. Each kit included additional graphics for the roof panel and the rear decklid. (Photo Courtesy General Motors LLC)

General Motors also produced a custom, underhood liner as an option for the would-be consumer looking to replicate the Jake Edition concept. It once more featured the Jake mascot in bright grey against a black background. *(Photo Courtesy General Motors LLC)*

To further integrate the look of the engine compartment into the car's overall theme, the factory LS3 engine rail covers (black with red lettering) were replaced with custom covers finished in carbon flash with yellow lettering. (Photo Courtesy General Motors LLC)

The interior of the Jake concept featured several subtle styling additions. Most notable was the yellow stitching against the ebony leather seats, on the leather shifter knob, and along the doors and dashboard. The car also received custom "Jake" floormats and an embroidered "Jake" on the center console armrest. (Photo Courtesy General Motors LLC)

The 2011 Jake Edition Grand Sport Corvette concept was raffled off by the National Corvette Museum after its appearance at the SEMA show. The money raised from ticket sales was used to help fund the NCM Motorsport Park, which opened in 2013. (Photo Courtesy General Motors LLC)

"Jake is more than the mascot for Corvette Racing; he personifies the Corvette spirit," said Dave Ross, Chevrolet Performance design manager, in a GM press release. "We designed this concept to demonstrate how any enthusiast could create his own Jake special model with parts available from any Chevrolet dealership."

In addition to the aforementioned options, the 2011 Corvette Jake Edition concept came equipped with an LS3 6.2L V-8 engine mated to a Tremec TR6060 6-speed manual transmission. It also included the following Chevrolet accessories: a racing pedal kit, a matte-black "Corvette" windshield header graphic, a full-width rear spoiler, an ebony interior with yellow stitching, and Jake-logoed center caps, center console lid, fender badges, and an underhood, tech-pattern engine cover.

"The Corvette has long inspired car enthusiasts to personalize it. The Jake concept shows one very unique way to do it," said Ross. "With the great variety of accessories and other parts available, there's virtually no limit to how you can make your Corvette stand apart from all others."

Although the Jake Edition concept may not be remembered as one of the true concept Corvettes of its generation, its introduction led to the development of many genuine GM-branded Corvette Racing accessories for the fifth-, sixth-, seventh-, and eighth-generation Corvettes.

The Jake mascot continues to be an integral part of the Corvette Racing program. It is recognized and celebrated by Corvette fans across the United States and around the globe.

The 2011 Corvette Z06X Track Car Concept

Where the Jake Edition concept provided consumers the opportunity to outwardly change the appearance of

The Corvette Z06X Track Car concept was presented alongside the Jake Edition Concept at the 2011 SEMA Show. The car, which was built in conjunction with Pratt & Miller, was designed to be a factory-produced, track-ready Corvette specifically geared toward the weekend racer. (Photo Courtesy General Motors LLC)

The finished conceptual design of the Z06X Track Car concept by Chevy designer Adam Barry is shown here. The car, which was assembled from Barry's drawings, was finished in low-gloss Icy White Metallic paint with exposed carbon fiber elements, including a carbon fiber raised hood, roof panel, and B-pillar panels as well as a carbon fiber wing. (Photo Courtesy General Motors LLC)

The Z06X concept was equipped with a variety of weight saving and safety features, including a shatter-resistant polycarbonate rear window, an SCCA-approved window net for the driver's door, an SCCA-spec roll cage, a fire suppression system, a driver's drink system, and lightweight racing wheels. (Photo Courtesy General Motors LLC)

After its appearance at SEMA, the Z06X toured racetracks around the country. As a hybrid of the production Z06 and the GT race car, it was a powerhouse on the racetrack that left Corvette enthusiasts clamoring for more. Despite receiving an overwhelmingly positive customer response, the car was never produced. (Photo Courtesy General Motors LLC)

their cars to commemorate the Corvette Racing program, the 2011 Corvette Z06X Track Car concept showcased how racing hobbyists could use Chevrolet's portfolio of performance parts to transform their Z06 Corvette into a full-on race car. Although this concept started life as a stock 2011 Z06 Corvette with the 1LZ equipment package, the Z06X ended up being anything but stock.

Like the Jake concept, the 2011 Corvette Z06X Track Car concept was developed by Corvette Chief Engineer Tadge Juechter and Dave Ross in cooperation with Pratt & Miller Engineering and Fabrication, the engineering wing of the Corvette Racing program since its inception in 1999. Per Ross in *Road & Track* magazine, the Z06X Track Car concept was "a classic case of form following function. The exterior color and accents were carefully selected to enhance the Corvette's racing-influenced design, but there's nothing superfluous in the Z06X's design—everything is there for a reason."

At the heart of the car was the production Z06's 7.0-liter LS7 V-8 engine fitted with a special low-restriction intake kit and a larger radiator with accessory cooler. The chassis came set up with the Z07 performance package and included Brembo carbon-ceramic brakes, an enhanced suspension with coilover struts and camber plates, mono-ball control arm bushings, adjustable anti-roll bars, and special lightweight alloy wheels wrapped in Michelin racing tires: 285/30R19 up front and 335/25R20 in the rear.

The body of the Z06X concept borrowed elements

In 2014, Corvette Product Manager Harlan Charles shared his vision for a seventh-generation Stingray based on the 2011 Z06X Track Car concept. It is generally believed that the Z06X provided the foundation for the 2019 Corvette ZR1, the purpose-built, production track car that enthusiasts had been demanding for nearly a decade.

from Corvette's CFZ Carbon Fiber package, which was first introduced on the 2011 Z06 Carbon Limited Edition Corvette. The package included a carbon fiber front splitter, rocker extensions, a raised carbon fiber hood, carbon fiber headlamp housings from Specter Werkes/Sports, and an adjustable full-width rear spoiler. Additionally, the Z06X included an adjustable carbon fiber rear wing for greater downforce and a polycarbonate rear window for reduced weight. Most of the exterior was finished in Icy White Metallic paint save for the rear fascia, which was finished in flat black. The car also received special "Z06X" badging and a black racing stripe down its center.

Inside the cockpit, the car was fitted with an SCCA-approved roll cage, window nets, a drink system, a fire-suppression system, an in-car camera, special racing pedals, and a racing seat equipped with a five-point safety harness. To help make the car as light as possible, the car's stereo, carpeting, and sound deadening were all deleted.

The 2011 Corvette Z06X concept debuted at the 2010 Specialty Equipment Market Association (SEMA) show in Las Vegas alongside the 2011 Jake Edition concept.

"Racing is an integral part of Corvette performance and technology," said Juechter at the car's unveiling. "This concept car represents a mid-point between our GT racer and the production Z06. It was prepared by the team responsible for our Corvette Racing C6.R race cars and features many performance parts owners can choose today."

The car was one of the highlights of that year's SEMA show. Initial crowd reaction and all subsequent feedback suggested that General Motors should greenlight the project immediately and move the Z06X from concept to production. Unfortunately, the timing still wasn't right within General Motors, and the decision was made to suspend the Z06X program, at least for the time being.

Fast-forward to 2014. During an interview with *Car & Driver* magazine, Corvette Production Manager Harlan Charles stated that he wanted to put the Corvette Z06X into production as a potential seventh-generation offering.

"The idea was a non-street-legal, factory-built track car, and that is something that we are considering would be a great thing to apply to the new Corvette Z06,"

Charles said. "I mean, that's something we could see in the future. We've got a lot of ideas, but nothing to show today, unfortunately."

While a genuine Corvette club race car was never commercially produced by Chevrolet, the evolution of the seventh-generation Z06 and ZR1 models incorporated many of the technologies previously showcased on the 2011 Z06X Corvette. These technologies included carbon fiber front splitters and rocker extensions, carbon fiber hood and roof panels, and in the case of the 2019 Corvette ZR1 at least, a factory-installed, adjustable high wing for improved downforce.

The 2014 Gran Turismo C7 Corvette Concept

For more than 60 years, Chevrolet has produced concept Corvettes to gauge public interest in new bodystyles, to showcase new/emerging technologies, and to expand the boundaries of automotive design. In 2013, the automaker introduced a special-edition, seventh-generation Stingray concept to commemorate the fifteenth anniversary of a video game franchise and to celebrate the release of its newest version: Grand Turismo 6.

The 2014 Gran Tourismo C7 Corvette Stingray concept was one of three Corvette "concepts" unveiled at the SEMA show in Las Vegas on November 5, 2013. Chevrolet transformed one of its newest Corvettes, the seventh-generation Stingray coupe, to closely match the Stingray Concept showcased in the GT6 game.

Although no modification was made to its factory powertrain, the 2014 Gran Turismo C7 Corvette concept's exterior was upgraded with a laundry list of race-inspired options, including a carbon fiber rear wing, a vented hood, a full aerodynamic body kit, and a custom grille, all of which provided better downforce at higher speed and enhanced the car's high-performance appearance. (Photo Courtesy Kolecki Photography)

In a world where high-end sports cars inspire video games, the creation of the actual 2014 Gran Turismo C7 Corvette concept was inspired by its likeness in the game "Gran Turismo 6." The concept was a re-creation (in great detail) of the computer-rendered model developed in cooperation with Chevrolet and the programmers at Polyphony Digital. (Photo Courtesy Kolecki Photography)

Its exterior was finished in a custom matte blue paint and featured many unique styling elements, including yellow-tinted headlamps, a custom carbon fiber hood, a removable carbon fiber roof panel, larger 19-inch wheels up front and 20-inch wheels in the rear, a carbon fiber front splitter, carbon fiber rockers, and a carbon fiber rear wing. The car's custom grille, front fender outlets, and rear-quarter ventilation duct inlets were each appointed with brushed-aluminum accents.

The interior received a pair of upgraded competition sport seats paired with four-point racing harnesses for both the driver and the passenger. A flat-bottom steering wheel was also included (a feature that resurfaced as a standard option on the 2016 Corvette Stingray). The dashboard, seats, door panels, and leather-wrapped safety bar were finished in brownstone with orange stitching. The rest of the interior was trimmed in dark grey and carbon fiber accents.

Chevrolet developed the 2014 Gran Turismo C7 Corvette Stingray concept in cooperation with Polyphony Digital, the company that developed the Gran Turismo video game franchise. While the concept car remained unaltered mechanically (it included the stock LT1 engine and a 6-speed manual transmission), Polyphony Digital worked closely with Chevrolet engineers to ensure that the Corvette showcased in the game accurately performed and handled like its real-life counterpart.

The 2014 Corvette Atlantic and Pacific Concepts

In addition to the Gran Turismo concept, Chevrolet presented a pair of "East Coast versus West Coast" Stingray concepts at the 2013 SEMA show. The look and feel of each car, appropriately named the Corvette Stingray Convertible Atlantic concept and the Corvette Stingray Pacific concept, respectively, was influenced by the region of the country and the culture it represented.

The 2014 Corvette Stingray Atlantic concept design package was inspired by the luxuries found on private jets. It came finished in Blade Silver paint with Carbon Flash Metallic accents. Its interior was wrapped in suede. It had premium carpeted floor mats, custom sill plates, a glass windscreen between the seats, and an embroidered armrest featuring the Stingray logo. (Photo Courtesy General Motors LLC)

The track-inspired 2014 Corvette Stingray Pacific concept design package came finished in Torch Red paint accentuated by full-length black racing stripes and a carbon fiber roof panel. Additional carbon fiber trim adorned the car's interior, along with a pair of Competition Sport seats and a flat-bottom steering wheel. It also included the immensely popular Z51 performance package. (Photo Courtesy General Motors LLC)

The Stingray Convertible Atlantic concept was a luxury GT-styled convertible finished in unique Blade Silver paint. It featured several sophisticated styling enhancements, including a new front splitter, rocker extensions, and a rear lower diffuser, as well as custom headlight surrounds, molded splash guards, a Carbon Flash Metallic rear license plate holder, and unique hood accents. The car sat on custom chrome five-spoke wheels: 19x8.5 inches out front and 20x10 inches in the rear. Each wheel featured a center cap with the "Stingray" script.

The Atlantic concept's interior came finished in suede-wrapped trim and included a wind screen mounted between and behind the seats, custom floor mats, an embroidered center armrest with the Stingray logo, and door sill plates. It also included a custom set of matching luggage.

The Corvette Stingray Pacific concept was a track-focused performance coupe that looked more aggressive in its Torch Red exterior and full-length black racing stripes. It came equipped with a carbon fiber hood (painted to match the car) and an exposed carbon fiber weave on the removable roof panel. A satin-black front splitter and rocker panel extensions added to the car's low, aggressive stance. Finishing off the look were 19-inch front and 20-inch rear wheels finished in satin black with red pinstriping around their perimeter, a rear spoiler covered in Carbon Flash Metallic paint, and Carbon Flash emblems on the nose, fenders, and rear fascia.

The interior trim of the Pacific concept was also adorned in carbon fiber. The cockpit also featured a pair of Competition Sport seats finished in red leather, a flat-bottomed steering wheel wrapped in carbon fiber flash, red and black accents throughout, and a pair of black embroidered "Stingray" floor mats that showcased the seventh-generation emblem as well as the name.

Like every generation of Corvette that came before it, the 2020 Mid-Engine Stingray started with design drawings, clay models (seen here), and extensive wind-tunnel testing. The black marks along the model's A- and B-pillars represent air movement around the car's body. This information was used to modify the design to maximize aerodynamics.

Outside the dramatic variations in styling, the most notable difference between the two cars was that the Pacific concept came equipped with the Z51 performance package. In addition to a 5-hp increase over the base engine (460 hp versus 455 hp), the Z51 included a dry-sump oil system, improved cooling and braking systems, and an electronically controlled limited-slip differential in the rear. Also, in keeping with the West Coast race culture, the Pacific concept was equipped with a 7-speed manual transmission.

"One of the design goals for the Corvette Stingray was to provide customers with the flexibility to tailor the car to their personality," said Kirk Bennion, Corvette exterior design manager. "The Atlantic and Pacific Design Packages were designed to showcase how the Stingray could be configured as a luxury sport GT car or as a high-performance motorsport car."

During the final weeks of the 2013 SEMA Show, Chevrolet officials hinted that the Corvette Stingray Atlantic and Pacific concept car packages might become special-edition packages, provided customer feedback from the show was favorable enough to warrant their inclusion. Although neither was offered to consumers for the 2014 model year, Chevrolet offered slightly modified versions of both packages as special editions in 2015.

The Road Ahead: Dreams of the Next Generation

It has been more than a decade since Chevrolet introduced a genuine Corvette concept car to the world. Although the evolution of the eighth-generation Stingray was well documented via countless spy photos, videos, and leaked CAD images posted across the internet beginning from 2014 on, General Motors shared virtually no official information about their new mid-engine Corvette until they were prepared to unveil the finished product on July 18, 2019.

Despite the high level of secrecy during its design and development, it is obvious that the mid-engine Stingray was the effort of many talented designers and engineers, especially Kirk Bennion and Tadge Juechter, to say nothing of the dozens even hundreds of others who participated in its creation. Still, the car evolved in a vacuum for nearly a half decade, leaving the world at large to speculate as to what the next-generation Corvette would look like and how it would handle, perform, etc.

Years before Chevrolet released any information about its new Corvette to the public, images of a highly stylized mid-engine sports car began circulating in publications like *Car and Driver* magazine. Interestingly, many of these images, even the earliest examples, contained

Officially known as a Powertrain Development Vehicle, this 2018 Mid-Engine Test Mule was used at the Milford Proving Grounds to evaluate GM's latest version of the 6.2-liter LT2 engine prior to its introduction in the 2020 Mid-Engine Stingray. This car was wrapped in vinyl to help camouflage it from photojournalists eager to catch a glimpse of the (then) future eighth-generation Corvette.

accurately rendered design elements found on the final production model. As the years advanced, so did the accuracy of the drawings being published. By the time Chevrolet announced the car's official unveiling in July 2019, there were many who were convinced that General Motors had already secretly revealed their car through this virtual medium.

It begs the question: Was Chevrolet disseminating bits of information about its new Corvette across the internet to pique the interest of enthusiasts? Was the development of the mid-engine Corvette carefully orchestrated to create virtual consumer feedback on a global scale? Were the sketches, drawings, and computer renderings of the mid-engine Stingray the 21st century equivalent of the concept cars showcased at venues like GM's Motorama all those years ago?

We'll likely never know, at least not for certain, but it certainly feels right.

What we do know is this: Despite facing production delays due to COVID-19 in 2020 and material shortages in 2021, the eighth-generation Corvette Stingray continues to be one of the most sought-after Corvettes in the history of the brand. Should its popularity continue to grow (and all indications are that it will), there'll likely be future generations of Corvettes as-yet unimagined. Just as it has always been, it will once more be up to the designers, the engineers, the *dreamers*—one of whom might be reading this book right now—to draw inspiration from the past as they conceptualize the Corvette of the future.

The eighth-generation Mid-Engine Corvette Stingray is the culmination of nearly 60 years of determination by many of the Corvette's most talented designers and engineers. Its arrival in 2020 would have thrilled Harley Earl, Zora Arkus-Duntov, and Bill Mitchell, none of whom, regrettably, were still alive to witness its unveiling on July 18, 2019.

Additional books that may interest you...

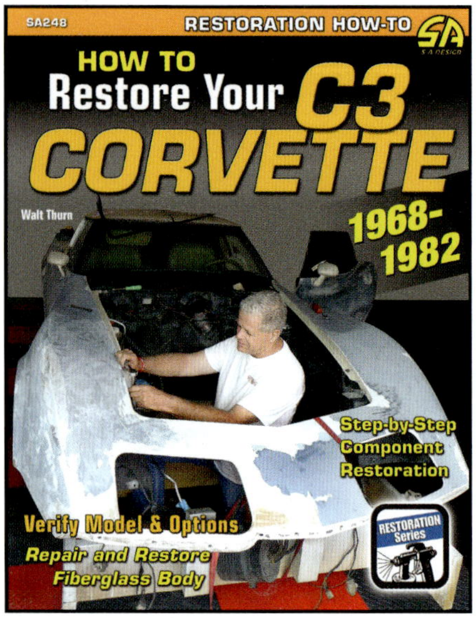

HOW TO RESTORE YOUR C3 CORVETTE: 1968–1982
by Walt Thurn
Hands-on restoration techniques for all major component groups are explained in exceptional detail for professional results, including suspension, engine, interior, body, paint, brakes, steering, electrical, and interior. Special coverage is devoted to restoring the birdcage frame and the fiberglass body. If you've been looking for the authoritative guide for restoring your 1968–1982 Stingray, you've found it. 8.5 x 11", 176 pgs, 493 color photos, Sftbd. ISBN 9781613250372
Part # SA248

How to Install Corvette Interior Kits
by Fred Mattson
Frustrations from installing an aftermarket interior kit are over with this easy-to-follow, illustrated, step-by-step book that shows how to achieve professional results. A first-of-its-kind book, it walks you through the steps of how to properly install seat upholstery, door panels, carpet, headliners, and troubleshoot those pesky fitment issues. 8.5 x 11", 176 pgs, Sftbd. Part # SA519

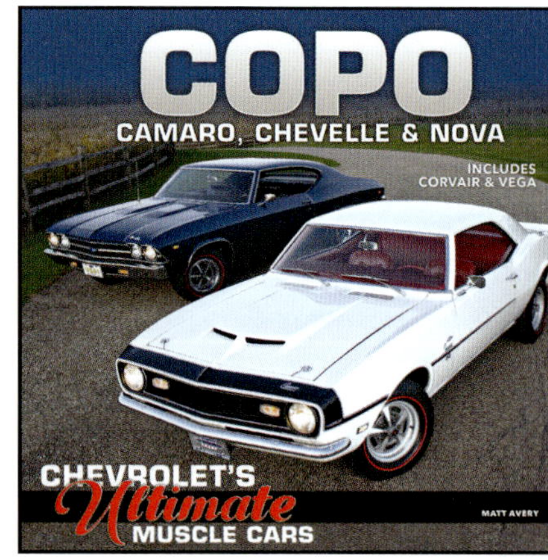

COPO CAMARO, CHEVELLE & NOVA: Chevrolet's Ultimate Muscle Cars
by Matt Avery
Chevy muscle car aficionado and author Matt Avery retraces the history of the COPO program and the creation of these premier muscle cars. He has scoured archives and tracked down owners and personnel involved in the program to deliver a comprehensive story and complete guide to the COPO cars. 10 x 10", 204 pgs, 400 photos, Hdbd. ISBN 9781613253915
Part # CT620

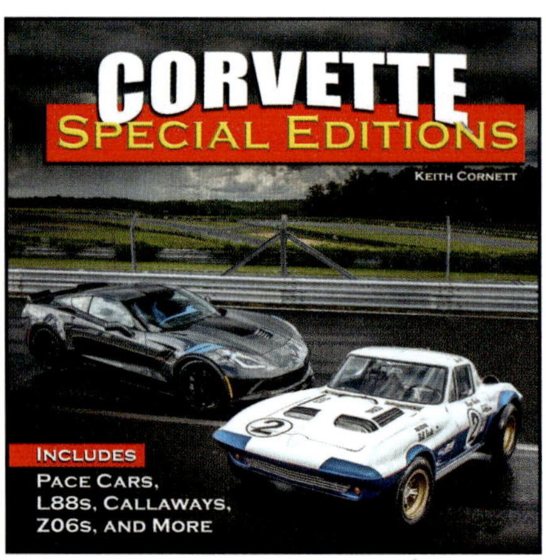

CORVETTE SPECIAL EDITIONS: Includes Pace Cars, L88s, Callaways, Lingenfelters, Z06s, and More
by Keith Cornett
Keith Cornett of CorvetteBlogger.com compiles a murderer's row of special-edition Corvettes in this first-ever compilation on the subject. This book is an encyclopedia of information, as you will learn about some of the rarest Corvettes on the planet. 10 x 10", 192 pgs, 481 photos, Hdbd. ISBN 9781613253939
Part # CT622

Check out our website:

CarTechBooks.com

✓ Find our newest books before anyone else

✓ Get weekly tech tips from our experts

✓ Featuring a new deal each week!

Exclusive Promotions and Giveaways at www.CarTechBooks.com!

www.cartechbooks.com or 1-800-551-4754

Get the latest from CarTech on facebook!